The Oneida Indians in the Age of Allotment, 1860–1920

The Civilization of the American Indian Series

The Oneida Indians in the Age of Allotment, 1860–1920

Laurence M. Hauptman
L. Gordon McLester III

University of Oklahoma Press : Norman

Also by Laurence M. Hauptman and L. Gordon McLester III
(coedited) *The Oneida Indian Journey: From New York to Wisconsin, 1784–1860* (Madison, Wis., 1999)
Chief Daniel Bread and the Oneida Nation of Indians of Wisconsin (Norman, 2002)

The Oneida Indians in the Age of Allotment, 1860–1920 is Volume 253 in The Civilization of the American Indian Series.

Library of Congress Cataloging-in-Publication Data

Hauptman, Laurence M.
    The Oneida Indians in the age of allotment, 1860–1920 / Laurence M. Hauptman, L. Gordon McLester III.
        p. cm.— (The civilization of the American Indian ; v. 253)
    Includes bibliographical references and index.
    ISBN 0–8061–3752–5 (alk. paper)
    1. Oneida Indians—Land tenure. 2. Oneida Indians—Education. 3. Oneida Indians—Claims. 4. Native allotments—United States—History. 5. Off-reservation boarding schools—United States—History. 6. United States. General Allotment Act (1887) I. McLester III, L. Gordon. II.Title. III. Series.

    E99.O45.H38 2006
    977.5004'975543—dc22

                                                    2005055951

1 2 3 4 5 6 7 8 9 10

Contents

Illustrations

Chief Cornelius Hill (1834–1907)
Dennison Wheelock, c. 1911
Laura Minnie Cornelius Kellogg, 1911
Oneida women lace workers, c. 1917
Oneida National Band, c. 1921

Map

The Wisconsin Oneida Indian Reservation under the Buffalo Creek
Treaty of January 15, 1838, and Amended United States–Oneida
Treaty of February 3, 1838   *Frontispiece*

Charts

Preface

This is the third volume in a continuing series on the history of the Oneida Nation. In 1988, Syracuse University Press published *The Oneida Indian Experience: Two Perspectives,* which provided an overview of these Native American peoples' history. In 1999, the University of Wisconsin Press published *The Oneida Indian Journey: From New York to Wisconsin, 1784–1860,* which described the pressures on these Indians during their treaty period, the reasons for their migration out of the Empire State, and their adjustment to their new home in the Badger State. The present volume contains interdisciplinary essays and community perspectives on another critical period. Professional historians join twenty-two voices of the Oneida community—tribal attorneys, educators, folklorists, genealogists, linguists, local historians, and tribal elders—to throw light on this vital but misunderstood era.

The current book has several unique features. First, the project is a joint one between the academic community and a Native American nation. Indeed, this collaborative project goes back a quarter of a century. Second, one of the editors and many of the authors in this volume are Oneida scholars, respected elders, community leaders, and tribal officials. Third, the editors of this volume recognize the importance of the continuing cultural, economic, kinship, legal, and political ties that bind the major Oneida Indian communities—Wisconsin Oneida, Oneida of the Thames (Southwold, Ontario), and Oneida, New York.[1] Although the Wisconsin Oneida community is today approximately three times larger than the two other communities combined, the other two communities both affected and still affect what happens in Wisconsin and cannot be completely separated in any treatment. Therefore, the editors have included an analysis of two major New York Oneida–initiated federal court cases—*United States v. Elm* (1877) and *United States v. Boylan* (1920). These two federal court decisions are reproduced in Part V of this book. The editors have included an article on Oneida Indian schooling in Canada, which stands in comparison with specific treatments of Oneida education at three Indian boarding schools in the United States. Fourth, despite the growing literature on the Dawes General Allotment Act of 1887 and its impact on American Indian nations, in the editors' opinion no historian has yet put federal policies into the full context of tribal life during this major era in American Indian history. By including numerous Oneida voices both past and present, along with analysis by both Indian and non-Indian scholars, the editors have attempted to fill this void.

This book features the rich historical record collected by the Oneidas themselves. The Oneida Nation of Indians of Wisconsin (ONIW) has one of the more documented histories of any Native American community. Their early post-contact history in New York has been preserved on fifty microfilm reels, *Iroquois Indians: A Documentary History,* edited by Francis Jennings and William N. Fenton, a project that was sponsored under the auspices of the Newberry Library in Chicago.[2] Because of their early involvement with white missionaries and attendance at mission schools as well as their significant presence at federal Indian boarding schools, the Oneidas also left behind extensive writings in the English language. The autobiography of Chief Cornelius Hill, the most important Wisconsin Oneida of the late nineteenth and early twentieth centuries, and the writings of his prominent daughter, Josephine Hill Webster, a remarkable entrepreneur who organized the women's lace-making guild, are made available for the first time. To explore the diverse impact and legacies of the federal boarding school experience, the editors have also transcribed and set forth here the oral histories of tribal elders presented at the Oneida Indian history conferences. Since some of the controversies of the past have present-day legal implications, the editors have also included a memoir written by Oneida tribal attorney Loretta Webster, who successfully worked for the return of tribal lands that had been lost in the age of allotment.

In addition to these Oneida voices, the editors have included selections from the rich oral histories collected by the Oneidas themselves during the New Deal. Working with anthropologists Morris Swadesh, Floyd Lounsbury, and Harry Basehart, the Wisconsin Oneidas established their Works Progress Administration (WPA) Language and Folklore Project. This collaborative effort produced an Oneida orthography for the first time; a vast body of other linguistic data on Iroquoian languages; an Oneida hymnal, which is still used on the reservation to the present day; and a voluminous collection of stories on every aspect of the Oneida experience.[3] For this book, the editors have selected representative Oneida WPA stories on the era from 1860 to 1920: concerning allotment policies under the Dawes General Allotment and Burke acts, boarding school days, the Civil War, cultural achievements by Oneida men and women in music and lacework, the impact of land loss, and tribal leadership.

Historians have long made use of the impressive materials collected by WPA projects. For example, first-rate scholars such as Theda Perdue and, more recently, David La Vere have effectively mined Grant Foreman's monumental WPA Indian-Pioneer History of Oklahoma; however, this project was dissimilar to the WPA Oneida Language and Folklore Project (OLFP).[4] Although both were part of the Federal Writers Project of the New Deal, Foreman did not have a linguistic focus. Unlike most of the Indian-Pioneer History of Oklahoma interviews, all the interviewers at Oneida were tribal members who collected and transcribed stories provided by other tribal members. Although there was a select number of interviewers, the storytellers provided a diverse cross section of the community.

La Vere has rightly warned that the use of elders' memories of specific events many decades old is fraught with danger.[5] Nevertheless, the editors believe that these interviews, placed side by side with scholars' analyses of the archival record, give the fullest picture of the Oneidas of this era. The records found concerning the allotment period in the National Archives confirm much of what was found in the WPA Oneida Language and Folklore Project; consequently, the oral record cannot be simply dismissed.

In 1950, the anthropologist Robert Ritzenthaler labeled the period from 1880 to 1930 the "transitional period" in Oneida history. He insisted that it was marked by "active cultural metabolism" caused by three main influences: (1) the Dawes General Allotment Act, (2) the federal boarding school educational policies, and (3) "the increasing interaction with the whites and absorption of white culture."[6] The editors decided to broaden the time period in order to include the Civil War, an event that had a shattering impact on individuals and a devastating effect on the Wisconsin Oneida community.

Despite Ritzenthaler's and other scholars' emphasis on the destructive forces at work (and there were many, as noted in this book), the editors have attempted to show that the Oneidas were not mere victims. They actively debated their future and developed entrepreneurial skills and legal strategies that have served them right down to the present day. They challenged their status under American law and sought compensation for land loss in federal court cases. Moreover, many Oneidas used their boarding school experiences to their own advantage and were not simply casualties of the institutions' rigid discipline and assimilationist agenda.

The book's end date is 1920. In that year, the acting commissioner of Indian affairs wrote that "practically all of the [Wisconsin] Oneida lands have been allotted, there being only approximately 150 acres unallotted."[7] In the same year, the Oneidas, in *United*

States v. Boylan, won their first federal case to protect their remaining lands in New York State, a decision that still influences Oneidas in pursuit of their claims right down to the present day. Thus, 1920 marks a low point for Oneidas in holding onto their Wisconsin lands as well as a new beginning in their quest for justice.

The editors have followed guidelines set forth in Mary-Jo Kline's *Guide to Documentary Editing,* prepared for the Association for Documentary Editing; nevertheless, wherever possible we have adopted a less intrusive policy of editing for the WPA stories. No attempt has been made to correct grammar, misspellings, or erratic punctuation except where necessary for the clarity of meaning. Scholars in need of more precision should consult copies of the originals on file in the Oneida Cultural Heritage Department, Oneida Nation of Indians of Wisconsin, Oneida.[8]

Notes

1. A fourth Oneida community exists at the Six Nations Reserve at Ohsweken, Ontario. They are largely descendants of Oneidas who followed Mohawk Joseph Brant and joined the British in the American Revolution, going into Canada after the war. They have less political ties to the other three major Oneida communities (Wisconsin; Southwold, Ontario; and New York) since these three communities are largely descended from the majority of Oneidas who joined the American Army in the Revolution.

2. Francis Jennings, William N. Fenton, et al., eds., *Iroquois Indians: A Documentary History of the Six Nations and Their League* (Woodbridge, Conn.: Research Publications, 1985), 50 microfilm reels.

3. For an early analysis of the first project under Swadesh and Lounsbury, see Jack Campisi and Laurence M. Hauptman, "Talking Back: The Oneida Language and Folklore Project, 1938–1941," *Proceedings of the American Philosophical Society* 125 (December, 1981): 441–48. A second project, under the direction of the late anthropologist Harry Basehart, followed the first project described in this article. See Herbert Lewis, ed., *Oneida Lives* (Lincoln: University of Nebraska Press, 2005).

4. Theda Perdue, *Nations Remembered: An Oral History of the Cherokees, Chickasaws, Choctaws, Creeks and Seminoles in Oklahoma, 1865–1907* (Norman: University of Oklahoma Press, 1980); David La Vere, *Life among*

the Texas Indians: The WPA Narratives (College Station: Texas A&M University Press, 1998).

5. La Vere, *Life among the Texas Indians,* xiv.

6. Robert E. Ritzenthaler, *The Oneida Indians of Wisconsin,* Public Museum of the City of Milwaukee Bulletin 19 (November 1950): 13.

7. E. B. Meritt to Edward E. Browne, November [received November 10], 1920, #91018-20-313 (Oneida), CCF 1907–1939, BIA, RG75, NA.

8. Mary-Jo Kline, *A Guide to Documentary Editing* (Baltimore: Johns Hopkins University Press, 1987).

Acknowledgments

The editors would like to thank the Oneida Nation of Indians of Wisconsin's Business Committee for supporting and promoting the historical conference that led to the publication of this volume. We would also like to thank Ms. Sherry Mousseau, principal of the Oneida Turtle School, and her staff for hosting the historical conference of August 14–16, 2003, in which 90 percent of the material in this volume was presented. Over two hundred people attended this historical conference held at a most beautiful facility, an Oneida elementary school run exclusively by the ONIW Education Department. The Oneida Cultural Heritage Department graciously allowed the editors the right to reprint an excerpt written by Loretta Webster for their publication *Oneida Land Returned* (2003). They also provided a genealogy of the Doxtator family and gave the editors full access to the rich WPA Oneida stories housed in their collection.

Dr. Herbert Lewis recovered a second series of Oneida WPA stories that had been warehoused at the University of Wisconsin and made helpful suggestions about which stories to use in this volume. Former Oneida tribal attorney Gerald Hill gave the editors insights into law and tribal politics in the age of allotment. Our friends Roy Black, Barbara Hollingshead, and David Jaman provided the editors with good cheer, excellent wit, and technical expertise during a difficult time. We would also like to acknowledge our editors at the University of Oklahoma Press for encouraging this project: John Drayton, Jo Ann Reece, Chuck Rankin, and Alessandra Jacobi. Most important, the two editors would like to thank their wives, Ruth and Betty, who for too many years have put up with their husbands' obsessions with Oneida history.

Abbreviations

ARCIA   Annual Reports of the Commissioner of Indian Affairs, U.S. Department of the Interior
BIA   Bureau of Indian Affairs
BL   Beinecke Library
Cong.   Congress
CCF   Central Classified Files
CCHS   Cumberland County Historical Society, Carlisle, Pa.
CWPR   Civil War Pension Records
DNR   Wisconsin Department of Natural Resources
FVR   Fox Valley and Western Railroad
GBAR   Green Bay Agency Records
GPO   U.S. Government Printing Office
LC   Library of Congress, Washington, D.C.
LM   Oneida Office of Land Management, ONIW.
MSS   Manuscript Collection
NA   National Archives, Washington, D.C.
NSTB   National Surface Transportation Board
NYSA   New York State Archives, Albany, N.Y.
NYSL   New York State Library, Manuscript Division, Albany, N.Y.
OIA   Office of Indian Affairs
OLFP   Oneida Language and Folklore Project, ONIW.

ONIW   Oneida Nation of Indians of Wisconsin, Oneida, Wis.

OR   U.S. War Department, *The War of the Rebellion: A Compilation of the Official Records of the Union and Confederate Armies*, 128 vols. Washington, D.C., GPO, 1880–1901.

RG   Record Group

SAI   Society of American Indians

sess.   session

SHSW   State Historical Society of Wisconsin (now WHS), Madison

Stat.   *U.S. Statutes at Large*

WHC   Wisconsin Historical Collections

WHS   Wisconsin Historical Society (previously SHSW)

WPA   Works Progress Administration

YU   Yale University

The Oneida Indians in the Age of
Allotment, 1860–1920

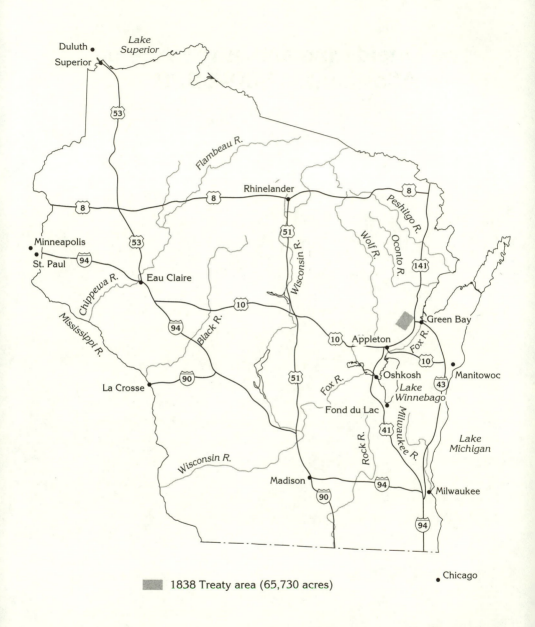

Duluth •

Lake Superior

Superior

{53}

{8}   Rhinelander   {8}

Flambeau R.   *Peshtigo R.*

{51}   *Wolf R.*   *Oconto R.*

Minneapolis •   {53}   {141}

St. Paul •   {94}

Chippewa R.   Eau Claire   {10}   Green Bay •

{94}   *Black R.*   {10}   Appleton   *Fox R.*

Wisconsin R.   {10}

Mississippi R.   {51}   Oshkosh   {43}   Manitowoc •

La Crosse •   {90}   *Fox R.*   *Lake Winnebago*

Fond du Lac •   {41}

Milwaukee R.   *Lake Michigan*

Wisconsin R.   *Rock R.*

Madison •   {94}   Milwaukee •

{90}

{94}

• Chicago

▨ 1838 Treaty area (65,730 acres)

The Wisconsin Oneida Indian Reservation under the Buffalo Creek Treaty of January 15, 1838, and Amended United States–Oneida Treaty of February 3, 1838

1

Introduction

One Hundred Years in Wisconsin

In August 1921, the Oneida Nation of Indians of Wisconsin (ONIW) celebrated the one-hundredth anniversary of its migration from New York to the Green Bay area. Bringing Indians together from all over the Midwest, the event was a tribal effort to show off the progress that the Oneidas had made over the century. The festivities were coordinated by a sizable contingent of Carlisle and Hampton graduates inculcated with the view that tribal progress was equated with cultural, legal, political, and social integration, namely, that Indians should take on the characteristics of the white world.[1]

In January 1922, the Hampton Institute school newspaper, the *Southern Workman,* reported on this celebration and printed a revealing description of Oneida, Wisconsin, showing the impact of allotment policies and the overall federal program of educational assimilation. The reporter, Caroline W. Andrus, had just toured reservations in the West. She explained what had happened to the Wisconsin Oneidas since the passage of the Dawes General Allotment Act of 1887:

> Oneida can hardly be called a reservation now. Nearly all the land has been allotted, the Government school and agency abolished,

and one clerk left in charge of the few Indians who cannot manage their own affairs. Last August the Oneidas celebrated the one hundredth anniversary of their coming to Wisconsin from New York. An occasion of this sort makes one realize that, no matter how slow progress may seem at times, vast change has taken, and is still taking place. The Oneidas are practically all citizens now, and their vote is an important factor in local elections. They occupy a number of such offices as town treasurer, town assessor, and road supervisor, active in the work of the school boards, and are making themselves felt in many ways.[2]

After describing the rich soil and excellent farms that some of the Oneidas tilled, she then indicated that others "have gotten so deeply in debt since they began to pay taxes that they lost their land, and a large number of white farmers had moved in." Andrus claimed that this dispossession "has proved a wholesome lesson, and has brought the loser to a realizing sense of the value of property." She added: "Some who have lost their allotments have gone to work and acquired other land." Andrus went on to "justify" the loss of the tribal estate: "The Indian, like the rest of mankind, prizes more highly that which he acquires by the sweat of his brow than that which he receives without effort."[3]

This description of Oneida was hardly what community observers had seen in 1860. Then, the nearly eleven hundred Oneida Indians of Wisconsin had a reservation of sixty-five thousand acres, which they owned in common. By the start of the Civil War, they had begun to overcome the trauma of their relocation from New York State to the West.

The Oneidas could look back with pride to their first four decades in Wisconsin because of their remarkable accomplishments. Under the steady, firm hand of their brilliant principal chief Daniel Bread, they had survived their removal to the West and had adapted to their new surroundings. They had withstood new removal pressures pushing for them to leave Wisconsin for the Indian Territory. These pressures continued unabated even after Andrew Jackson's presidency and were steady and frequent, made by various Indian agents as well as by territorial and state officials, until the Civil War. In spite of these efforts, the Oneidas established their tribal council of twelve and a principal chief as their governing body, built schools and churches, started productive farms, and celebrated every Fourth of July with both their Indian and non-Indian neighbors. Although not American citizens, they saw themselves as valuable allies of the United States.[4]

The world they carved out on the Wisconsin frontier was not without problems, however. These included internal political tensions dating back a half-century to their days in New York. The descendants of the Oneidas' First Christian Party, on one hand, and Orchard Party, on the other, had an uneasy truce that was slowly coming apart by the Civil War. Moreover, the Wisconsin Oneidas faced rapidly developing pressures from Green Bay mills, timber interests, and shingle processors who lusted after the hardwood forests then on the Oneida reservation.[5]

The Civil War and the aftermath of the Dawes General Allotment Act of 1887 were to change the Oneidas of Wisconsin beyond recognition. The war years weakened the Oneidas immensely. They now faced the third major crisis in their history—allotment. The first had been the American Revolutionary War era, a time of troubles when the Iroquois Confederacy split apart and the Oneidas were dispossessed of over five million acres of lands in the twelve years immediately following the Treaty of Paris in 1783. The second had been the Oneida migration from New York to Wisconsin between 1820 and 1838 caused by white land and transportation pressures. The third now was federal, state, and local efforts to convince the Oneidas by persuasion, schooling, or coercion to accept fee simple title and end their separate reservation existence.

Part I illustrates the devastation of war. The Civil War helped depopulate the reservation of its young men and shattered the lives of many who returned from battle. The home front was weakened by two major smallpox epidemics and by increasing pressures put on the Oneidas by the surrounding white population seeking Indian forest resources during and immediately following the war.[6] Questions concerning the Oneidas' legal status arose first in New York, when one veteran of the Civil War, Abraham Elm, decided to vote in a congressional election in 1876.[7]

Part II illustrates the federal Indian boarding school system, which was also founded after the Civil War. These schools were inspired by a veteran of the conflict, Captain Richard Henry Pratt, the founder of the U.S. Indian Industrial School at Carlisle, Pennsylvania, and by the head of the Freedmen's Bureau, Samuel Chapman Armstrong, the founder of the Hampton Institute, a largely African American school. These were extraordinary but controversial experiments in educating Indian youth. Both men had a profound effect on Oneidas—of whom 500 attended Carlisle between 1885 and 1918, and 193 attended Hampton between 1886 and 1923.[8] Under Pratt, Carlisle—less than forty miles from Gettysburg—was largely based on a military disciplinary model of conduct. Pratt's "Carlisle experiment" became the model for most other federal Indian boarding schools from 1879 to 1904, including one founded at Oneida in 1893 that closed in 1918.

Part III illustrates how Carlisle, although mostly known for promoting athletics, also emphasized military band and classical music, which, Pratt felt, encouraged discipline and Western culture. Out of Carlisle's martial music sprang an internationally famous band that influenced the development of reservation ensembles, described in three WPA stories. Moreover, vocal styles were brought from Hampton and combined with traditional hymn singing.

The importance of these experiences is highlighted in an extensive treatment of these schools in Parts II and III. Some, such as Dennison Wheelock, whose life is described in Part III, could never fully be accepted as a result of his ideas inculcated at Carlisle. Others such as Josephine Hill Webster, whose life is also described in Part III, became a community leader and an accomplished businesswoman with a sense of noblesse oblige.

By 1920, Wisconsin Oneidas had been dispossessed of almost all of their reservation. Part IV of this book focuses on how the land was lost. This section also analyzes the origins of allotment at Oneida. On February 8, 1887, Congress enacted the Dawes

General Allotment Act. Allotments were made in 1891 to Oneidas on the Oneida Reservation and patents were issued in June of the following year; however, the Indians could not alienate their individual lands since the act contained a twenty-five-year trust clause. Heads of Oneida families were allotted ninety acres of land; orphans under the age of twenty-one and single persons over twenty-one were each allotted forty-five acres; and minors received twenty-six acres. The only tribal lands not allotted were those reserved for churches, cemeteries, day schools, or those set aside for the future government boarding school.

After the Burke Act of 1906 allowed for the end of trust restrictions on most allotments, Oneida lands became subject to taxation, which resulted in impossible tax burdens, many fore-closures, and subsequent tax sales of property. Previously, in 1903, the Wisconsin state legislature had established the towns of Oneida in Outagamie County and Hobart in Brown County out of former Oneida tribal lands. Now the pressures became extreme. Impoverished Oneidas and those inculcated with the boarding-school mindset, believing that the reservation system was about to end, began taking their fee patents and selling them for the "quick money." Land speculators, in collusion with the Indian agent and, on occasion, a few Oneidas themselves, set out to separate the Indian allottees from their allotments. The final blow occurred in 1917, when a federal competency commission recommended that the trust period end the following year on almost all the remaining allotments. This meant that nearly all of the former original reservation lands were subject to tax burdens and/or could be alienated. Thus, by the New Deal, a majority of the nation's 3,078 members had been forced off their limited land base and were scattered, with large Oneida popula-tions in Milwaukee, Chicago, Detroit, and Minneapolis.[9]

Recently, historians have focused on the highly adaptive native community responses to outside pressures in this time period.[10] They have gone beyond what historian Emily Greenwald termed the "dispossession narrative," which treats American Indians simply as victims without describing the creative methods they developed and used to survive.[11] Greenwald focuses her attention on the Nez Perces and Jicarilla Apaches, both far distant from Oneida, Wisconsin. To her, despite being "politically and culturally marginalized, Indians were not inert." She added: "Sometimes they used tried and true strategies; at other times they innovated. In either case, Indians responded to new contexts on their own terms."[12]

The Wisconsin Oneidas' voices were not silent; they were diverse during this period. They demonstrated cultural and political adaptability. They held fast to their views of tribal sovereignty, pushing their Kansas claims and their belief that New York State had stolen their lands in the years between 1785 and 1846. As in the past with the likes of Rev. Samuel Kirkland at the Hamilton-Oneida Academy and with Rev. Eleazar Wheelock at Moor's Charity School, they sent their children off to learn the white man's ways in the hope of gaining insights in dealing with the dominant society that was crowding in upon them. In the post–Civil War era, the off-reservation equivalents had names such as Carlisle, Flandreau, Hampton, Tomah.

Although the boarding school system was often harsh and destructive to many Indians, Oneidas included, many of these Wisconsin Oneidas drew ideas and values from their experiences at boarding school. Some returned with certain agricultural, industrial, and leadership skills, and many benefited from the contacts and friendships they made with Indians from other native communities. Some of these boarding school students did not return to Oneida, Wisconsin; but others did, some to found and work at a federal Indian boarding school at Oneida where they were employed until the school's demise.

Despite the incredible land loss and the sizable acculturative pressures that they faced, the Oneidas fought back, as Parts III, IV, and V describe. The Oneidas have slowly rebounded from the 1920s onward. A detailed analysis of the incredible Oneida turn-around mentioned in the Afterword is beyond the scope of the present volume. The Oneidas' pursuit of justice, from the 1920s to the present, is the focus of the next installment of this planned four-volume history of these Wisconsin Iroquoian peoples.

Notes

1. *Souvenir Program, Oneida Indian Centennial, August 5–7, 1921,* pamphlet file, State Historical Society of Wisconsin (SHSW), in Bibliography as Wisconsin Historical Society (WHS).

2. Caroline W. Andrus, "Changing Indian Conditions," *Southern Workman* 51 (January 1922): 26.

3. Ibid.

4. Laurence M. Hauptman and L. Gordon McLester III, *Chief Daniel Bread and the Oneida Nation of Indians of Wisconsin* (Norman: University of Oklahoma Press, 2002), 43–126.

5. Ibid., 126–40.

6. Ibid., 136–62.

7. *United States v. Elm,* U.S. District Court, Northern District of New York—Albany, Case No. 15,048, 25 Fed. Cas. 1006–1008, December 24, 1877 (see Part V).

8. See the articles by Barbara Landis and Thelma Cornelius McLester in Part II. For the best treatment of Carlisle, see Genevieve Bell, "Telling Stories out of School: Remembering the Carlisle Indian Industrial School, 1879–1918." (Ph.D. dissertation, Stanford University, Palo Alto, Calif., 1998). For the best treatment of Hampton, see Donal F. Lindsey, *Indians at Hampton, 1877–1923* (Urbana: University of Illinois Press, 1995). For an overview of the American Indian boarding school experience in this period, see David Wallace Adams, *American Indians and the Boarding School Experience, 1875–1928* (Lawrence: University Press of Kansas, 1995).

9. Laurence M. Hauptman, *The Iroquois and the New Deal* (Syracuse: Syracuse University Press, 1981), 70–87.

10. One study that emphasizes Native American entrepreneurial skills during this dismal age is Brian Hosmer, *American Indians in the Marketplace: Persistence and Innovation among the Menominees and Metlakatlans, 1870–1920* (Lawrence: University Press of Kansas, 1999).

11. Emily Greenwald, *Reconfiguring the Reservation: The Nez Perces, Jicarilla Apaches and the Dawes Act* (Albuquerque: University of New Mexico Press, 2002), 5–6. Greenwald cites various examples of this narrative: D. S. Otis, *The Dawes Act and the Allotment of Indian Lands* (1934; reprint, edited with an introduction by Francis Paul Prucha, Norman: University of Oklahoma Press, 1973); J. P. Kinney, *A Continent Lost, a Civilization Won:*

Indian Land Tenure in America (Baltimore: Johns Hopkins Press, 1937); Loring Benson Priest, *Uncle Sam's Stepchildren: The Reformation of United States Indian Policy, 1865–1887* (New Brunswick, N.J.: Rutgers University Press, 1942); Leonard A. Carlson, *Indians, Bureaucrats, and Land: The Dawes Act and the Decline of Indian Farming* (Westport, Conn.: Greenwood Press, 1981); and Janet A. McDonnell, *The Dispossession of the American Indian, 1887–1934* (Bloomington: Indiana University Press, 1991). Greenwald suggests that Melissa L. Meyer's work started to break away from this dispossession model: *The White Earth Tragedy: Ethnicity and Dispossession at a Minnesota Anishinaabe Reservation, 1889–1920* (Lincoln: University of Nebraska Press, 1994).

12. Greenwald, *Reconfiguring the Reservation,* 153.

Part I

The Civil War

period of Oneida relocation from New York and adjustment to the Wisconsin setting and well into the age of allotment. Doxtator's life was shattered by the many infirmities that resulted from his military service in the Union Army. The article is followed by three WPA stories that focus on Cornelius Doxtator and his family, Oneida involvement in the Civil War, and this Indian nation's overall military service to the United States.[2]

Notes

1. For more on the Oneidas in the Civil War, see Laurence M. Hauptman, *The Iroquois in the Civil War: From Battlefield to Reservation* (Syracuse: Syracuse University Press, 1993), 67–84.

2. George and Paul C. Doxtator, Cornelius's sons, also served in the Fourteenth Wisconsin Volunteer Infantry. In the early years of the twentieth century, Paul—as one of the leaders of Oneida's "Indian Party"—opposed the fee simple patenting of trust lands and was a strong critic of the Federal Competency Commission of 1917 (See Hauptman, Part IV).

Introduction

General Aspects

For the Wisconsin Oneidas, the Civil War was a major disaster. Estimates of Oneida enlistment in the war range from 111 to 142 out of approximately 1,100 reservation residents. At least 46 of these volunteers for the Union were killed, went missing in action, or died of disease while at war. Moreover, the Oneida Indian Reservation in Wisconsin was ravaged by major smallpox epidemics, one that raged in 1862 and another in the second half of 1864 and early 1865.[1] White communities that suffered in the war were soon replenished with immigrants, but the Wisconsin Oneida Indian community experienced a 4–5 percent population decline, which had severe and debilitating repercussions well into the future. With the loss of so many of their men ripe for tribal leadership, the Oneidas faced a crisis after the Civil War at a time when allotment pressures were mounting. Whereas there had been only a few white settlers on the west side of the Oneida Reservation in the 1850s, after the Civil War the Oneidas found themselves surrounded by an aggressive non-Indian world desirous of their lands and forest resources.

The following article focuses on Cornelius Doxtator, a private in F Company, Fourteenth Wisconsin Volunteer Infantry, the most important Oneida unit in the Civil War. His life spanned the

2

Cornelius Doxtator

An Oneida Veteran of the Civil War

Laurence M. Hauptman and L. Gordon McLester III

Cornelius Doxtator was one of the more prominent Oneida Indians of the nineteenth century. His long life intersected with many of the major events affecting his people in this period—pressures to leave the Oneida homeland in central New York; migration, settlement, and adjustment in Wisconsin; efforts to press claims as well as to prevent tribal removal to Indian Territory; participation in the American Civil War; attempts to hold onto the chiefs' council in the postwar era; the allotment of the Oneida Indian Reservation; and tribal dispossession after the Burke Act of 1906. The focus here falls on two aspects of this important Oneida's life, namely, Doxtator's participation in the American Civil War and the conflict's impact on his and other Oneidas' lives.

Private Doxtator's war did not end with General Lee's surrender at Appomattox Courthouse. Until his death in 1911, Doxtator suffered physically and psychologically in part from conditions brought on or aggravated by his wartime service. Moreover, Doxtator's role in the war has taken on a life of its own, becoming part of an Indian legend. According to Oneida tradition, Private Doxtator helped recover the body of the famous general James

Birdseye McPherson, the highest ranking Union officer killed in action during the Civil War.[1]

Cornelius Doxtator (Dockstader) was born on the Oneida Indian Reservation in Madison County, New York, sometime between 1817 and 1819.[2] Doxtator was a descendant of prominent Oneida warriors of the late eighteenth and early nineteenth centuries: Honyerry and Hanyost Dockstader, distinguished officers in General Washington's Patriot Army in the American Revolution. Cornelius Doxtator was named after another Oneida relative who had fallen in the Battle of Chippawa fighting on the American side in the War of 1812.[3] During the Black Hawk War in the early 1830s, Cornelius, despite his youth, served as a cadet under Colonel William Dickens's command and acted as a scout around nearby Fort Howard. Before, during, and after this initial military service, Doxtator attended the Episcopal school at Duck Creek, which had been founded by Chief Daniel Bread and the missionary Solomon Davis soon after the bulk of Oneidas arrived in Wisconsin (then Michigan Territory) in the late 1820s.[4]

In 1839, Cornelius married Susan Doxtator, a distant cousin who had been born at Oneida, New York, around 1818. Cornelius and Susan Doxtator had ten children: George (Button), Abram, Paul, Mary Jane, Lucretia, Henry Duke, Cornelius Kemper, Edward, Daniel, and William. Two of their sons—George (Button) and Paul—served in Company F of the Fourteenth Wisconsin Volunteer Infantry. Susan's father, George, appears to have been very active in tribal politics and was an ardent supporter of the hereditary Oneida chiefs council before the nation established an elected system of sachems and councillors in 1879. Because Cornelius Doxtator was an educated man and many of the Old Chiefs council were not literate in English, young Cornelius assisted the chiefs by drafting documents and serving as an official representative to Albany, Madison, and Washington, D.C. His obituary described him as having been "a prominent member of his tribe," who had "represented the tribe before the Indian Department at Washington."[5]

Cornelius Doxtator enlisted along with another Oneida, George Powlas, at Fond du Lac on February 3, 1864, filling the quota for

Oakfield, Wisconsin, under the Enrollment Act of March 3, 1863.[6] His enlistment must be understood in the context of wartime exigencies. Because fewer recruits were coming forward, Congress passed the Enrollment Act, making every able-bodied male citizen and resident alien who had filed for naturalization aged twenty to forty-five eligible for the draft. Wisconsin was divided into six draft districts, coinciding with congressional districts. Each district acquired a set of federal draft officers—a provost marshal, a commissioner, an examining physician, and a board of enrollment. The enrollment boards were to make up lists of eligible conscripts for military duty, leaving off those they considered exempt on physical or other grounds. Once a man's name was drawn, he had ten days in which to report for duty, furnish a substitute, or buy exemption by paying a $300 fee. The War Department assigned each congressional district a quota based on a percentage of its eligible males minus the number of men who had already served in the army. A district would be given fifty days to fill its quota, and conscription would be a last resort in case of a shortfall after other methods—bounties, substitutions, and commutations—failed to meet the quota.[7]

Since there was substantial resistance to conscription in Wisconsin, the bounty system became the chief means of stimulating volunteering.[8] Districts competed for volunteers by offering greater bounties. Although not conscripted, Private Doxtator received a bounty of sixty dollars to enlist.[9] Most Oneidas were poor farmers, attracted not necessarily by flag-waving patriotism. Some followed their fathers' and grandfathers' footsteps into American military service; nevertheless, many were attracted by military bounties provided by towns, counties, the state of Wisconsin, and the federal government.

From 1860 through 1863, the Oneida economy was in shambles. Agriculture, largely of a subsistence level, had been the basis of the Oneida economy before the Civil War. Oneidas had supplemented their farming with hunting game, fishing in Duck Creek, and gathering wild berries. Leasing land to whites and selling timber became increasingly important. During the early 1860s, the Oneidas suffered two smallpox epidemics, two years of drought, severe winters leading to livestock losses, and they even witnessed a June frost. One annual report of the commissioner of Indian affairs during the war indicated that many Oneidas were destitute and that school-age children did not have clothes to attend the Indian school. Hence, for the Oneidas, military service, despite the risk, became a way out of a desperate economic condition. War bounties and the substantial relief efforts of the Quakers in early 1864 enabled the Oneidas to survive.[10]

Doxtator had another reason to enlist besides financial exigencies. His son Paul had enlisted one month before at Green Bay, and it may be suggested that Cornelius's paternal instincts came into play, perhaps to watch over his eldest boy. It was no coincidence that, upon enlisting, Cornelius was assigned to the same company as Paul, Company F of the Fourteenth Wisconsin. One month later, in March 1864, Cornelius's son George (Button) enlisted and was also assigned to F Company.[11]

Cornelius Doxtator—along with Henry Stephens and John Danforth, both of whom enlisted in March 1864—claimed to be forty-five years of age, by far the oldest Oneidas in the unit.[12] These three men, the elders, had the responsibility of watching over the young warrior-recruits in service, much as in earlier war parties of the seventeenth and eighteenth centuries. As one of the few Oneida Indians during the Atlanta Campaign who could both read and write English, Doxtator, who had faithfully served his Indian nation prior to the war, had the added responsibility of being the interpreter for the Indians, making the Oneidas' concerns known to their commanding officer.[13]

In the winter of 1864, the Fourteenth Wisconsin, which had excelled in holding the center of the Union line at the Battle of Shiloh in 1862 as part of the Army of the Tennessee, received veterans' furlough. In an effort to fill its decimated ranks to the original strength of 970 men, the adjutant general's office in Madison began recruiting new soldiers for the regiment. The Fourteenth was supposed to rendezvous at Camp Washburn in Milwaukee at the end of the furlough. Because of severe winter snowstorms that blocked the rails and impeded travel, many of the new recruits for the regiment failed to reach Milwaukee when

Chart 1
The Oneida Indian Soldiers of F Company,
Fourtheenth Wisconsin Volunteer Infantry

Antone, Abram	Johnson, Peter
Archiquet(te), Aaron	King, Adam
Archiquet(te), John	King, Nicholas
Archiquet(te), Solomon	King, Simon
Baird, Thomas	Nimham, Anthony
Bread, Daniel	Nimham, James
Chrisjohn, Daniel	Powlas (Powless), Anton[y]
Coulon, Henry	Powlas (Powless), George
Danforth, Cobus F.	Powlas (Powless), Moses
Danforth, John	Powlas (Powless), Peter I
Doxtator, Cornelius	Powlas (Powless), Peter II
Doxtator, George S.	Silas, Abram
Doxtator, Jacob S.	Silas, Isaac
Doxtator, Paul C.	Skenandore, Jacob
Hill, Abram	Stephens, Henry
Hill, Abram C.	Thomas, Thomas
Hill, David	Webster, Augustus
Hill, Henry	Webster, Edgar E.
Hill, Lewis	Webster, Lewis B.
James, Antoine (Anthony)	

Source: Descriptive muster rolls (Blue and Red Regimental Books,
SHSW) and regiment books (RG94, NA).

the furlough expired. Those who showed up on time included
thirty-four Oneidas who were sent to the Red River Division at
Vicksburg. Major Asa Worden remained behind in Milwaukee to
collect the stragglers, mostly Company E and a smattering of
troops from most of the other companies of the regiment.[14]

Among the latecomers were fifteen Oneidas, including Cornelius
and his two sons. Their "reward" for being delayed was to be
assigned to Worden's battalion of the Seventeenth Army Corps in
southeastern Tennessee. According to E. B. Quiner in his classic
Military History of Wisconsin (1866), this battalion "subsequently

joined General Sherman's Grand Army at Ackworth in the month of June, and performed gallant service against Atlanta."[15]

General Sherman's Division of the Mississippi, the so-called Grand Army of the West, contained between 100,000 and 112,000 of the best troops in the Union Army. Sherman's forces were led by three field commanders—generals James Birdseye McPherson, George "The Rock of Chickamauga" Thomas, and John M. Schofield. The Fourteenth Wisconsin, as part of General Francis Preston Blair's Seventeenth Corps, was part of McPherson's Army of the Tennessee. McPherson, a self-made man from Ohio, a West Pointer, and a friend of General Sherman, had between 23,000 and 25,000 men in his army. Although brilliant and a former professor of military science at West Point, he did not have the great field reputation of Thomas. Blair, a Missouri congressman, was from a prominent Maryland political dynasty, brother of President Lincoln's postmaster general.[16]

During this Atlanta Campaign, which lasted from May to September 1864, 4,423 Union and 3,044 Confederate soldiers were killed. In July and August alone, over 62,000 were hospitalized, one in every three federals each month. Many of those Union troops were not killed directly by Confederate bullets but later died of wound infections, dysentery, typhoid fever, and other diseases.[17]

General Joseph E. Johnston's 60,000–65,000 soldiers from the Confederate's Army of Tennessee and the Army of Mississippi tried to stymie Sherman and his generals. On June 18, 1864, the bulk of Johnston's Confederate troops began moving into newly constructed defensive positions along the ridgeline just west of Marietta, Georgia. Centered at Kennesaw Mountain, the Confederates' position rose to nearly seven hundred feet high.[18] The F Company Oneidas were then ordered to move around the Confederates' west flank, where fighting soon broke out. The Indians served as skirmishers on one side below the ridge. The firefight that resulted led to the wounding of Daniel Bread (not the Oneida principal chief of the same name). Bread was permanently disabled as a result of his wounds.[19] Confederate General Johnston then commanded General John Bell Hood to move his corps from the right to the threatened left flank, near a farm owned by Peter Valentine Kolb. Hood poorly planned his next move and did not reconnoiter. On June 22, 1864, outnumbered and with limited intelligence gathered, Hood, nevertheless, ordered his 11,000 Confederates to advance on the Union positions, coming within five hundred yards of the federal line. Outnumbering the Confederates, Union General Joseph Hooker then ordered his forty-cannon battery to open up.

The result was the Battle of Kolb's Farm.[20] Union forces opened up with a devastating barrage of canister, forcing Hood's forces to retreat. Hooker's infantry then followed up the victory. Historian Albert Castel has dubbed the battle a "one-sided slaughter." Hood's mistakes cost the Confederacy 1,500 men killed, wounded, and missing, while Hooker suffered less than 250 casualties at most; however, one of them was Oneida private Simon King who was shot "in the head while lying on the ground at Kennesaw Mountain" that same day.[21] Johnston skillfully regrouped after Hood's failure, and five days later, the Confederate general defeated General Sherman's army at the Battle of Kennesaw Mountain. In Sherman's worst defeat, the Union suffered more than 2,000 killed, wounded, and missing, whereas Confederate forces under General Johnston this time took 450 casualties.[22]

Although Private King was killed, the remaining Oneidas were held back, on duty along the Western and Atlanta Railroad guarding the "vital iron lifeline by a sudden enemy thrust to or above Big Shanty."[23] While the Battle of Kolb's Farm was being waged on the evening of June 22, Private Cornelius Doxtator and his Oneida comrade Henry Stephens were detailed to haul water back to camp for cooking. Both men had been put in charge of cooking for the company.[24] Private Elisha Stockwell, Jr., of the Fourteenth Wisconsin described this routine:

> I have spoken of our camp. Our camp was wherever we stopped. We had no tents, would stack arms, and the ground was our bed and the sky was our cover. We often slept with our belts on and gun by our side, ready to fall in at a moment's

warning. Two men were detailed to go back into the rear, where they could get wood and water, to make coffee and boil the beef when we got beef, and bring it up to us at the front.[25]

In the distance, Private Doxtator could probably make out the noise of Hooker's batteries pummeling Hood's defeated force. Instead of being wounded or killed by the Confederates' minié balls or canister, Private Doxtator, nevertheless, suddenly experienced excruciating pain. He was accidentally pierced in the groin by a protruding stick encountered in the dark. He later described it in affidavits as a severe injury, confirmed by three separate Oneida comrades in his company:

> I am the identical Cornelius Doxtator in affidavits who was a private in Company F, Fourteenth Regiment Wisconsin Infantry Volunteers during the late War of the Rebellion and who made an application for a pension under the laws granting pensions to disabled soldiers etc. I hereby solemnly swear that while we were on a march to reach Kenesaw [sic] Mountain when near Rome Ga. sometime in June A.D. 1864 we camped for the night and myself with others were sent for water to cook for the company; and on our return to the camp, night being dark, I ran against a stick, the end there of being in the ground, with the other end some distance above the ground. I ran against said stick, which struck me in my privates producing a severe rupture and breach. Said rupture and breach have continued ever since, and is now very severe and troublesome. I further declare that while in the service of the United States and line of duty as a soldier, I contracted chronic catarrh and the small pox [sic] and from said diseases I have suffered ever since. For these injuries and diseases, I pray that my claim may be considered, and all matters be referred to Malcolm Sellers of Fort Howard, Brown County as my attorney of record.[26]

Despite his painful injury, Doxtator was not treated by doctors in the field hospital, and he went off to pioneer duty the next day.[27] Undoubtedly, Doxtator had other things on his mind. Perhaps embarrassed by the nature of his injury, he did not immediately disclose it to his commanding officer when he reported back to camp. To him, his injury was not comparable to those of others. After all, seven Oneidas in Company F perished during the Civil War. Two died of specific diseases (typhoid fever and dysentery), three died from unknown causes, and two were killed in action.[28]

A month later, General McPherson was killed. In attempting to repair a gap in the Union line, the general ran into Confederate skirmishers. The general's body was then stripped of his watch, sword, belt, field glasses, and dispatch book.[29]

A Union order went out to secure the general's body. In his Civil War pension application, Private Cornelius Doxtator repeatedly claimed that he served as "a volunteer to rescue the body of General McPherson on the 22nd day of July 1864 from within the lines of the enemy from which service he was granted a furlough to visit his family."[30] The U.S. Bureau of Pensions investigated Doxtator's assertion and found that Private George Reynolds, a non-Indian of Company D of the Fifteenth Iowa Volunteer Infantry, severely wounded at the time, reached the dying general. Reynolds "was chiefly instrumental in recovering his [McPherson's] body going with two of his staff officers pointing out the body and assisting in putting it in an ambulance" while "under heavy fire from the enemy [and] while his wound was still uncared for." Consequently, Private Reynolds was awarded the Gold Medal of Honor, now known as the Congressional Medal of Honor.[31]

Doxtator's claim can be disputed in other ways as well. At times, he gave an alternate explanation for his furlough:

[of] about 15 Indians in my Co. and regiment, I was the only one who could speak English and almost everything had to be done through me as interpreter. We got to Atlanta and I understood that we were to remain there a month. I had heard from my family that they were sick and destitute. I had not received any pay yet and I went to General [Francis Preston] Blair and told him and he gave me a furlough of 30 days. I had only been home about 8 days when I was taken sick with small pox. I had been in the service about 8 months when I got furloughed.[32]

Moreover, at the time of McPherson's death, F Company Indians were pinned down by Confederate fire. On the afternoon of June 22, 1864, the Fourteenth Wisconsin were engaged in repulsing a Confederate advance in what is generally referred to as the Battle of Bald Hill. They had been on picket duty when the Confederates attacked. Along with Companies E and F and the Eleventh Iowa Volunteer Infantry, they dug in, holding "the small fort on the hill and the immediate line of works connected with it." Lieutenant Colonel J. C. Abercrombie of the Eleventh Iowa later wrote in his official report: "Many acts of bravery were performed by officers and men of the regiment which might be mentioned did time and opportunity permit."[33]

Other evidence also suggests that Private Doxtator was not involved in the rescue of McPherson's body. Three of Cornelius Doxtator's Oneida comrades in arms in Company F, including his son George, dictated affidavits to the U.S. Bureau of Pensions in support of their fellow Oneida's pension application or pension increase. Not one of them mentioned the private's rescue of McPherson's body, a fact that would have been worthy of description. Instead, they described Doxtator's run-in with a stick and his injury to his "private parts." These statements were repeated by the soldier's neighbors at Oneida and by his physician who had tended to his medical needs for thirty-five years. Equally revealing, there is no letter from his son Paul in the pension records to confirm this important event. It should be noted that Paul was given a furlough to return home in October 1864, about the same time his father was also allowed to go back to Oneida, Wisconsin.[34]

After the "rescue," Private Doxtator participated in the siege of Atlanta, the decisive Union victory that spelled the beginning of the end for the Confederate States of America. After reporting for duty in August through mid-October during those momentous days of the war, Doxtator is listed as a "deserter" from November 1864 onward.[35] It should be pointed out that the word "desertion" was used for AWOL (absent without leave) during the Civil War. The U.S. Bureau of Pensions accepted Doxtator's affidavits that he had been given official furlough to return home in the fall of 1864 and that, while home, he had contracted smallpox, which delayed his return to his unit until he was officially mustered out with a general discharge in May 1865.[36] There is also evidence that, while recuperating, Doxtator remained loyal to the Union cause. He later claimed that he went to Madison after he recovered from smallpox but was rejected because of poor health. There is evidence that he helped in recruiting Oneida soldiers for the war effort while back on the reservation during his convalescence.[37]

Then what can explain the story concerning this highly respected Oneida's rescue of General McPherson's body? There are several explanations. This unfortunate Oneida clearly suffered for decades as a result of his Civil War service. Historian Eric T. Dean has written about the aftermath of the conflict, suggesting that veterans in general suffered from high rates of what today we call post-traumatic stress disorder. "Artillery and high explosives produced a number of psychiatric casualties in the Civil War that seemed at times almost identical to the hysterias, mutism, and uncontrollable shaking produced by the barrages on the Western Front in World War I." Dean added, pointing out one battle of the Atlanta Campaign: "The demoniacal appearance of the men—enraged, blackened faces, screaming, firing their rifles in a frenzy, grappling in hand-to-hand combat—was matched by the surreal aspect of the battlefield, its smoke, smell, noise, confusion, and havoc."[38]

At the aftermath of the Battle of Kennesaw Mountain, numerous Union and Confederate bodies lay for two days in the steaming Georgia sun before a truce was finally arranged. The rapidly putrefying corpses were later described by federal Colonel Melancthon Smith: "a most revolting appearance, as black as negroes [sic]—enormously swollen, fly blown, emitting an intolerable stench."[39] A month later, at Peachtree Creek near where McPherson had fallen, Private Stockwell described the scene: "one place where the dead Rebs were piled three deep, and they were scattered quick thick as far as we could see through the woods, which was [sic] quite thick."[40]

Indeed, the death of McPherson was a defining moment in the entire Atlanta Campaign, one that became indelible in Private Doxtator's mind, which was failing by the mid-1880s. The general's death became his touchstone, his badge of honor for serving in the "Grand Army of the West." To Americans of the postwar generation, McPherson and his heroic death took on legendary proportions. To include oneself in the legend would give more meaning to one's postwar existence, which was a miserable one at that, filled with chronic illness and extreme poverty. Yet, as a survivor of the war, Private Doxtator was undoubtedly affected by embarrassment describing how and where he was injured, the same day his fellow Oneida, Simon King, paid the ultimate sacrifice.

In the fifteen years after the Civil War, Doxtator still commanded respect in the Wisconsin Oneida community. He served as a representative to Washington, as a delegate opposing Chief Cornelius Hill's and Reverend Edward Goodnough's efforts in the late 1870s to establish an elected tribal government, to replace the hereditary chieftainship system put in place on the Oneidas' removal to Wisconsin in the 1820s. Much like traditionalists of the past, Doxtator viewed elected systems with apprehension.[41]

By the late 1880s, the U.S. Bureau of Pensions had awarded him a pension, since the affidavits and other supporting evidence had erased the false charges of his desertion and verified everything that Private Doxtator claimed, with the exception of the McPherson story. He was described in the records as an upstanding moral man by his Oneida comrades and his Oneida neighbors, his white doctor, and his white attorney. As a survivor of the hell known as the Civil War, however, he continued to bear the physical and psychological scars of the conflict.

His Civil War pension record documents that he had suffered from smallpox, had a "continuous pain in the head above the eyebrows," had limited vision, was going deaf, had severe rheumatism, gasped for breath being affected by a myriad of respiratory problems, suffered from a hernia with a perforation the size of "a small orange," and showed the initial signs of dementia. He could do no manual labor and was totally dependent on his Oneida neighbors and relatives.[42]

In 1893, Henry Smith, his neighbor, and William Doxtator, his youngest son, wrote to the Bureau of Pensions:

> We are acquainted with the above claimant Cornelius Doxtator late a private Company "F," Fourteenth Wisconsin Vol's. That we personally and well know his financial and physical condition, that financially he is without property either real or personal from which any income is derivable, that he has no income from any source whatsoever, that no person is legally bound to support him nor to contribute to the same, that he has no income property or support. That physically he is totally and wholly incapacitated for the performance of any and all manual labor, that his physical condition is such that he is almost an entire charge on his friends, that he is nearly blind, and has to have assistance to get around, that he is entirely dependant on others for support and maintenance, and that he is support[ed] by the contributions of friends and relatives who are not legally bound to contribute to the same, if not for their assistance he would be a charge on public charity of his friends and relatives, we would ask that under the circumstances that his claim for pension be taken up out of its order made special and settled at as early a date as possible, we are positively sure if any claimant who has claim pending knew of the destitute and helpless condition of the claimant there would be no fault found with such action being taken.[43]

Similar observations of Doxtator's health were made by at least three other Oneidas—Moses Coulon, Elizabeth Johnson, and Louis Hill.[44]

The Civil War took more than 620,000 lives. It also had a long-standing psychological effect on individuals such as Private Doxtator. The survivors of the war had to recall the horrors of the battlefield; the guilt of surviving while comrades in arms had been killed in action; the sight of body parts, amputations, and other aspects of the primitive conditions of field hospitals; the stench of decaying bodies on the battlefield; the miserable conditions in rain-filled trenches with their putrid smells. All these and more Private Doxtator remembered all the time his bones ached from chronic rheumatism. Added to this, Doxtator had to contend with the U.S. Bureau of Pensions, an agency that made the Office of Indian Affairs, later renamed the Bureau of Indian Affairs, look both benevolent and efficient! Although Doxtator was to secure a pension under the act of 1890, the munificent sum of twelve dollars a month raised to twenty dollars in 1907, for over a quarter of a century he had to fight his way through the red tape of this insensitive process. He even hired Malcolm Sellers, a white attorney from Fort Howard, in the long drawn out effort to secure and then increase his pension.[45]

The Civil War veteran's problems compounded in the last two decades of his life. Joseph C. Hart, the controversial Indian agent at Oneida and superintendent of the local boarding school there, became his legal guardian after Cornelius's wife died in 1887 and the Civil War veteran's health continued to fail. In 1906, according to his son Paul, a deed "was issued by the Department of the Interior for forty-five acres of [Father's] Corneil [sic] Doxtator land in favor of William Larson." Perhaps taking advantage of Doxtator's advanced age and ill health at the time and ignoring Paul's power of attorney, the transaction went through. After complaining to the Interior Department, the family was successful in canceling the Larson deed. However, later on, this same trust patent land was deeded away without the consent of Cornelius Doxtator's heirs. The controversy over these lands continued well into the 1920s.[46]

By the time of his death in 1911, Cornelius Doxtator was described as suffering from "senile decay."[47] The only saving grace for this good but pathetic man was that he could no longer remember what he and his people had experienced in the last four decades of his life.

Notes

1. Laurence M. Hauptman, Oneida field notes, 1977–2003. Hauptman heard Private Doxtator's story told on separate occasions over the years, in

Wisconsin and in Washington, D.C., including by two Oneida community historians and an Oneida Civil War reenactor.

2. Judy Jordan, comp., "Descendants of Cornelius Dockstader," Genealogical Records, Oneida Cultural Heritage Department, ONIW; Toni Jollay Prevost, *Indians from New York in Wisconsin and Elsewhere* (Bowie, Md.: Heritage Books, 1995), 83; Cornelius Doxtator's Civil War pension file, Certificate No. 82.104, Civil War Pension Records (CWPR), War Department Records, RG94, NA. Employing the 1900 federal census, Prevost suggests that Doxtator was born in 1817; Doxtator's CWPR puts his birth in 1818; Oneida tribal records have the year of his birth as 1819.

3. Jordan, "Descendants of Cornelius Dockstader."

4. *De Pere News,* October 18, 1911, obituary.

5. Ibid.; Jordan, "Descendants of Cornelius Dockstader." Cornelius Doxtator's Claim to U.S. Bureau of Pensions, January 15, 1898; Guardian's Application (Joseph S. Hart) for Reimbursement, November 23, 1911, both in Cornelius Doxtator's CWPR, RG94, NA.

6. Blue and Red Regimental Books, Company F, Fourteenth Wisconsin Volunteer Infantry, SHSW. The same is also found in the Regimental Books, F Company, Fourteenth Wisconsin Volunteer Infantry, Records of the Adjutant General's Office, RG94, NA.

7. For a fuller treatment of the Civil War recruitment in Wisconsin, see Hauptman, *Iroquois in the Civil War,* 70–73; Richard N. Current, *The History of Wisconsin: The Civil War Era, 1848–1873* (Madison: SHSW, 1976), 311–35; Frank L. Klement, *Wisconsin and the Civil War* (Madison: SHSW, 1963), 33–42; E. B. Quiner. *Military History of Wisconsin; Record of the Civil and Military Patriotism of the State, in the War for the Union* (Chicago: Clarke Publishing, 1866), 139–49.

8. For instances of draft resistance in Wisconsin, especially from Milwaukee to Green Bay in the eastern part of the state, see Eugene C. Murdock, *One Million Men: The Civil War Draft in the North* (Madison: SHSW, 1971), 30, 41; James W. Geary, *We Need Men: The Union Draft in the Civil War* (DeKalb: Northern Illinois University Press, 1991), 40, 105; Current, *History of Wisconsin,* 2:332.

9. Cornelius Doxtator's Compiled Military Service Record, Records of the Adjutant General's Office, RG94, NA.

10. ARCIA (1865): 43, 443–44. Joseph Powless Diary, 1863–1865, University of Wisconsin Area Research Center, Green Bay.

11. Blue and Red Regimental Books, Company F, Fourteenth Wisconsin Volunteer Infantry, SHSW.

12. Ibid.

13. Affidavit of Cornelius Doxtator, November 22, 1887, in his CWPR, RG94, NA.

14. Quiner, *Military History of Wisconsin,* 606–609.

15. Ibid., 608.

16. Although perhaps too critical of General Sherman, by far the best account of the Atlanta Campaign is Albert Castel's *Decision in the West: The Atlanta Campaign of 1864* (Lawrence: University Press of Kansas, 1992).

17. James O. Breeden, "A Medical History of the Later Stages of the Atlanta Campaign," *Journal of Southern History* 35 (1969): 54–56; Robert W. Athearn, "An Indiana Doctor Marches with Sherman," *Indiana Magazine of History* 49 (1953): 410; Oscar O. Winther, *With Sherman to the Sea* (Baton Rouge: Louisiana State University Press, 1943), 122.

18. For Johnston and his army, see the treatment in Thomas L. Connelly, *Autumn of Glory: The Army of Tennessee, 1862–1865* (Baton Rouge: Louisiana State University Press, 1971). See also Castel, *Decision in the West,* 291–324.

19. Daniel Bread's Compiled Military Service Record; Daniel Bread's medical records; Daniel Bread's CWPR no. 102,617, all in RG94, NA.

20. Castel, *Decision in the West,* 291–99.

21. Widow's application [Evalina King], Simon King's CWPR no. 67, 448, RG94, NA.

22. Castel, *Decision in the West,* 303–324.

23. Ibid., 301.

24. Affidavit of Cornelius Doxtator, June 15, 1893; Affidavit of Henry Stephens, July 21, 1888; Affidavits of George S. Doxtator, August 11, 1891, August 19, 1899; all in Cornelius Doxtator's CWPR, RG94, NA.

25. Byron R. Abernethy, ed., *Private Elisha Stockwell, Jr., Sees the Civil War* (Norman: University of Oklahoma Press, 1958), 87–88.

26. Affidavit of Cornelius Doxtator, May 4, 1887, Cornelius Doxtator's CWPR, RG94, NA. Henry Stephens, George S. Doxtator, and Henry Coulon, Oneidas all in Company F, confirmed the accident: Affidavit of Henry Stephens, July 21, 1888; Affidavits of George S. Doxtator, August 11, 1891, August 19, 1899; Affidavits of Henry Coulon, September 12, 1891,

June 15, 1893; Affidavit of Henry Coulon and George S. Doxtator, April 12, 1905; all in ibid.

27. Affidavit of George S. Doxtator, August 19, 1899; Cornelius Doxtator's Declaration for Original Invalid Pension, February 25, 1890, in ibid.

28. Blue and Red Regimental Books, Company F, Fourteenth Wisconsin Volunteer Infantry, SHSW.

29. Castel, *Decision in the West,* 398–402; Elizabeth J. Whaley, *Forgotten Hero: General James B. McPherson, the Biography of a Civil War General* (New York: Exposition Press, 1955), 159.

30. Affidavit of Cornelius Doxtator, August 1885; Cornelius Doxtator's Original Invalid Pension Claim, November 29, 1887, in his CWPR, RG94, NA.

31. General Francis Preston Blair General Order No. 8, commendation of Private George J. Reynolds, July 26, 1864, in ibid.

32. Cornelius Doxtator, Original Pension Claim, December 16, 1885; Affidavit of Cornelius Doxtator, November 29, 1887, in ibid.

33. *OR,* ser. 1, vol. 38, pt. 3, pp. 599–600.

34. Blue and Red Regimental Books, Company F, Fourteenth Wisconsin Volunteer Infantry, SHSW.

35. Cornelius Doxtator's Compiled Military Service Record, RG94, NA.

36. "The charge of desertion removed. He was absent without leave from Oct. 20, 1864 to April 20, 1865." R. C. Drum (U.S. adjutant general) to Commissioner of Pensions, June 12, 1889, in Cornelius Doxtator's CWPR, RG94, NA.

37. Affidavit of Cornelius Doxtator, August 1885 (stamped August 20, 1885); Cornelius Doxtator's Original Claim for a Pension, December 16, 1885; Affidavit of Cornelius Doxtator, January 25, 1888, all in ibid. Deborah B. Martin in her history of Brown County quotes Provost Marshal E. C. Merrill of Wisconsin: "the Oneida Indians, always a warlike people, organized a company of sharpshooters under command of Cornelius Doxtator." Besides reinforcing stereotypes about the Oneidas, either Martin or Merrill misidentified Doxtator as being in the Third Wisconsin. We believe that this was the same Cornelius Doxtator of Company F, Fourteenth Wisconsin, which would confirm at least part of his story. Deborah B. Martin, *History of Brown County, Wisconsin: Past and Present* (Chicago: S. J. Clarke, 1913), 1:209.

38. Eric T. Dean, Jr., *Shook over Hell: Post-Traumatic Stress, Vietnam and the Civil War* (Cambridge, Mass.: Harvard University Press, 1997), 46–69.

See also the article on Wisconsin veterans by James Marten, "Exempt from the Ordinary Rules of Life: Researching Postwar Adjustment Problems of Union Veterans," *Civil War History* 47 (2001): 57–70.

39. Quoted in Castel, *Decision in the West,* 323.

40. Abernethy, *Elisha Stockwell,* 92–93.

41. See Lavinia Elm's "They Had Been to School" (OLFP.ONIW), reprinted in Chapter 3. Petition of Oneida chiefs to Secretary of the Interior Carl Schurz, July 17, September 8, 1879; letter of Cornelius Doxtator and George Doxtator to E. Stephens, U.S. Indian Agent, October 6, 1879; Cornelius Doxtator to Carl Schurz, January 14, 1880; all in microcopy 234, reel 335, OIA, GBAR, RG75, NA.

42. Cornelius Doxtator's Original Claim for a Pension, December 16, 1885; Doxtator's Claim for Invalid Pension, February 25, 1890; Doxtator's Affidavits of January 25, August 11, 1888, September 17, 1890, March 2, 1892; Doxtator's Invalid Pension Application, May 4, 1889, April 3, 1901; Bureau of Pensions Surgeon's Certificate, April 3, 1901; Affidavit of Dr. Israel Green (Doxtator's Green Bay physician), September 14, 1885; Acting Commissioner Bureau of Pensions to Edward Doxtator, July 24, 1907; all in Cornelius Doxtator's CWPR, RG94, NA.

43. General Affidavit Henry Smith and William Doxtator, February 11, 1893, ibid.

44. Affidavits of Moses Coulon and Elizabeth Johnson, January 1891; Affidavit of Louis Hill, August 2, 1899, all in ibid.

45. Affidavit of Malcolm Sellers, August 2, 1894, in ibid.

46. Paul C. Doxtator to Senator Robert LaFollette, May 29, September 6, 1917, May 13, 1918, in the file Indian Affairs—Oneida, 1912–1923, LaFollette Family Papers LC. Protracted investigations concerning Cornelius Doxtator's allotment continued well into the 1920s; see no. 91141-09-312 (Oneida), parts 1, 2, 3, CCF 1907–1939, BIA RG75, NA.

47. Paul and Henry Doxtator to U.S. Commissioner of Pensions, June 29, 1907; Joseph C. Hart to Bureau of Pensions, November 23, 1911; both in Cornelius Doxtator's CWPR, RG94, NA.

Three Oneida WPA Stories

Editors' Note: The following WPA story describes the Doxtators as educated Oneidas who had served the nation even before the Civil War.

They Had Been to School

Lavinia Elm

The Doxtators were educated. Cornelius Doxtator and Thomas Doxtator and Mary Ann Doxtator were graduated from some large school where they attended in some white community. This Cornelius knew quite a good deal concerning law. He used to always be writing and getting letters from [Wisconsin] Governor [William] Dodge. He used to also write to Washington D.C. asking the officials different things in regards to Oneida claims. He had a hobby of taking a letter out of his pocket in a hurry if he met anyone, saying, "I just got a letter from Governor Dodge."

But Thomas Doxtator learned how to interpret, so he used to interpret in church and he was considered a very good interpreter. And Mary Ann Doxtator had taken the study of nursing, and she used to take care of the sick. She even went among the white people nursing, and working until she got quite old.

Editors' Note: The following WPA story recounts an Oneida oral tradition about their service in the Union army and its impact.

The Civil War

Thomas Elm

About the time of the war which started in sixty-one [1861] and which ended in sixty-five [1865], during that time an eagle stayed around where the Oneidas were. When the fighting got furious, the eagle would be flying around above. After the war he had only a few feathers left. It was from being grazed by many bullets in the fight. Now I don't know who brought him back, but at present he stands so big and proud in Madison. Before they would receive an order to meet the enemy, he would be flying above. He must have been telling them of the coming events. While the battle is raging, every so often he would surprise them with his appearance from the thick clouds of smoke. It is said, that it was noticeable that he had lost a lot of his feathers. This is the tale told by those who had been there.

Editors' Note: The Oneidas have proudly served in the U.S. military since the American Revolution.

Oneida Soldiers

Thomas Elm

Oneidas were always brave men[.] [T]here were now five wars that the President had and each time the Oneidas took part in his favor. The first war was when Washington fought against England [American Revolution]. They helped him. And the war of 1812, and when the French [possibly the Undeclared War with France, 1797–1800] fought against this country, and when Lincoln fought against the South and the Spanish [American] war with this country and the last war [World War I] when they went across the seas to fight. And which ever side the Oneidas were on was always the winner. The war of 1861, was when the Oneidas showed their true fighting spirit[.] [S]ome of them were not of age but they volunteered in the army and some of them went in place of white men who could pay them seven hundred dollars to go in their place. And they fought to the end of the war until they were discharged[.] [A]s long as these old soldiers lived[,] they were drawing pensions. But now they are all dead.

Editors' Note: Despite the pride the Oneidas had in their significant service in the American military, their separate status as an Indian nation remained in peril even after their enlistment in the Civil War. The Oneidas witnessed what had befallen their Wisconsin Indian neighbors the Winnebagos (Ho-Chunks), who were removed from the state for the fourth time in 1874. Since the late colonial period, the Oneidas always tried to educate their children in two worlds—to preserve their traditions and to learn the new ways of the whites. As migrants from central New York to north-central Wisconsin, they were masters of adaptation. With the poor level of education found at the reservation schools in the 1870s and not able to provide the basic wherewithals for their children, the Oneidas began sending their boys and girls away to be fed, clothed, and educated. A few received scholarships to Lawrence University in Appleton by the late 1870s. By the mid-1880s, Oneida children were recruited in great numbers to attend Carlisle and Hampton. With the expansion of the federal Indian boarding-school system, they went to Flandreau, Haskell, and Tomah. Their own government school, founded at Oneida in 1893, became a "feeder school" to these much larger institutions until its closing in 1918.

Part II

Boarding School Days in the Age of Allotment

Introduction

Captain Pratt and His Legacy

Richard Henry Pratt, a former Union cavalry officer, helped shape federal Indian educational policies after the Civil War. Pratt later served on the Trans-Mississippi frontier during the Red River War of 1874–1875. At the end of this Indian war, he brought a group of Plains Indian prisoners to Fort Marion at St. Augustine, Florida. Subsequently, he was permitted to release the prisoners from their shackles and close confinement and to allow them to work for the local white community. He also began an experiment, namely, teaching these Indians English and other basic skills.[1]

In 1878, Pratt was assigned to Hampton Normal and Agricultural Institute in Hampton, Virginia, and he took some of these former Indian prisoners with him to further their so-called mental and manual training. Hampton had been founded ten years earlier by General Samuel C. Armstrong for the educational needs of ex-slaves. Soon after, with Armstrong's backing, Pratt went west to recruit additional Indian students. Until 1912, the federal government underwrote this Indian educational experiment at Hampton, a largely black institution. In all, 193 Oneidas were to attend Hampton until 1923. Some of the more prominent Oneidas of the twentieth century—such as nurse Lavinia Cornelius and businesswoman Josephine Hill Webster—attended the school (see

McLester, Part II). Moreover, the vocal traditions brought back from Hampton directly affected the Wisconsin reservation community.[2]

Pratt's belief in the success of his plan led him to push for his own separate Indian industrial school. Unlike Armstrong, Pratt had a long acquaintance with the Indian world. He approached Secretary of the Interior Carl Schurz, the noted German American intellectual and fellow Civil War veteran, about a school for Indians. Schurz gave him permission to use the abandoned military outpost at Carlisle, Pennsylvania. To Pratt, segregating Indians on reservations was wrong, extremely damaging, and he considered the old Indian ways totally outmoded and unsuitable for the age. U.S. citizenship and total Indian integration into American society had to be the goal.[3]

Washington policy makers believed in the necessity of bringing "civilization" to the Indians, a multifaceted plan to absorb them into American society as quickly as possible. This policy had its roots in the earliest days of the republic. Historian Frederick Hoxie has dubbed this late-nineteenth- and early-twentieth-century version of this plan "the campaign to assimilate the Indian." This so-called Americanization process included encouraging missionary activities on reservations (although Pratt was no friend of any missionary association) in order to stamp out "paganism"; the exposure of the Indians to white Americans' ways through compulsory education and sending children—boys and girls— off the reservation to boarding schools; the eventual destruction of the reservation system and the allotment of reservation land to individual Indians to "instill" personal initiative, required by the free enterprise system; and, finally, in return for accepting land-in-severalty, the "rewarding" of U.S. citizenship. Reform groups such as the Indian Rights Association, the Women's National Indian Association, and the Lake Mohonk Conferences of Friends of the Indian pushed this agenda because they felt these policies were essential to force the Indian to bridge the gap from "barbarism" and "savagery" to civilization. Behind their policy proposals was the seldom challenged assumption that it was possible to "kill the Indian but save the man."[4]

The establishment of an elaborate countrywide system of federal boarding schools was integral to these paternalistic and misguided racial assumptions. However, there were other reasons for the establishment of these schools and for Oneida attendance at these faraway institutions. The Oneidas' exposure to Western education was hardly a new idea. Presbyterian missionary Samuel Kirkland had started his educational efforts as early as the 1760s, which led to the establishment of a school for Oneidas in central New York. By the 1790s, Oneidas were attending Kirkland's Hamilton-Oneida Academy (later Hamilton College) and Eleazer Wheelock's Moor's Charity School (later Dartmouth College). Under chiefs Daniel Bread and Jacob Cornelius, an Episcopal- and Methodist-affiliated school was established in Wisconsin by the mid-1830s.[5] By the 1870s, Oneidas were being educated in four day schools (later six) on the reservation; by the late 1870s, several Oneida students were also sent to study at Lawrence University in Appleton, Wisconsin.[6] Thus, by the time Carlisle opened in 1879, the Oneidas, unlike many other Indians, had long been familiar with Western education.

Privately run mission schools on the Oneida reservation in the post–Civil War era were totally inadequate to meet either the white societal goals of absorbing the Indians or the reservation community's aspirations to educate their children. The schools were overcrowded, poorly equipped, and largely underfunded by these eastern missionary societies. The curriculum was limited at best. The federal Indian agent's report in September 1875 revealed much about the woeful state of education on the reservation: "These schools are schools in name only, although there is some improvement the past few years; but it matters not how efficient teachers they may have, no one can make good or even passable scholars of pupils who can come or stay away at their pleasure." The Indian agent indicated that only sixty out of four hundred school-age children were in daily attendance. The annual reports of the Indian agent over the next decade show that the limited attendance of students at these schools was not simply caused by parents' resistance to Western schooling but, among other things, was a result of the extreme poverty faced by the Oneidas in the decades after the Civil War. School-age children had to work in the fields for family survival.[7] In one report in 1884, the Indian agent blamed the children's lack of attendance on the size of the reservation and the poverty found at Oneida. The Indians were "scattered over a reserve of nearly three townships of land, in extent, and in many cases are too far situated from the schoolhouse to attend." He added that attendance was also affected because "the children are provided with an insufficient amount of clothing to protect them from the inclemency of the weather."[8]

It was no coincidence that, in the same year, Captain Pratt began recruiting Oneida students for his new school at Carlisle, Pennsylvania. The school's campus could take these children out of their extreme poverty, feed and clothe them, and concentrate them in a place far away from what Pratt considered the "evils" of the reservation system. The Oneidas, (see Landis, Part II) were one of the larger and more influential Indian student populations at Carlisle. Approximately five hundred attended the school from 1885 to 1918, and they ranked fourth in tribal affiliation, behind the Chippewas, Sioux, and Senecas at Carlisle. There, they excelled in the classroom, in debating societies, in vocal and band ensembles, and on the gridiron. Some, such as the musical composers and bandmasters Dennison Wheelock and James Wheelock, achieved international attention, while others, such as Dr. Josiah Powless and nurse Nancy Cornelius, achieved recognition in the health sciences.

Although Pratt's aim was to remove the Indian "from the blanket," his formula had other results both intended and unintended. Pratt's ideas (see Cornelius, Part II) became the bases of other federal Indian schools, such as the Oneida Boarding School, and Pratt's trained Carlisle graduates were employed nationwide. They served as teachers, bandmasters, disciplinarians, matrons, and laborers at these schools.

In the same year as the Dawes General Allotment Act, the federal government began to make plans for the construction of a "large boarding-school for their [Oneida] use, which will be of immense benefit to them."[9] A church history of the Oneidas

published in 1899 ties the school's founding to the federal allotment policy:

> Soon after the passage of the "Dawes Allotment Act," a com-
> mission, appointed by the President, came to the reservation to
> explain the provisions of the law and to induce the Oneidas to
> take advantage of the same. At a council with the Indians this
> matter was thoroughly discussed, and, as one of the induce-
> ments to take their land in severalty, the commission agreed to
> recommend to the President and Secretary of the Interior, that a
> boarding school be established on the Oneida reservation. This
> recommendation was favorably considered, and in the allotment
> of lands that soon followed, a tract of land near the center of the
> reservation was reserved for a school farm.[10]

The federal Indian agent's report of 1888 indicated that the
Oneidas had been seriously divided over accepting allotment
under the Dawes Act, but that they had reached consensus on
establishing a federal Indian boarding school on the reservation
and unanimously voted "one year's annuities to aid in erecting
the building." The federal Indian agent indicated that the push
had come from the Oneidas' large attendance at faraway
"Indian industrial and training schools, which shows the interest
manifested by these Indians in education."[11] Until its closing in
1918, the U.S. Indian Industrial School at Oneida, Wisconsin
(commonly known as the Government School or the Oneida
Boarding School), became a "feeder" school; children would
prepare there to go on to off-reservation boarding schools, most
notably Carlisle, Hampton, Tomah, Flandreau, and Pipestone.

The ultimate aim of the schools was to transform the Oneidas.
The schools separated children from their families and exposed
young people—girls and boys—to regimentation, harsh discipline, even physical abuse. Oneida critics of the Indian boarding
school system such as Laura Minnie Cornelius Kellogg (see
Stovey, Part III) described the harshness of the system, revealed
also in the excerpt from John Skenandore's WPA story. Moreover, a class system emerged on the reservation. Oneidas, who

Chart 2

Government Off-Reservation Schools Established Prior to 1900

Location	Date of opening
Carlisle, PA	November 1, 1879
Chemawa, OR	February 25, 1880
Chilocco, OK	January 15, 1884
Genoa, NE	February 20, 1884
Albuquerque, NM	August 1884
Lawrence, KS (Haskell Institute)	September 1, 1884
Grand Junction, CO	1886
Santa Fe, NM	October 1890
Fort Mohave, AZ	December 1890
Carson, NV	December 1890
Pierre, SD	February 1891
Phoenix, AZ	September 1891
Fort Lewis, CO	March 1892
Fort Shaw, MT	December 27, 1892
Perris, CA	January 9, 1893
Flandreau, SD	March 7, 1893
Pipestone, MN	February 1893
Mount Pleasant, MI	January 3, 1893
Tomah, WI	January 19, 1893
Wittenberg, WI	August 24, 1895
Greenville, CA	September 25, 1895
Morris, MN	April 3, 1897
Chamberlain, SD	March 1898
Fort Bidwell, CA	April 4, 1898
Rapid City, SD	September 1, 1898

Source: ARCIA, 1879–1900.

did not attend these elite schools, resented the growing power of the large Carlisle-Hampton contingent in the community, as reflected by the time of Oscar Archiquette's WPA story. These Carlisle-Hampton graduates were separated from the others within the Oneida community by their educational attainments and economic successes.

Most of the stories of Oneida elders collected by the WPA or more recently in the last two decades show another side of these schools. The federal Indian boarding school system provided food, clothing, shelter—basic needs for impoverished youngsters. Many Oneidas themselves were employed in these schools, and not just at the Oneida Boarding School. The schools also helped train the future leaders of the nation. It is ironic that, although the boarding schools—as well as the residential schools training Oneidas in Canada (see Antone, Part II)—were intended to "destroy the Indian but save the man," they did things that at times reinforced Indian identity and aided Native peoples in developing new strategies for survival. Indian cultures were never static, and new forms of cultural expression such as the bands and vocal groups were encouraged by this training. From the post–Civil War era through to World War II, Indian marching bands (see Part III) were features at Indian community events from New York to California. The success of Carlisle's athletes brought pride to reservation communities faced with a myriad of problems in the age of allotment; however, there were many other less visible influences of these schools on Oneida life.

In an 1890 appeal for financial assistance for her Oneida charges, teacher Jemima Wheelock, a recent Carlisle graduate, wrote about the horrendous conditions faced by the children in her one-room reservation schoolhouse. In the process, she clearly demonstrated skills she had learned at the Pennsylvania Indian school, namely the ability to communicate with non-Indians and to raise funds off the reservation for the betterment of her young students:

I am working hard and I can only laugh when I think of how many times I've got to make fire through the coming winter. The school-house was in a bad condition when I came, and I especially dreaded to pull the wood out of the snow, for there was no woodshed; but I will tell you how I managed to build a wood-shed, and to get other things I needed, I called on a Judge at Green Bay and I told him what I wanted. I was a stranger, mind you, but to my luck I drew a paper from this Judge, which introduced me to the most prominent people of Green Bay. I went to all three banks of Green Bay and I collected enough money to build a woodshed and without any trouble, and now I have a nice woodshed and a storm house built. I bought two new doors and had all the windows fixed. The woodshed will hold about ten cords of wood and now I can laugh again, because I will not have to dig the snow for my wood. I had three carpenters to work for me. I feel as though I was the mother of my four children. Christmas is coming soon and I would like to give something to every one of my scholars, but there is nothing to give.[12]

The Carlisle newspaper praised Jemima for being "courageous and energetic" and added its own appeal to send boots, shoes, and warm clothing to the school. Thus, although the schools emphasized competitiveness and the value of material success, they also stressed a sense of noblesse oblige, namely, that every-one should take personal responsibility to help the less fortunate and "uplift" them. It is no wonder that one Oneida—Sarah Smith King, a Carlisle graduate—writing to Richard Henry Pratt on his eightieth birthday in 1920, bemoaned the fact that Carlisle had closed and sadly stated that she "had hoped that my oldest boy could attend that dear old school."[13]

Notes

1. David W. Adams, *Education for Extinction: American Indians and the Boarding School Experience, 1875–1928* (Lawrence: University Press of Kansas, 1995), 36–45.

2. Ibid., 44–51. For the best work on the history of the Indian educational "experiment" at Hampton, see Lindsey, *Indians at Hampton Institute;* also Terence J. O'Grady, "The Singing Societies of Oneida," *American Music* 9 (Spring 1991): 69–70; David W. Adams, "Education in Hues: Red

and Black at Hampton, 1878–1893," *South Atlantic Quarterly* 76 (Spring 1977): 159–76.

3. Francis Paul Prucha, *The Great Father: The United States Government and the American Indians* (Lincoln: University of Nebraska Press, 1984), 2:694–700. For Pratt's own writings, see his *Battlefield and Classroom: Four Decades with the American Indian, 1867–1904,* ed., Robert M. Utley (New Haven, Conn.: Yale University Press, 1964).

4. Frederick E. Hoxie, A Final Promise: The Campaign to Assimilate the Indians (Lincoln: University of Nebraska Press, 1984), 56; Adams, *Education for Extinction,* 55–70. See also Francis Paul Prucha, ed., *Americanizing the American Indian; Writings by the "Friends of the American Indian," 1880–1900* (Cambridge, Mass.: Harvard University Press, 1973).

5. Hauptman and McLester, *Chief Daniel Bread,* 99–116. For Kirkland's Oneida educational experiment, see Walter Pilkington, ed., *The Journals of Samuel Kirkland* (Clinton, N.Y.: Hamilton College, 1980).

6. One of these students was Fred W. Cornelius. ARCIA 1879, 160.

7. Ibid., 1875, 369.

8. Ibid., 1884, 177.

9. Ibid., 1887, 228.

10. The Episcopal Church Mission to the Oneidas, *Oneida: The People of the Stone: The Church's Mission to the Oneidas* (Episcopal Church of the Holy Apostles, 1899), 43.

11. *ARCIA,* 1888, 240.

12. *Indian Helper,* December 26, 1890.

13. Sarah Smith King to Richard Henry Pratt, Dec. 1, 1920, in the file "Richard Henry Pratt on His Eightieth Birthday" (1920), Carlisle Indian School Papers, U.S. Military History Institute, Carlisle Barracks, Army War College, Carlisle, Pa.

4

Oneidas at Carlisle Indian School, 1884–1918

Barbara Landis

The "t's" and "d's" and "b's" and "p's" are hard for the beginning Oneidas. They turn the tin-cups into "din-cups," and tables into "daples." Ponies are "bonies" and pigs are "bigs." They try so hard, however, that they soon will do better.

Indian Helper, November 14, 1890.[1]

The Oneidas may have had difficulty learning English at the Carlisle Indian School, but not compared to students from other tribes. The Wisconsin Oneidas came to Carlisle with generally more schooling than other Indian students. Their experience at the school also showed higher graduation rates, more students trained in the professions, and a determination to carry on the Carlisle philosophy after their return to their home community in Wisconsin.

At Carlisle, learning English was the basis for initiation into a program designed by the United States to wash away "Indianness." Founded in 1879 by Richard Henry Pratt as the first off-reservation boarding school exclusively for American Indians, Carlisle was set up in central Pennsylvania, far from the traditional influences of families on the reservations. Organizing the school's industrial and academic curriculum with the intention of training students for a trade or profession to take out into the dominant culture, Pratt subscribed to a program designed to transform the identities of his Indian charges. This program was based on the model of the Hampton Institute in Virginia, the school where Pratt was able to send a group of American Indian prisoners after their sentences were fulfilled at the Fort Marion Prison in St. Augustine, Florida. Having served as their jailer for three years, Pratt was able to convince a group of the prisoners to enroll at Hampton, one of the few schools that would accept Indian students.[2]

Pratt likened his program at Carlisle to Christian baptism, using the imagery of holding children under "until they are thoroughly soaked." To his initial program of academics and industrial training, he would add the influences of music, literature, drama, and later, sports. These ideas dominated U.S. educational policies concerning Indians during the post–Civil War era. The theory of cultural evolution was a popular idea during the thirty-nine years of the school's existence.[3]

According to the September 1884 *Morning Star,* a group of seven Wisconsin Oneidas arrived at the Carlisle School, a full five years after the first students came to the school from the Pine Ridge and Rosebud Sioux agencies. Among the group were Belinda Archiquette and Jemima Wheelock. Dennison Wheelock, along with his brother Charles, arrived the following year at the age of fourteen. Charles was the older of the two, with fifty months' previous schooling. Dennison had been in school six years prior to his enrollment at Carlisle.[4]

Several Oneida students had been enrolled in the short-lived Indian Boarding School at Martinsburg, Pennsylvania. The school was located a hundred miles west of Carlisle and began enrolling Indians in 1885. According to the December 1887 *Indian Helper,* Isaiah Doxtator, Angeline S. Baird, and Mary W. Parkhurst were enrolled there. By 1888 fifteen Oneidas were sent to Carlisle from the Martinsburg school, which had been "discontinued."[5]

Missionaries, agents, and alumni recruited students. Peter Powlas often recruited Oneida students from Wisconsin. Three years after his own time at Carlisle had expired, Powlas accompanied "a young army" of students destined to receive the benefits to which he was privy. He spoke at Carlisle's Sunday evening program extolling the virtues of the school. During that trip in September 1890, Peter Powlas brought Lucinda Kick, Melinda Metoxen, Lydia Powlas, Melissa Green, Ophelia King, Alice Powlas, Moses King, Isaac Metoxen, Martin Wheelock, Taylor Smith, Whitney Powlas, John Powlas, Chauncey Archiquette, Brigman Cornelius, and Isaac Johns with him from Oneida.[6]

In the summer of 1891, Mr. and Mrs. Campbell, who were teachers at Carlisle, arrived with twelve boys and fourteen girls from Oneida. Among them were two returning students—Dennison Wheelock and Josiah Archiquette—poised to enroll in Dickinson Preparatory School, which was affiliated with Dickinson College located about a mile west of the Carlisle Indian School. In September 1895 Marianna Burgess, editor of the weekly newspapers, and Dennison Wheelock brought in a group of Oneidas from Wisconsin. Of the fourteen boys and sixteen girls, nine were returning. Isabella Cornelius, an 1892 Carlisle graduate, recruited Oneida pupils in September 1897 and then left for Connecticut to teach public school. Later, Sarah Smith (King), class of 1897, returned home to Oneida for vacation and came back with seven boys and seven girls, including Caleb Sickles who would later enter the Dickinson Preparatory School.[7]

All students were typically enrolled at Carlisle for a period of five years and were assigned to a particular trade. For Chester Cornelius, that trade was printing.[8] For Edwin Schanandoah, it was managing the bakery.[9] On his way home to Oneida in August 1893, Benjamin Wheelock made a detour through Chicago to visit the Carlisle Indian School's exhibit at the Columbian Exposition. One of the harnesses that he had made in shop during his time at Carlisle was on display at the fair.[10]

A number of former Carlisle students returned to Wisconsin to teach at the Oneida Boarding School. One, Josiah Powless, reinforced Pratt's Carlisle philosophy for the Oneida school at a speech at the 1899 Farmer's Institute:

The Government has allotted land for each individual member of the tribe, which is a starting point for industrial training, if the Indian will look at the subject in the right light. We have passed beyond savagery and barbarism on our road to the height of civilization. Industrial activity should go hand in hand in the progress toward that point. We see the neat and tidy ways in which our pale-faced neighbors arrange their farms and how they accumulate property. One may ask where is the source of all this? It comes simply through economy and industrial training, backed by ambition.[11]

The timing of the Carlisle experiment dovetailed with federal allotment policies. At the Carlisle school, there were Dawes Bill meetings on Wednesday nights touting the supposed advantages of allotment. News of allotment reached the Carlisle school in September 1889, with the revelation that Julia Powlas was assisting the special agent in Oneida with the allotments.[12]

In addition to academic and vocational training, extracurricular activities contributed to the educational program at Carlisle. Students who found themselves on an academic track were expected to be able to debate the important questions of the day. Dennison Wheelock, a fluent Oneida speaker, wrote an essay published in the November 1887 *Helper,* disparaging the teaching of Indian languages. His article was an entry in a competition and he won first prize. The debating societies were not only relegated to the boys; girls had their own organizations founded on similar principles. The Susan Longstreth Literary Society also featured the art of recitation, exemplified by Belinda Archiquette's reading "in a graceful and easy manner" of "The Rising in 1776."[13] Debating societies were in vogue at the Oneida school as well, where sometimes the returned Carlisle boys "lead and keep the discussions going as late as eleven o'clock at night."[14]

Pratt initiated what became known as the Outing System. Instead of going home to the reservations during summers and vacations, Indian students were sent out into non-Indian homes where they lived with their Outing families and earned a minimum wage. They attended Sunday School and church with their non-Indian siblings. Indeed, Christian theology permeated the Carlisle program, and all students who enrolled came affiliated with a denomination, especially a Protestant sect.

In some cases, students were Out during the entire school year, attending public schools from their Outing homes. Students on Outing were required to save at least half their pay. Jemima Wheelock, from the first group to arrive, displayed her enthusiasm for proper learning in a letter written from her Outing home, chastising a local non-Indian boy's use of poor grammar. "How do you expect your Indians to talk good English when we often hear poor English?"[15] Much as the Outing system was designed to entrench Carlisle students in the dominant culture, they were not always exposed to the finest examples. Jemima's discriminating ear recounted the bad examples she heard at a camp meeting near her Outing home.

An unnamed Oneida boy's letter was published in July 1888 under the heading "Well Satisfied." He made a point to explain how kind the folks were, "although they never had an Indian before, so we are making a new friend."[16] In an interesting melding of altruism and Outing earnings, Dennison Wheelock responded to an appeal for help by the Indian agent at the Devils Lake Agency for his "starving Indians," by encouraging donations of Outing funds by his peers at the Carlisle school. In February 1890, Captain Pratt obliged by wiring funds to Agent Cramsie, taking special care to remind his colleague at the indigent North Dakota reservation of the Outing income of the successful Carlisle earners. Included with the funds was a note explaining that Carlisle netted twelve thousand dollars in savings for the students who were privileged to participate in that exemplary program.[17]

Martha Doxtator's Outing family lived in Richfield Springs, New York, the site of a sulfur springs park. The summer resort featured therapeutic baths and water. Martha's letter to the school described the park, the waters and baths as having "done me a great deal of good and I am very glad I had the chance to come here." Outing was not entirely unique to Carlisle but was a part of the Hampton program as well. The *Indian Helper* reported that Alfred Powlas stopped in Carlisle on his way home from Massachusetts to Hampton.[18]

The Carlisle experiment was designed to incorporate a program of academic and industrial training, and by the time the Oneidas arrived, many students had typically completed a program of four years' schooling. As a consequence, the Oneidas' English-speaking skills were more advanced than others, marking them as likely graduates. This is significant, since graduation rates were so low at Carlisle. Of a known population of almost 10,700 students, only 758 were graduated. Of these, 118 were Oneidas.[19]

One, Nancy Cornelius, went on to nursing school in Hartford, Connecticut, where she was graduated with honors. Cornelius cut short her nursing career in the East to return to Oneida to care for her mother who was suffering with eye trouble. Another Oneida, Isabella Cornelius enrolled in the State Normal School in New Britain, Connecticut, after having graduated from Carlisle in 1890. When she attained her degree in June 1896, she wrote to a friend that she was "proud of my sheepskin and red skin too."[20]

Later Superintendent Moses Friedman, successor to Pratt, reported on the outcome of students who had completed the Carlisle program. The Oneida track record was impressive. Edwin Schanandore was living in Carson City, Nevada, working in business. Mrs. Otto Wells (née Mary Parkhurst) and her husband were teaching at the Rainy Mountain School, Oklahoma. Martin Archiquette worked at the Menominee Boarding School. Leila Cornelius had been appointed to a position at the school in Fort Belknap, Montana. Carrie Cornelius took a position at the Hoopa Valley Agency school in September 1896.[21] Yet, there was another side as well. The school population was not immune to tragedy.

Ophelia Powlas was the first Oneida child to be buried in the Indian cemetery at Carlisle. The daughter of Peter Powlas, both of her parents were deceased at the time of her passing. She had arrived at the school on August 16, 1887, at the age of fifteen and died of pneumonia on February 21, 1891. Her funeral was officiated by the Reverend Doctor Wile of the Episcopal church in town. Peter Cornelius (married to Jemima Wheelock) died on February 19, 1897. Melissa Metoxen died of lung trouble in April 1897. Lilly Cornelius died in August 1897. Frank Green's obituary appeared in the July 1, 1898, issue of the *Indian Helper* as a warning to all who might entertain thoughts of deserting. He ran away by following the railroad tracks and was killed by a train.[22]

For those who survived, returning home marked a certain rite of passage. For some, it was the end of a successful run of promotions through the grades culminating in graduation. For others, going home meant the term of enrollment was up, and there was no certificate of achievement to justify five years of government expense. The sendoff was ceremonial, a time for pomp and circumstance, hymn singing, recitations, Bible quoting, testimonials, and memoirs. Pratt provided moral lessons, condemnations of the reservation system, and laments concerning the plight of students returning to the reservation. Among the students returning to the reservation was the Oneida Dennison Wheelock who, in August 1890, urged his Oneida schoolmates to do their best to excel in their newly acquired skills albeit in their old surroundings: "Unless our influence is great enough and good enough to have the Indians look up to us; unless we have sufficient education to stand before them and show by our good works and our talk that they are going to destruction if we have not enough education for this and enough courage for this, we had better not go home."[23]

Notes

1. The *Indian Helper* and the *Morning Star* were weekly and monthly publications, mostly four pages in length, of the Carlisle Indian school. They served a dual purpose of showcasing the printing trade and publicizing the school. For a complete listing of the school publications, go to www.carlisleindianschool.org.

2. Richard Henry Pratt, *The Indian Industrial School, Carlisle, Pennsylvania: The Origin, Purposes, and Progress and the Difficulties Surmounted* (Carlisle, Pa.: Hamilton Library Association, 1908; CCHS Publications, 1979), 5.

3. Ibid.

4. *Morning Star*, September 1884. For more on Dennison Wheelock, see Hauptman, Part II.

5. *Indian Helper*, December 1887.

6. Ibid., September 23, 1890.

7. Carlisle Indian School Records, CCHS.

8. *Morning Star,* October 1887.

9. Ibid., August/September 1887.

10. *Indian Helper,* August 27, 1893.

11. Ibid., March 24, 1899.

12. Carlisle Indian School Records, CCHS.

13. *Indian Helper,* February 14, 1890.

14. Ibid., February 13, 1891.

15. Ibid., September 2, 1887.

16. Ibid., July 27, 1888.

17. Ibid., February 14, 1890.

18. Ibid., September 8, 1893; October 4, 1895.

19. Bell, "Telling Stories out of School," 403.

20. *Indian Helper,* July 3, 1896.

21. Ibid., November 25, 1898.

22. Statistical documentation of the names found in the Carlisle Indian Cemetery has been organized as an unpublished database available to tribal historians, usually referred to as the Bell/Landis Cemetery Database. This database matches the names found on the headstones with a template of information housed in file no. 1327, RG75, NA.

23. *Indian Helper,* August 1, 1890.

5

Oneidas at Hampton Institute

Thelma Cornelius McLester

Hampton Institute, founded by General Samuel Chapman Armstrong in 1868, provided educational opportunities for both black freedmen and American Indians. Born in 1839, Armstrong was raised in Hawaii where his father was a missionary to native Hawaiians. It was there that he learned and never forgot his father's teaching methods. One such method was the addition of manual labor as a part of education. His father had once stated: "Manual labor to any teaching must accompany every school for native peoples, for without industry, they cannot be moral."[1]

Samuel Chapman Armstrong's original idea was to open up a school to prepare the recently freed black slaves to become teachers so that they could return to their communities and teach literacy skills to the largely "untutored" black population. This did not necessarily hold true for American Indian students, but Armstrong's beliefs were that both races eventually had to serve the same purposes, that is, to be trained and then return to their own communities to help their own people succeed. Extremely paternalistic in his views, Armstrong believed himself to be the vessel uplifting racial minorities to "civilization."[2]

Hampton became one of the premier industrial schools for racial minorities during the late nineteenth and early twentieth centuries; however, unlike the nearly 10,000 American Indians educated at Carlisle, Hampton educated 1,388 Native peoples from 1878 to 1923.[3] The school was primarily for blacks from its inception, and blacks and Indians resided in separate dormitories over the years. General Armstrong first became associated with blacks during the Civil War and this association continued when he headed up the Freedman's Bureau after the conflict ended. Noting the lack of adequate educational facilities for blacks, Armstrong persuaded the American Association of Missionaries of New York to purchase land in Hampton, Virginia, so that a school could be built.[4]

The Hampton Institute officially opened its doors to black students in April 1868. Two years later, the General Assembly of the State of Virginia issued a formal charter recognizing Hampton as an institution for learning, and General Armstrong was assigned by the Freedman's Bureau to work at Hampton.[5]

The first American Indians were admitted to Hampton in 1878. These students were Indian prisoners of war who had just been released after three years of incarceration at St. Augustine, Florida. As prisoners they had been under the authority and tutelage of Captain Richard Henry Pratt, and it was he who now sought to transform them through education. Their alleged crimes were simply their fight to preserve their tribal lands. The group consisted of seventy-five Indians representing the Arapahos, Cheyennes, Comanches, and Kiowas. While in captivity they were introduced to basic literacy skills, with the result that some of the younger Indian men, on their release, wished to pursue their education, although most chose to return to their reservations. Seventeen young Indian men were accepted at Hampton as an experiment, and thus began a new chapter. Shortly thereafter, Captain Pratt and his wife traveled to South Dakota and returned with Sioux Indians—forty men and nine women.[6]

From 1886 to 1912, Hampton received U.S. governmental funding—the set amount of twenty thousand dollars per year—for a total of 120 Indian students each year. A total of sixty-five tribes from across the country attended Hampton over a forty-six-year period. The total number of Indian students was 1,388, with the largest enrollment in 1889. The normal length of stay for students was three years. Only 11 percent of the American Indian student body there graduated from Hampton. The larger number received certificates in the various fields of vocational training.[7]

The first Oneida students at Hampton arrived in 1886. Between that year and 1923, 193 Oneidas attended the school. The largest number arrived between 1892 and 1901. In 1898 alone, 60 Oneidas were enrolled. Overall, the Iroquois, which included the Oneidas, had the second highest number of students—the first being the Sioux—in the school's Indian program.[8] The Oneidas who attended ranged in age from thirteen to thirty. Members of the same families left together for Virginia by train via Green Bay.

Hampton concentrated on building character, going beyond the academic, and promoting social, religious, and economic values. Hampton, unlike Carlisle, continually concentrated its studies on the academic rather than on athletics. This fact alone is important when making comparative studies between the two schools. For what was then promoted with a strong emphasis was the necessary schooling that was lacking in other institutions on or near Indian reservations. This was a vital step for Indian people in their ability to become competitive in an ever-changing society. Hampton's success was due to two elements: the thinking of Armstrong, followed by the school's financial underpinnings as a result of its influential board of trustees and the acquisition of governmental funds. Although it was an effort to rapidly acculturate American Indians, the school, nevertheless, provided a higher level of education than could be found on reservations of that day. It also became a training ground to teach reservation teachers.

The 1870 Hampton School catalog lists various courses. The first level—the Junior Class—consisted of arithmetic (long division and percentages), reading, spelling, grammar and sentence structure, as well as geography and history. The second level—the Middle Class—listed arithmetic and bookkeeping, spelling, English grammar and analysis of sentences, and the history of the United States. The third level—the Senior Class—listed algebra and geometry, language consisting of spelling, reading, rhetoric, and composition, physiology and botany, universal (world) history, and the history of England. There were in addition other offerings: instruction in mental arithmetic, penmanship, agriculture, house-work, and moral sciences.[9] There were also night classes, especially for those who were placed in preparatory classes. These students were not yet ready to enter academic classes because of their limited knowledge of the English language. Many of these students worked during the day at various jobs including at the school's farm. Although every student had to work in addition to attending classes, these preparatory students spent more time working than attending regular classes.[10] Moreover, much like at Carlisle, Hampton administrators promoted the "Outing System" to foster assimilation and allow the students to earn their own wages. These Outings usually took place during the summer months when there were no classes.

Oneida men, on their return to the reservation, became farmers, painters, carpenters, blacksmiths, and pursued other forms of general labor. Some entered federal service, teaching or working at Indian schools. Farming in particular was the most prevalent occupation during this period, and even prior to their children's leaving for school, some parents expressed a desire to have their sons learn more about farming while at school. Individual files of the Oneida students who attended Hampton showed that, on leaving Hampton, the primary occupations pursued by Oneida women were housekeeper, cook, laundry worker, and seamstress. There were also those who became teachers, teacher aides, and nurses. A few men and women were encouraged to go on to achieve advanced degrees.[11]

The life stories of four Oneidas who attended Hampton, found in the files of the Oneida Cultural Heritage Department, illustrate the great diversity of student experiences at this Virginia school.[12] The first student, a male who attended Hampton from 1897 to 1903, had spent three years at Haskell Institute and two years at the Oneida Boarding School before going east. After leaving Hampton, he worked as a farm laborer in the Green Bay area and as a logger in Amberg, Wisconsin. In February 1904, he wrote back to his teachers at Hampton, stating his regret at not having taken more from his schooling to "better my life" and "stand [up to] competition with the educated class of our country and . . . be somebody in this world."

A second Oneida male, who had attended Hampton from 1894 to 1898, wrote that he had been on four Outings working in Cornwall, Connecticut, and Sheffield, Massachusetts. After graduation, he became a painter and a farmer, and now he and his wife and two children were operating a fifty-two-acre farm, planting oats and potatoes. He mentioned that one of his children, a girl, was attending Carlisle.

A third Oneida male had attended Hampton sometime before 1896. He was somewhat disappointed in his Hampton schooling since the institution's manual training had not helped him move up to a trade. He insisted "that anyone can become a farmer, but we want the right skills for Oneida." Consequently, he sought advanced training at the University of Wisconsin in Madison, where he attained an agricultural certificate. In May 1896, this Oneida attended "Indian Day" at Hampton, where he was invited back to present a talk before the school assembly. Later, the same man, a descendant of a chief who had signed the Treaty of Fort Stanwix in 1784, became a chief himself at Oneida in 1925.

One Oneida woman who had attended Hampton from 1891 to 1895 listed her current occupation as housekeeping. Her experience in Hampton's Outing System had been a negative one. She indicated that she did housework for three different families. In one of these experiences, she was expected to work seven days a week. After church, she was supposed to go back to work. One Sunday, she remained for religious instruction after church services, and when she returned to her employer's residence, she was reprimanded for not returning right away.

The Oneidas' experience at Hampton had a significant impact on them long after graduation. In 1908, five Hampton graduates served as councillors in the newly created Township of Oneida, Wisconsin. Encouraged by Hampton school clubs, many of the Oneida graduates of Hampton joined the local YMCA and YWCA movements. Attendance at Hampton also encouraged students to develop charitable organizations to address social needs upon the students' return to their homes at Oneida. One society that had some of its origins at Hampton was the Oneida Welfare Society, also known as the Soup Society, whereby monies were raised to help members with their medical and funeral bills. The Oneidas were also influenced by the music they learned at Hampton. The long-standing tribal singing societies were now infused with gospel music traditions brought back from the Virginia school. Attendance at Hampton created the opportunities to meet American Indians from across the United States. Some of these friendships continued long after students left school and even led to marriage.[13]

There were other successful Hampton Oneidas, such as Josephine Hill Webster, who were looked on as leaders on their return to the reservation.[14] This of course was the premise General Armstrong had envisioned. His plan was to have both the blacks and the Indians become cultural missionaries, that is, return to their homes and communities to share their experiences as well as to lead their communities to "civilization." Many Wisconsin Oneida community members whose relatives attended Hampton have a more favorable assessment of the years their relations spent in Virginia, fifteen hundred miles from Wisconsin, than those Oneidas whose family members did not go off to school.[15] This favorable assessment can be explained in that during the last decades of the nineteenth century, Oneida students had little to no other alternatives for higher education beyond the local day and mission schools, both of which were limited. For example, there was no secondary level education offered locally, nor were there any opportunities to go beyond and attend any professional schools. The Oneidas of Wisconsin had no opportunities for work experience or opportunities to travel. The opportunities for attendance at Hampton—paid for partially by the federal government (through use of the tribes' own trust funds), along with other scholarship funds—increased the knowledge base of, in this case, the Oneida community of Wisconsin and was provided at an opportune time. Later on, public schools were opened on or near the reservation, which lessened the need for the boarding schools, but this did not occur until the early twentieth century and, more particularly, after American Indians had gained their citizenship.

Notes

1. Lindsey, *Indians at Hampton,* 2; Francis G. Peabody, *Education for Life: The Story of Hampton Institute* (Garden City, N.Y.: Doubleday, Page, 1918), xiii–xv.

2. Lindsey, *Indians at Hampton,* 50–53; Adams, *Education for Extinction,* 44–48.

3. Lindsey, *Indians at Hampton,* 58.

4. M. F. Armstrong and Helen W. Ludlow, *Hampton and Its Students* (New York: G. P. Putnam's Sons, 1874), 15, 21.

5. Lindsey, *Indians at Hampton,* 23–24.

6. Ibid., 26–30.

7. Ibid., 35.

8. Ibid., 202, 241.

9. Records of the Oneida Students Who Attended Hampton Institute, Cultural Heritage Department, ONIW.

10. Hampton School Catalog 1870, Cultural Heritage Department, ONIW.

11. Records of Oneida Students at Hampton, ONIW.

12. These stories are taken from ibid. The anonymity of the student records was a decision made by the author and the staff of the ONIW Cultural Heritage.

13. Ibid.

14. Thelma McLester, "Josephine Hill Webster," in Campisi and Hauptman, *Oneida Indian Experience,* 116–18.

15. Records of Oneida Sudents at Hampton. ONIW.

6

The Oneida Indian Boarding School

Judy Cornelius

As an inducement to accept land-in-severalty under the Dawes General Allotment Act of 1887, the Oneidas were promised that the federal government would establish a boarding school on lands on their Wisconsin reservation. The movement to create the Oneida Boarding School was prompted by Edward Goodnough, the highly influential Episcopal missionary on the reservation, who urged the creation of a centrally located government educational institution. At the time, besides mission schools run by the Episcopal and Methodist churches, there were "four or five scattered district schools sustained by the Government."[1]

In the spring of 1892, the construction of a school building commenced. Charles F. Pierce, a disciple of Richard Henry Pratt of Carlisle Institute and a man who had worked organizing an Indian boarding school among the Sioux, was soon appointed Oneida School superintendent. On March 27, 1893, the school opened on a 151-acre site.[2] The school was later described in an Episcopal Church mission publication:

The school is beautifully located on a high ridge across the Duck Creek from the Hobart Mission [Episcopal Church of the Holy Apostles], near the railroad station. . . . It can be seen from all directions, and its fine brick buildings, over which floats the American flag, present a beautiful as well as a patriotic scene. The Indian children are taken from their homes at the age of six years, and during ten months of the year are kept at the school where they are educated, clothed and cared for by the government without expense to the parents.[3]

Despite Carlisle's emphasis on removing Indian children from "the blanket" (namely, reservation life), the Oneida Boarding School was, nevertheless, influenced strongly by Pratt's experiment in Indian education. The coeducational Oneida Boarding School had a strong emphasis on vocational-agricultural as well as industrial education. There was a creamery, a working farm, and a blacksmith shop as part of the complex. Much of the focus was on encouraging the assimilation process of education. Carlisle recruiters came to the school each year to select the brightest and most promising scholars, or the finest musicians and athletes, among the students for Pratt's Pennsylvania Indian industrial school. It is important to note that in 1893, the year of the Oneida Boarding School's founding, several other federal Indian boarding schools were also established—Flandreau, Mount Pleasant, Pipestone, and Tomah. Although the course of study included "literary work," the focus of the curriculum for boys was largely tied to the school's farm, where they learned agricultural methods, "gardening, care of stock and the use of tools." Girls were "taught to cook, wash, iron, sew, knit, and do other branches of domestic work." After completing this course of study, the promising students were "eligible for promotion to the larger training schools, such as Carlisle, Hampton or Haskell."[4]

The school grew rapidly, and soon applications outran the institution's ability to accommodate the number of students seeking admission. At the time of the Oneida Boarding School's founding, there were 564 Oneida children of school age. By 1907, 225 schoolchildren, boys and girls between the ages of six and fourteen years, were attending the Oneida Boarding School. By this time, there were seven brick and twelve frame buildings in the educational complex. With the expansion of attendance and the construction of new facilities came an increase in school staff.[5] By 1900, there were twenty-one employees, including thirteen Indians in a variety of capacities. Seven years later, the school had a staff of twenty-five, including five Indian teachers. Among the Oneidas employed by the school in this period were school engineer Richard Powless and nurse Lavinia Cornelius, both graduates of Hampton Institute; teacher Alice Cornelius, a graduate of Carlisle; and boy's matron Hattie Metoxen.[6]

In 1898, Joseph C. Hart began his fourteen-year tenure as Indian agent for the Oneida. Hart was also appointed superintendent of the Oneida Boarding School in 1893; his wife served as teacher-administrator at the school. Hart's reports—found in the Commissioner of Indian Affairs' Annual Reports (ARCIA)—provide descriptions of the school and the student body. Although his administration was controversial and led to several official investigations of the school, Hart provided valuable information in his reports. In 1903, he reported:

> the boarding school has had a satisfactory year. The enrollment was 206, with an average attendance of 190. September is a busy month for a farming population like this, and the average for that month was only 166, as most of the boys big enough to work were busy at their homes. A class of 25 will be transferred to training schools September 1. Buildings are in good condition and have been kept in good repair. Instruction is given in such of the household duties as are suited to the age and strength of the girls, and in farming and gardening for the boys. The average age of pupils is 10 years, so that extended instruction in the trades is not practicable, and is left for the training schools that have facilities for such work, and to which our pupils are transferred at from 13 to 15 years of age. As in other years, basketry and beadwork have received some attention, but in these arts perfection rather than quantity has been the aim, and the work has been a test of neatness and thoroughness rather than a productive industry. There is one Government day school on the reservation with an average attendance of 20, and two mission day schools, with an attendance of 35. Several

Chart 3
Employees of the U.S. Indian Industrial School at Oneida, Wis., 1900 (also known as the Oneida Boarding School)

Name	Position	Salary	Sex	Race	Date of Original Appointment
Joseph C. Hart	Superintendent	$1,500	M.	W.	Apr. 7, 1893
Marilla S. Purman	Clerk	660	F.	W.	Feb. 14, 1900
Lucy P. Hart	Teacher	660	F.	W.	Nov. 7, 1887
Alice Cornelius	Teacher	600	F.	I.	Jan. 17, 1898
Mary E. Bonifant	Teacher	540	F.	W.	Sept. 4, 1894
Mary M. Shirk	Kindergartner	600	F.	W.	Mar. 20, 1895
Moses E. King	Industrial Teacher	400	M.	I.	Dec. 1, 1896
Bertha A. Macy	Matron	660	F.	W.	Jan. 10, 1899
Hattie Metoxen	Assistant matron	500	F.	I.	July 1, 1897
Florence Bonifant	Seamstress	480	F.	W.	Apr. 1, 1897
Minnie C. King	Assistant seamstress	240	F.	I.	Mar. 2, 1900
Phoebe Baird	Assistant seamstress	240	F.	I.	May 2, 1899
Melissa Reed	Laundress	400	F.	I.	May 2, 1899
Elizabeth Skenandore	Assistant laundress	240	F.	I.	July 10, 1896
Lydia Powlas	Assistant laundress	240	F.	I.	Dec. 11, 1899
Emma F. Smith	Cook	480	F.	W.	Oct. 4, 1895
Melissa Green	Assistant cook	240	F.	W.	July 10, 1896
George W. Haus	Farmer	600	M.	I.	Oct. 5, 1892
Richard S. Powless	Engineer	720	M.	I.	Oct. 1, 1899
Lavinia Cornelius	Nurse	480	F.	I.	Sept. 1, 1899
Jonathan E. Kennedy	Night watchman	360	M.	I.	Mar. 27, 1900

Source: ARCIA, 1900, 723.

Note: Twelve of the twenty-one employees were American Indians. Nine Oneidas of the twelve Indians listed attended either Carlisle (five) or Hampton (four). See Appendix A and Appendix B.

children attend the public day schools off the reservation, and 200 or more advanced students are now at the various Indian training schools.[7]

In 1907 Dennison Wheelock proposed that the Oneida Boarding School be converted into a day school. There were several meetings held by the community in the Episcopal Parish Hall and Epworth

Hall (Methodist); however, the consensus was to continue the boarding school. Laura Minnie Cornelius, Alice Cornelius's sister, became an outspoken opponent of Wheelock's proposal, insisting on the continuance of the Oneida Boarding School. Nevertheless, by 1908, the Bureau of Indian Affairs (BIA) began planning to phase out the Oneida Boarding School. With the shrinking land base of the Oneida Indian Reservation caused by the increased issuance of fee simple patents, it was only a matter of time before the school's demise.[8]

From 1907 onward, government officials debated the future of the school. Much of the pro-closing position maintained that Oneida Indians should be integrated into the nearby public school districts as rapidly as possible. Although the pro-closing argument was based significantly on federal cost savings, the school's operating budget was always inadequate and was in line with other Indian boarding schools at the time. Moreover, Bishop Reginald H. Weller of the Fond du Lac diocese wrote on behalf of maintaining the school.[9] While the debate intensified, the reservation land base was shrinking as a result of allotment policies, especially after 1906. In 1917, the process was further sped up by the establishment of the federal McLaughlin Competency Commission.

The school was finally closed in 1918 with a few staff provided by the BIA to maintain the grounds and the livestock. Over the next six years there was much controversy over whether to turn the boarding school into a day school, use it for an agricultural training center or canning factory (advocated by Laura Cornelius), or convert it into a hospital for tuberculosis patients (suggested by Dennison Wheelock).

On several occasions the Oneidas officially protested the closing of the school. There were several meetings of the tribal council to discuss and take action on the Oneida Boarding School. A resolution, passed at a general tribal council meeting on June 17, 1919, reads: "whereas the desire of the Oneida Indians is, that a school shall be maintained for the education of their children and their children's children." Another tribal council meeting held on May 23, 1921, contained a petition prepared by Joseph Smith and signed by tribal chairman Martin Archiquette, one of the more

Chart 4
Oneida Schoolchildren Attending Schools
on the Reservation, 1910

	Capacity	Enrollment
Oneida Boarding School	140	141
Oneida Day School No. 1	50	50
Oneida Day School No. 2	60	60
Hobart Mission Day School (Episcopal)	30	30
Advent Mission Day School (Methodist)	25	21
Totals	305	302

Note: The total Oneida population in 1910 was 2,301, with 692 children of school age. The vast majority, but not all, of the remaining children not attending schools on the reservation were at Carlisle, Flandreau, Hampton, Haskell, and Tomah. This chart is based on a letter from C. F. Pierce, supervisor of Indian Schools, to the commissioner of Indian affairs, August 8, 1910, in ARCIA 1910. Pierce had previously been the first principal at the Oneida Boarding School and had served as superintendent at Flandreau as well.

prominent Oneida graduates of Carlisle, and tribal secretary Isaac N. Webster, a Hampton graduate:

> We, the undersigned Oneida Indians, residing upon the Oneida reservation respectfully request you to stop the sale of the Oneida School plant and agency office. We further petition you to re-open the school as many Oneida children are without a school to attend and many more of them are going to other Indian schools at a great expense to their parents.[10]

The school and property were eventually purchased by Murphy Land and Investment Company on October 1, 1924, for $21,794 and were quitclaimed to the Catholic Diocese the same day for $1.00. They were then turned over to what became known as the Sacred Heart Seminary. Shortly after the school was purchased, the Catholic Diocese set up another coed boarding school.[11]

According to one Oneida elder, Prudence Doxtator, she was the only Oneida who attended during 1927. Doxtator shared with me that there were about three or four non-Indians from the Oneida area who attended this school, which subsequently changed its focus and its name to the Sacred Heart Seminary, becoming a training school for Catholic priests.

In the early 1980s, the Oneida Nation of Indians of Wisconsin began to pool all of its resources and formed a task force to work with the Catholic Diocese to bring the property back into tribal hands.[12] In 1984 the Oneida Tribe came to an agreement with the Catholic Diocese to purchase the property for the price of $800,000. In the 1990s, the school building was named the Norbert Hill Center, in memory of Norbert Hill, Sr., who had been the chairman of the tribe and one of the negotiators of the task force who helped bring the property back into Oneida hands. Today, the current tribal leadership, the Oneida Business Committee, along with the Tribal High School, Head Start program, day care, education offices, internal audit, and a host of other programs operate from this property. It is a fitting tribute to the Oneidas, who struggled to keep this property for the purpose of educating their children and their children's children, a wish they expressed back during the chaotic years between 1908 and 1924 when they fought to keep this property.

Chart 5
Wisconsin Oneida Children in School, 1918

Non-Reservation Schools	217
Oneida Boarding School	154
Five District Schools	141
Mission Day Schools	34
Total	546

Source: Memorandum of June 3, 1919, in ARCIA 1919.

Note: The Oneida Boarding School closed in 1918. There were 898 Indian children of school age. Consequently, 352 Oneida schoolchildren were not attending school.

Notes

1. Julia K. Bloomfield, *The Oneidas* (New York: Alden Brothers, 1907), 335.

2. Ibid., 336.

3. *Oneida: People of the Stone,* 44–46.

4. Ibid., 45.

5. Bloomfield, *The Oneidas,* 336–38.

6. Ibid.; *Oneida: People of the Stone,* 44–46. The statistics about enrollment and staff at the Oneida Indian Boarding School are from ARCIA 1893–1918; from tribal records found in the Oneida Office of Land Management, ONIW; and from the Records of the Oneida Indian Historical Society, Oneida, Wis.

7. ARCIA 1903.

8. See the article on Dennison Wheelock by Laurence M. Hauptman, Part III, and also Stovey, Part III.

9. Bishop Reginald H. Weller to Commissioner Cato Sells, December 21, 1914, in the Records of the Oneida Indian Historical Society, Oneida, Wis.

10. Resolution of June 17, 1919, and petition of May 23, 1921, both in Records of the Oneida Indian Historical Society, Oneida, Wis.

11. Ibid.

12. Interview of Prudence Doxtator, August 14, 2003, Oneida, Wis.

7

The Origins of Residential Schooling among the Onyote'a:Ka of the Thames, 1840–1920

Eileen Antone

In 1840, when part of the Oneidas/Onyote'a:ka Nation moved to the banks of the Thames in Delaware Township, London District, Upper Canada, they were familiar with formal Western education. Therefore, on settling in this new community, a school was established almost immediately. In 1843 under the direction of the Wesleyan Missionary Society, Oneida No. 1 School became the first educational institute for the Onyote'a:ka children. The school was located across the road from the River Road Methodist Church, which was situated on the site of the present-day United Church cemetery. In the early years, the people of this new community recognized the necessity that their children should learn to read, write, and do arithmetic. The first teacher was Abraham Sickles, an Onyote'a:ka from their own community. He taught all the subjects using the Onyote'a:ka language, which enabled the children to learn quickly.[1]

From 1842 to 1844, a federal commission surveyed aboriginal education in Canada. This Bagot Commission Report recommended that the aboriginal people had to acquire "industry and knowledge" if they were to become valuable members of society. Much of the report had an assimilationist focus. It became "the cornerstone for an Indian residential school system."[2]

In 1847 Egerton Ryerson, the Methodist head of education in Upper Canada, authored a report on Indian affairs, recommending that "the education of Indians consist not merely of training of the mind but of a weaning from the habits and feelings of their ancestors and the acquirements of the language, arts and customs of civilized life." Ryerson also suggested that there be a partnership between government and church, and that the schooling be of a religious nature. The education of Indian children was to be in separate schools away from the white population and away from their own Indian reserves.[3]

The education of aboriginal people in Canada was also affected by an act passed in 1857. This act was a plan for Indian enfranchisement. Amerindians rallied to reject the act.[4] Nine years after Canada became a nation in 1867, the British colonial laws of the day were combined to form the 1876 Indian Act, which is still in existence today. This act relegated the indigenous peoples of Canada to the status of minors and treated them as wards of the state.[5]

The origins of residential schools among the Onyote'a:ka began within a decade of their migration to Canada. It was during the mid-1840s that Peter Jones, an Ojibwa Methodist minister, moved to the Muncey and Chippewa community across the river from the Onyote'a:ka of the Thames settlement. Although Reverend Jones was a Methodist minister, he had another vision for the First Nations people. Jones envisioned an educational system that would teach the children to survive as Native people and to develop skills in order to protect what little bit of land they still had left.[6] In one letter, he wrote: "It is also our intention to select from these schools the most promising boys and girls, with a view to giving them superior advantages, so as to qualify them for missionaries and school teachers among their brethren."[7] He felt that if there was a formal institute run by the First Nations people, Native children would have a better chance of survival.

Reverend Jones dedicated his work at Muncey to this goal. He began the arduous task of obtaining funds to begin the Mount Elgin Indian Residential School. With much exhausting travel through Upper Canada and England, he managed to collect enough funds to have a manual labor school open in December 1849 on the Chippewa Reserve. With the exception of a three-year closure from 1864 to 1867, this residential school remained open until 1946, teaching many generations of Onyote'a:ka children.

Due to his failing health, Reverend Jones was unable to continue the work he had started. The school was taken over by a non-Native minister, Rev. Samuel Rose, who had problems as an administrator because of his "ignorance of Indians." Instead of Christian Indian tutelage, as envisioned by Jones, "white people fed, clothed, trained, and preached to the students in English."[8] The masses of Indian missionaries, teachers, and interpreters that Peter Jones had prayed for did not come forward. Thus, the school never fulfilled Jones's original vision. Although the Mount Elgin Residential School was close to the Onyote'a:ka community, many of the reserve's children were sent also to the Mohawk Institute in Brantford, a residential school that had opened in 1834, which continued to operate until 1970. In later years Onyote'a:ka children were also sent as far away as Sault Ste. Marie Shingwauk Home Residential School, and to Brandon Manitoba.[9]

Even though Mount Elgin Residential School continued to exist under the direction of non-Native people and Onyote'a:ka students attended this facility, the Onyote'a:ka people continued to have their own one-room school with Methodist mission support. Throughout the early years both Native and non-Native teachers were employed as staff for this school. While Rev. Peter Jones was working to establish the Mount Elgin labor school, Rev. Richard Flood of the Church of England established an Anglican mission at Onyote'a:ka in 1847.[10] It was not until about 1878 that a Church of England school was started. This school would become known as Oneida No. 2. On January 27, 1882, a third school was opened. This school was built for and by the people to educate the children of this community who were not within walking distance of the other two schoolhouses in this settlement. The third school became known as Oneida No. 3. Its first schoolteacher, Elijah Sickles, was an Onyote'a:ka community member. As a result of problems of funding the operations of these schools, all the schools at Onyote'a:ka eventually came under the control of the Canadian Department of Indian Affairs and Northern Development.[11]

Notes

1. Grafton Antone, ed., *Oneida 1990 Sesquicentennial: In Our Stories along the Thames River* (Brantford, Ont.: Woodland, 1990).

2. D. Napier, "Sins of the Father," *Anglican Journal* (May 2000), at www.anglicanjournal.com/126/rs/index.html.

3. Ibid.

4. M. Brant-Castellano and J. S. Milloy, "A History of Indian Education through the Experience of Iroquois Indians," in *School Days: An Exhibition on the History of Indian Education* (Brantford, Ont.: Woodland Indian Cultural Education Centre, 1984), 11; Olivia Dickason, *Canada's First Nations: A History of Founding Peoples from Earliest Times,* 3rd ed. (Toronto: McClelland and Stewart, 2000).

5. B. Richardson, *People of Terra Nallius* (Vancouver, BC: Douglas and McIntyre, 1993), 15.

6. Donald B. Smith, *Sacred Feathers: The Reverend Peter Jones (Kahkeweaquonaby) and the Mississauga Indians* (Toronto: University of Toronto Press, 1987), 193.

7. Quoted in S. R. McVitty, "The Story of Seventy Years of Progress," *Missionary Bulletin* 16 (1920): 160–208.

8. Smith, *Sacred Feathers*, 214.

9. McVitty, "Seventy Years of Progress," 176.

10. C. F. Pascoe, *Two Hundred Years of the S.P.G.: An Historical Account of the Society for the Propagation of the Gospel in Foreign Parts, 1700–1900* (London: Society for the Propagation of the Gospel in Foreign Parts, 1901), 172.

11. Inez Philips, "Our Stories—Inez Philips' Memories of Her Father Freeman Doxtator," in Antone, *Oneida 1990 Sesquicentennial*; McVitty, "Seventy Years of Progress," 4. See also Eileen M. Antone, "The Educational History of the Onyote'a:ka Nation of the Thames," *Ontario History* 85 (December 1993): 309–20.

8

Three Oneida WPA Stories

Editors' Note: Boarding schools such as Carlisle also created schisms within Indian communities and class divisions as shown in the following WPA story.

Carlyle Students with Bicycles

Oscar Archiquette

There were a group of Oneida Indians came back from Carlyle Indian School in Pennsylvania. When they came back they bought bicycles and they rode all over the Reservation and one day they met another young man with a bicycle and they gave him an awful licking, and somebody asked, why did they lick him. They said, because he is good for nothing and has a bicycle too.

Editors' Note: The great Oneida athletes at boarding schools brought great pride to Oneidas in the age of allotment as shown in the following WPA story.

Football

Moses Elm

It has been long time already, that the Oneidas have been famous for playing football. They used to go to different schools for the

Indians. They were big fellows these Oneidas that were on the team of different schools such as, Carlisle, Haskell, Chilocco, Flandreau, Tomah, and Riverside California. These that I am going to call their names were some of the best players in their day: Jonas Metoxen, Martin Wheelock, Joel Cornelius, Tom Skenandore, Alex Parkhurst, Samson Cornelius, Chauncey Baird, Wilson Charles, Philip Cornelius, Johnie House, Persell Powles, and Chauncey Archiquette. And not very long ago playing football for different schools were men and their names were as follows: Ben Greene, Emerson King, Ben Skenandore, Charles Baird, Frederick Skenandore, Frank Summers, Guy Elm, Emerson Metoxen, Lynas Skenandore, William Metoxen, Reuben King, Layton Skenandore, George Peters, George Hill, Joel Wheelock, Hugh Wheelock, La Front King, Elijah Smith, Wilson Charles Jr, Clarence Powles and Norbert Hill. This man's name I mention before Wilson Charles Jr, was the best football player and all around athlete. He was almost as good as the famous of all time all around athlete, Sac and Fox [and Potawatomie] Indian James Thorp[e]. The Carlisle Indians were the best team of all Indian schools teams. They tried to beat all the best white men's teams of the universities and colleges. They used to travel all over the United States and Canada. Some of these players were able to be placed on the All American Teams.

Editors' Note: The following WPA story shows the emotional and physical pain that some students experienced at the boarding schools.

The Oneida Boarding School

John A. Skenandore

I must have went to our old mission school a very short time as when my parents took me to [the Oneida] Government School[.] I still didn't understand a word of English. And that was the place where I had many hardships. We were not allowed to talk in our own language [and] so we had to hide ourselves before we could have any fun and talk as we liked. And then our disciplinarian caught us at it many times and gave us a whipping each time, and sometimes we were punished by carrying in wood at the boiler house which heats all the buildings. We were made to haul twenty five sticks a piece on our shoulders and there were times when we had to haul from quite a distance. We were made to work half a day and went to school the other half[.] [T]he children that went to school in the morning had to work in the afternoon. As I said I didn't understand [a] word of English[,] so I just guessed when I did went to school[.] [T]he teacher made lots of funny noises in her mouth which didn't mean a thing to me but finally the boy next to me told me in our language that she said that I was supposed to come to school in the mornings and that I could go back to the building.

So I went out and it happened I met Ben Green as I got out[.] [H]e too was sent out. He said the teacher told him that we were to go home and come back the next morning. We were just glad and started out straight across the woods and went home. The teacher must have meant that we go back to the boys building [dormitory] and come back to school the next morning. Ben was further advanced in English than I was, so he partway [partially] understood what the teacher said but she did not tell us to go all the way home. Our parents brought us back to school early the next morning and they must have explained for us as we were not punished. I still got another mishap the very same day[;] that time I was walking towards the boys quarters when I met the disciplinarian[.] [H]e stopped me and rattled off a lot of his stuff which I didn't understand a word and just could not answer. To my surprise he slapped me with both hands [on] both sides of my face and I stooped down to hide my face[.] [T]hen he pounded my head with his fist, but that didn't knock the English into my head. At that time I only wished he was still alive after I grew up. We were hungry a lot there but the reason was that they only put on just so much food to the one table and some of the boys were as greedy as pigs. So if a boy was not a fast eater he would never get enough to eat. I was going to that school when I was twelve years old, the time I met an accident. The way this happened as I have said before we were made to work half a day and the other half school. We were detailed to work different places and certain time[s] we were changed about. At that time I was detailed to work in the laundry and all the machinery was run by steam. I must have worked in this laundry about two weeks with a very mean boss who was always scolding, and she was so very big, weighed about three hundred pounds[,] so it was not very pleasant to get a scolding from her. A boy was sent to this laundry when I was at work, with his bed clothes to do his own washing as he was troubled with his kidneys and gets [his] bed wet at nights. This made her very angry and one day she took all his clothes off and put him in a washer[,] closed it up and even turned on the steam a little and turned the washer by hand. When she opened and took the boy out[,] the boy was so scared that I thought sure he went crazy. From that time on[,] I was so scared of her and she made me very nervous. There was two of us boys running these machines, but one day when my friend had gone after some coal from the boiler house, I was setting by the window watching the machinery when I saw that the ringer was at a standstill[.] [T]his made me very nervous and I rushed a tubful of bed clothes over to the ringer. First I took a sheet and doubled it nicely and put it into the ringer. Just as I got this inside the ringer[,] the sheet was snatched off my hands and my left hand had to go along with the sheet. It all went so quick that it seems like just a wink of my eye and there I was with my left hand off. It didn't bleed until after I had some clean towels wrapped over it[.] [T]hen the boss came and took more towels and wrapped more on my arm before she lead me out through the door. By the time we got to the door[,] I could only see a little light ahead of me, but as soon as we got through the door and got the fresh air, everything cleared up[,] seems to feel so good no pain of any kind, and she lead me and walked about seven hundred feet to the school hospital. It wasn't until we got to the hospital then [that] they tied my arm to keep from bleeding. And then I was taken in[to] bed until they got a woman[,] a Government doctor. She then put me under ether as she had to saw off about two inches of the bone so as to stitch the flesh over the bone. I didn't feel any pain for three days[,] only from my shoulder down it was numb. After the third day the pain came on and that's what made me cry a little. She had to saw my arm off twice[.] [T]he first time she forgot to tie one of the cords and infection set in so she had to do it all over again. I must have been just about still alive after all the suffering this woman gave me. And [she] still did a very poor job after it was all knitted. I lost a good many days of school and my class-mates left me behind in class. I was so weak from lack of blood that my bed was placed near lots of windows so as to get plenty of sunlight and fresh air. It took sometime before I was able to get up from bed and I had to start way back and practice how to walk and I had to be very careful not to hurt my arm[.] [T]ime came when I was able to go outside and play with the boys by the hospital. I have never forgotten the funny feeling I got when I thought I was strong enough to run around with the boys. . . . I hurt this arm many times before I got used to it. I finally got back to school and I was very discouraged to learn that my class had left me so far behind. I had been in school long enough but my parents did not tell me to work hard in school and never told me what I could do with a good education so I just had my own way and every chance I got I stayed out of school and much rather work. I was nineteen years old when I quit school altogether and my father was getting quite old[,] so I did the farm work then. While I was out west I have tried a day of school but my eyes failed me as I went one week in school and was sent two weeks in the hospital. And [I] had no one to buy me eye glasses which would have helped me a lot in day school. I often wonder why the Government never offered any kind of reward for all the damages it has done to me[.] [T]hey didn't even as much give me a good job and I have asked many times for some kind of a settlement. If I was only playing when this happened[,] I would not expect a thing but I was put to work among the machinery at the age of twelve. . . .

9

Contemporary Oneida Elders Reflect on Their Boarding School Experiences

Editors' Note: The following four stories by contemporary Oneida elders show the more positive side of the federal boarding school experience.

My School Days

Prudence Bennett Doxtator

I started school at St. Joseph's School at Oneida. When I was twelve years old [around 1927], my father passed away. I was then sent to the Guardian Angel Boarding School, which had been formerly known as the Oneida Boarding School. I was with five or six other Oneida students at the school. The school was operated by the Catholic Diocese and the teachers were all nuns. I was allowed to go home on weekends or I stayed at Josephine Webster's house. While at the Guardian Angel School, I had a music teacher by the name of Sam Bill who lived in a mansion on Quincy Street in Green Bay. I would be invited to his home periodically. Mr. Bill would also come by train to give music lessons when I was home. My mother paid for the lessons by cleaning his shirts. I finished the eighth grade and was graduated from St. Joseph's. I then attended the Tomah Indian School in

Tomah, Wisconsin, for a year and a half. I worked two hours everyday in the dining room and attended classes the rest of the day. The students were furnished with shoes and clothes, if needed, but were also allowed to wear their own clothes from home. We were bussed to town for church services and for shopping. We were allowed to go to the movies. Oneidas worked at Tomah—Eli and Mercie Hill and Lavinia Cornelius. "Miss Lavinia," as she was called, was a nurse and she was very stern. I worked for another nurse, a Miss Hughes, to obtain spending money. At Tomah at the time, there was no restriction on speaking our Oneida language. In my sophomore year, I left Tomah for Flandreau Indian School in South Dakota. My mother had a job as a cook at Flandreau until she became ill and had to return home to Oneida. At Flandreau, I worked in the campus hospital for a year. I belonged to several clubs, played on the basketball team, and was a member of the choir traveling to nearby communities to perform. I liked it there. There was plenty of food. You could always volunteer at the hospital as a nurses' aide if you got lonesome. There were not many Oneidas at Flandreau. Lillian and Rose Smith were my friends from Oneida. I also chummed around with two Sioux girlfriends. We were allowed to speak our own Indian languages and there was always plenty of food. The only prejudice I witnessed was when I went with my friends one day into town and I saw a big sign in a store window: "No blankets allowed." Nevertheless, I liked Flandreau and I believe it did a lot of us good to go there. After I graduated, I stayed for a while at Flandreau and worked in the campus hospital before returning home. After I came home, I worked in a grocery for thirty-five years and in the Oneida Tribal Library for twenty years.

My School Days

Marie Hinton

My father took us—I was three years old and my brother Amos who was five—to the government school [Oneida Boarding School]. Those days, we were told to change our ways and not be Indians all our lives. At the time, there was no kindergarten there and so I had to find things to do at the school. I would sit in the playroom or hang out with a kind lady at the laundry. This same lady would always watch over me and feed me since I missed my brother who was in class. I had a friend but she was sent off to Keshena [Indian Boarding School]. At the school while I stood by a nice picket fence, I remember seeing my grandparents pass by. I was at the school when the influenza epidemic [1918–1919] hit. The classrooms were filled with cots of the sick. When I was six, the government school closed. I went to live with my grandparents David and Louisa Christjohn. I went to the St. Joseph's School until the third grade. For a brief time I attended the Bethany Mission School in Wittenberg, Wisconsin, but I eventually went back to St. Joseph's School at Oneida. At St. Joseph's I was made fun of because I spoke Oneida and could hardly speak English. I did not like it there. My aunt Marie Webster took me to Mt. Pleasant, Michigan, where she worked as a matron in the Indian school there. Marie Webster's husband worked as the disciplinarian in the same federal Indian boarding school. My brother Amos and I attended school at Mt. Pleasant [Indian Boarding School]. I was happy there. I did not have to walk to school in cold weather or eat cold sandwiches. I then went to Flandreau government school where I stayed two or three years. You had to make a contract to attend a government school. Most students didn't have the right to go home as children do today; however, I was allowed to return home after the school year ended since my aunt and uncle worked at the school. I then went to Haskell Indian School in Kansas and I attended from the tenth to the twelfth grade; however, I did not graduate. I lived in a cottage and worked in the laundry and kitchen while going to school. On weekends, I worked for the staff doing housework. The reason I did not graduate from Haskell was that I went on "Outing." For three years I worked in Kansas City. This was the time of the Great Depression. I came home and I had found that things had changed. I moved to California and went to nursing school while doing odd jobs here and there. I later moved to Milwaukee and went to school there. I then moved back home to

Oneida. I received my bachelor's degree from the University of Wisconsin Green Bay and a teaching certificate from Mt. Scenario College. In the meantime, I was teaching the Oneida language in the Oneida school system and working in developing curriculum on the Oneida language and working on an Oneida dictionary that has recently been published.

My School Days

Mary Schuyler Metoxen

I started school when I lived in Menasha, Wisconsin. I attended kindergarten through the third grade there. My family then returned to the Oneida Reservation and I continued my schooling at the Elm Hill School and then grade school at Chicago Corners, where I completed the eighth grade. I then attended Washington Jr. High School in Green Bay going by bus everyday. The Bureau of Indian Affairs had made arrangements with the Green Bay School District to have Oneidas attend this school and then go on to East High in Green Bay. I completed my sophomore year at East High. I then went on to Flandreau Indian School in South Dakota since I had been skipping school at East High. I did not like East High and hardly went there, preferring instead to go downtown and bum around. My mother then asked if I would like to go to Flandreau and I agreed. She got busy and helped get me into Flandreau. At Flandreau, I spent half a day in class and in my studies and the other half I spent either working in the kitchen or the craft area weaving rugs. I enjoyed weaving rugs on the big loom. The rugs were then sold and the money was used for more art supplies for the school. The food at the school was good and I was treated well. I chose to work in the kitchen, which was considered cook's training. I worked in uniform in tea-room training, doing all the cooking, serving the school staff, and cleaning up afterwards. I also worked in the school laundry. The girls had to wash their own clothes as well as those of the boys. I guess the boys did not know how to wash their clothes! Our daily schedule included getting up at 6:00 A.M., dressing and making beds and reaching the dining room for breakfast by 7:00 A.M. Lunch was served at noon and supper at 5:30. All students needed to be in bed by 9:00 P.M. Bells rang for all things—wake up, meals, bedtime. On weekends we could go into town. We could go downtown to see a movie that cost twenty-five cents. You could go to stores or restaurants as long as you had money. You had to be back by supper. All students needed to sign out and sign in on your return. In the evening, you could visit and play in a set aside area, the oval. Every other Saturday night, there was a dance in the school gym and movies in the auditorium. I can't say I was treated badly. You could be punished if you got off track and you were punished by being restricted to the school buildings. When I returned to Oneida, I became the cook for the first Head Start Program on the reservation. I worked with my aunt, Irene Moore [first woman to be Oneida Tribal Chairperson] at Head Start. I then worked cooking for the tribal elders in the Meals-on-Wheels Program. I enjoyed every bit of it.

My School Days

Purcell Powless

I started at St. Joseph's [Catholic] School at Oneida and went through the fourth grade. When I was twelve, I was sent in 1937 to Pipestone [Government Boarding School] in Minnesota. My uncle Eugene along with his girlfriend drove me and my older brother John there. I didn't realize what I was getting into and that we were [to be] left there. I only realized that when I didn't see the car anymore. After two weeks, I realized that we were there to stay. My brother John ran away from the school, but I remained. Oneidas worked at Pipestone. My relatives Sherman Baird and Lilian Powless Baird worked there. Sherman worked as a custodian in the powerhouse and Lilian was the head of the laundry. Sherman was a really nice guy. When I was sent as punishment to the powerhouse, he let me smoke. Anderson Cornelius' sister Delia was a baker at the school and her daughter was a cook at the school. Pemberton Doxtator was a night watchman there. Life at the school was good compared to home. No chores. I didn't have to cut kindling wood for the stove. We had steam heat. We had nice warm beds. We didn't have to get up and haul water. We had pretty good food, three meals a day. It was like going into the military. I received new clothing—shoes, shirts, jackets for winter. At home I had to work on my father's thirty-acre truck farm, my grandfather's homestead. I had to do my chores before I could go swimming in Duck Creek. At school I worked in the laundry or on the school farm where I cleaned the barn, fed the cattle and picked the corn. We worked half-a-day and the other half we attended classes. I hear they forbade our language at these schools, but it didn't affect me since I didn't know my language. The Winnebago [Ho-Chunk] and Sioux spoke their language in small groups at the school and yet no one bothered them at the time [1930s]. I stayed at the school during holidays and went home during the summer months. I returned to the school in the fall by train. Although there were bullies at the school, I had no problems with the five or six tribes represented there. I had no problems with the Chippewas and Sioux [most of the student population at the school]. I went on to Flandreau [Government Boarding School] when I was about fourteen or fifteen years of age. At Flandreau, it was similar to Pipestone. I worked half a day and went to high school the other half. I worked in the kitchen, dairy or laundry. Sometimes I worked for local farmers to earn spending money. The students at Flandreau were older, some nineteen or twenty years of age. I never went home on holidays and looked forward to presents [money] from home. After graduation from Flandreau, I joined the Merchant Marines. I then was an iron worker for thirty-seven years, living in Milwaukee and Chicago during some of those years. I moved back to Oneida around 1960. I blame Norbert Hill, Sr. [former Oneida tribal chairman] for getting me mixed up in tribal politics. In the old days, clan mothers ran things. I worked with the ladies of the tribe—Irene Moore, Amelia Cornelius, Anna John, Alma Webster, Priscilla Mander. These good people served the Oneidas well long before bingo operations, casinos. . . .

Editors' Note: Despite the overwhelming criticisms over the past four decades by scholars and contemporary Native Americans about the historical impact of the federal Indian boarding school system, the Oneida student experiences at these schools were diverse. While an overall national policy was set in Washington, there were many variables. These included why the students were sent to these schools in the first place, when they attended, where they were sent, and the local quality and cultural sensitivities of administrators and teachers at these schools. To treat these children merely as victims, unable to cope or respond to the circumstances, belies their strength and the fact that some of these American Indian youngsters became major leaders of their nations—politically, economically, and culturally—in the decades that followed allotment.

Oneida Indian adults were to speak with more than one voice during this critical era in their history. They debated the future direction of the tribal estate—whether to accept or reject allotment and later fee simple title. Some turned to rallying the nation by pursuing compensation—money and land—from New York State based on claims dating from as far back as the 1780s and 1790s. Others turned inward, becoming more devout Episcopalians or Methodists, to anchor them in most difficult times. Still others joined together in efforts to save the government school; improve health facilities; and/or oppose the federal, state, and local push to extend Oneida fee simple title. On the cultural and economic side, Oneida women formed a lace-making guild, one that received national attention and provided supplemental income to their struggling families; while Oneida men became professional musicians, some establishing ensembles that entertained at every reservation function and fostered community pride and identity.

Part III

Oneida Voices in the Age of Allotment

Introduction

Some Oneida Families

Three families at Oneida, Wisconsin—the Corneliuses, the Hills, and the Wheelocks—produced four distinct cultural, economic, and political responses to the Oneida plight in the age of allotment. Chief Cornelius Hill (1834–1907) was the first great Oneida leader to be born in Wisconsin, and his autobiography appears in print here for the first time. As a youth, Hill spent five years at Nashotah House, an Episcopal seminary, where the priests inculcated him with a deep religious faith. Because of his intelligence, his English language skills, and his early and recognizable leadership abilities, Hill was made chief by his teenage years and given the name Onan-gwat-go, or "Big Medicine." Even before the Civil War, he was making his mark in tribal politics. He served as treasurer of the tribe and conducted the tribal census in 1856.[1]

One of the greatest influences on the life of Cornelius Hill was Reverend Edward A. Goodnough, the Episcopal missionary and teacher among the Oneidas who served the Indian nation from 1853 until his death in 1890. Goodnough acted as spiritual adviser and father figure to the young chief. Hill frequently defended the missionary, who was often intrusive in tribal politics and who strongly questioned allotment as a quick solution to Oneida problems and poverty.[2]

By the late 1860s and into the early 1870s, Hill opposed the leadership of Chief Daniel Bread, the principal chief of the Oneidas, who had reluctantly come to the conclusion that allotment was inevitable and could not be prevented.[3] With the death of Hill's longtime chief rival Bread in 1873, the forty-year-old Hill took a more visible role in Oneida politics. The following year, as a member of the council of chiefs, Hill drafted a petition to the New York legislature asking that state officials recognize Oneida claims—specifically Oneida reserved fishing rights under state treaties.[4] Although he did not succeed in this particular endeavor, he was to lead a revolution in tribal politics a short time later.

After more than ten years of bitter tribal debate, the Oneidas adopted an elected system in 1878 and 1879 and replaced their council of chiefs, which had been established fifty years earlier. The result was an elected system comprised of a sachem and councillors in place of the chiefs. Hill was elected sachem for four years, and John Archiquette, A. P. Cornelius (who replaced Daniel Ninham in a second vote in 1879), Henry K. Cooper (secretary), William Cornelius, Baptist Doxtator, Jacob Hill, and James A. Wheelock were elected as tribal councillors.[5]

Chief Hill and his supporters blamed the council of chiefs for not protecting the timber on the reservation from both whites and Indians, who were stripping the trees and cutting and hauling off logs "without permission from any one." Hill claimed that the new elected government could stop these illegal operations, and this could be accomplished by issuing certificates to individual Indians who desire to "improve and cultivate the land or lot, as shall be assigned to them." This should be done "before the General Government gets ready and sees fit to apportion our lands by allotments." Hence, although an early opponent of allotment, by 1879 Hill also saw that allotment was inevitable.[6] It is important to note (see Part II), that only when the Oneidas were promised a federally operated and funded government boarding school, one proposed by Hill as early as 1879, did tribal members vote for allotment.

On February 8, 1887, the Dawes General Allotment Act was signed into law. When the act was applied to the Oneidas in 1891 and allotments made the following year, each head of an Oneida family received ninety acres, single persons over twenty-one years of age and orphans under twenty-one were given forty-five acres each, and each minor was allotted twenty-six acres. Lands were also reserved for tribal cemeteries, churches, day schools, and the government boarding school established in 1893. Unlike many other Indian communities under the Dawes General Allotment Act, there were no "surplus" Indian lands available to be sold off and thrown open to white settlement (see Oberly in Part IV).

Chief Hill was not merely an accomplished Oneida political leader. A devout Episcopalian, he turned more and more to spiritual matters after the allotment of the Oneida reservation began in 1892. In 1895, he became a deacon of the Episcopal church. On June 24, 1903, in a ceremony attended by three bishops, twelve clergy, and numerous Indians, he was ordained a priest, the first Oneida to be so honored. Hill, in the well-attended ceremony, repeated his vows in the Oneida language. In one description of the 1903 ceremony, Julia K. Bloomfield wrote:

> Chief Onan-gwat-go [Onuhkwastkó or Big Medicine], now the Rev. Cornelius Hill, was at the time of his ordination in his sixty-ninth year, and is said to have resembled the portraits of some of the old chiefs that hang in the State Historical Society at Madison, Wisconsin. He is tall and straight, with quiet, cordial manner, thoroughly self-possessed, and with a genial smile that wins the friendship of all with whom he comes in contact. There is a bronze tinge to his face; his hair is iron-gray. He has a wife who has not yet learned to speak English, and eight children. His children are receiving a good education; after finishing the schools at Oneida, at Hampton, and other Indian schools away from the Reservation. Though the Rev. Cornelius Hill will have a missionary stipend, it is only the small sum of $150 per annum; so his main support must come from his well cultivated farm.[7]

Much of Hill's later life as an Episcopal cleric confirms the findings of recent scholarly writings on Native clergymen in the post–Civil War era. Writing on the Presbyterian Native clergy, Bonnie Sue

Lewis has emphasized that they "saw in Christianity a universal message of hope and the appreciation of values that were at the heart of their own cultures." Lewis added that, with "the authority of ordination, Indian ministers maintained traditional leadership roles and cultural values." The Native clergy's most important skill was "their ability to speak to Native concerns, to interpret Native existence in terms of Indian and Christian concepts, and to provide for their people continuity, meaning, and hope in changing circumstances."[8] Hill, who replaced his mentor Goodnough (who had died in 1890), served precisely this role among the Oneidas. As an ordained clergyman, not as an assistant or catechist to Goodnough, the chief could be the bridge between the Indian and white worlds.

The historical importance of the two largest Oneida reservation congregations—the Episcopal and Methodist churches—is in need of a book-length study. The later life of Hill, the most prominent voice of the first generation of Oneidas born in Wisconsin, clearly shows the significance of Christianity among the Oneidas through the age of allotment, as a way of grappling with the crises all around them in the age of allotment.

One of Hill's greatest legacies was his extraordinary daughter Josephine. Instead of her father's political and religious focus, Josephine Hill Webster (1883–1978) became the leader of one of the more successful economic experiments in modern Iroquois history. She headed the Oneida Indian Lace Association, comprised of reservation women, that lasted well into the 1940s. Josephine Hill attended the U.S. Grant Grammar School and Lincoln Institute in Philadelphia, as well as the Hampton Institute in Virginia, where she was graduated with honors in 1904. There she met her future husband, Isaac Webster, who himself became prominent in tribal politics after World War I.[9]

The lacework experiment originated from the work of Episcopal missionary Sybil Carter, a close associate and friend of Bishop Henry Whipple, who suggested to the prominent cleric the need to establish art programs and self-sufficiency efforts among Indian women. In 1890, Carter began teaching lacework to Ojibwa Indians on the White Earth Reservation in Minnesota. This experiment provided Indian women with wage work by reviving cut work and bobbin lace (pillow lace), a seventeenth-century northern Italian tradition that by the late nineteenth century was dying off. Encouraged by Bishop Whipple and reformers of the Lake Mohonk Conference of Friends of the Indian, Carter established lace classes among the Ojibwa as well as among the Arapaho, Hopi, Kiowa, Mission, Oneida, Onondaga, Seneca, Sioux, Paiute, and Winnebago Indians. In 1904 Carter founded the Sybil Carter Indian Lace Association, a philanthropic effort whose members included the elite of the New York metropolitan area—the Cuttings, Mortons, Reids, Vanderbilts, Frelinghuysens, and Roosevelts. This association lasted until 1926.[10]

In 1899, an Oneida Episcopal Church publication indicated that the reservation women had taken to this project, that seventy-five were participating and had "made over 500 pieces of lace, including 600 yards of lace edging in strips of two and three yards each and many doilies. This brought them in a cash return of about $425." The Oneida women undertook two kinds of lace-work: braid lace, which was of needlework, and pillow or bobbin lace. Despite the newness of lacework, the publication made clear, these same women had adapted their traditional skill at making Iroquoian moccasins and corn-husk dolls to this new endeavor. Now forming a guild and working at home and at the Episcopal church, they earned money for their family's survival. The women in the guild had specific but very distinct responsibilities. Some did the lacework, others carefully packed the lace for eastern shipment, others sold the lace at county and state fairs throughout the Midwest. This cooperative functioned much like the traditional Iroquoian women's societies that had influenced so much of tribal life in New York.[11]

After Josephine Hill's graduation from Hampton Institute, she returned to Oneida and directed the lacework project from 1908 onward. Initially she worked with the Sisters of Charity in a project that included more than eighty workers, half of whom were employed in cut work and half on bobbin lace. Even after the Sybil Carter Lace Association ended its formal existence in 1926, Webster and these Oneida women continued to fashion their lace and sell their creations. One of their masterpieces is at the Cathedral of St. John the Divine in New York City.[12]

In order to demonstrate "their excellent work made into useful and salable articles" for their New York patrons, the Oneida women held a major exhibition of their lacework in July 1912. A picnic, with a concert performed by the Oneida Band, was incorporated into the program. A representative of the Sybil Carter Lace Association reported on the exhibit. She commented on the quality of music performed and on the Oneida old men "who loved to talk about the day 'when my father came from New York State.'" The exhibit, which was held in the Webster homestead, drew the following comments from the reporter:

> What the Lace Industry is meaning to the Oneidas today, is an important consideration. That it is the only permanent industry by which an Indian woman may become self-supporting without leaving the Reservation, is a strong appeal, for the Reservation is home and the love of it is no mere sentiment. That the women have made intelligent use of the instruction given them is proven by their good work and the interest which they take in it. One has but to visit the homes of the workers, to see what it means to them in their efforts to supplement the meagre income from their none too profitable land.[13]

The Oneida lacewokers' guild lasted long after the women lost the financial support of their New York City backers, when the Sybil Carter Indian Lace Association stopped operations in the 1920s. The Oneida women continued to fill orders and win recognition, especially locally in the Midwest at Christmastime, in their sales of lace handkerchiefs, pillow and dresser scarves, table runners, bedspreads, women's lace collars, and luncheon sets. These efforts provided extra money to their families during the worst days of the Great Depression. Webster, a true entrepreneur, also served as Oneida postmistress for two decades, from 1934 until 1953. She died in 1978.[14] Today Oneida women have begun to revive this lacework endeavor since it is seen as an integral part of modern Oneida cultural traditions.

Dennison Wheelock (1871–1927), a member of a second leading family (one named after Eleazar Wheelock, the missionary and founder of Dartmouth College), is today a controversial figure at Oneida, Wisconsin. Wheelock was one of the greatest of American Indian musicians (see Hauptman, Part III). However, Wheelock's second career, which began in 1906 (that of tribal attorney), put him on the firing line in Oneida politics since some of his ideas ran counter to those of many within his community. He advocated and promoted an assimilationist path that stressed Oneidas' becoming U.S. citizens, fully integrated and not living apart on their reservations, and accepting personal responsibilities for their own affairs rather than depending on Washington. His ideas were largely shaped by his education at Carlisle where he came under the direct influence of Captain Pratt. Indeed, Wheelock was part of a newly emerging educated elite that greatly influenced the Indian world in the age of allotment (see Hauptman, Part III).

Largely separated from his people from 1885 to 1906, and from tribal politics, Wheelock was "Mr. Carlisle" among the Oneidas. He was one of the school's most illustrious graduates because he had become an internationally famous musical composer, musician, and band and concert orchestra conductor. Wheelock and Carlos Montezuma, the noted Indian physician and journalist, were among the Carlisle superintendent's favorites. In effect, they became Pratt's surrogate sons, corresponding with their "father" extensively for over four decades. Moreover, many of Wheelock's brothers, sisters, and cousins attended Carlisle. Wheelock met his wife there; Paul Wheelock, his first son, was born there and then died in infancy at Carlisle when Dennison was employed there. Pratt frequently promoted Dennison after his graduation in 1890—from his personal assistant to bandmaster to professor of music.

Wheelock, like Pratt, believed that the Indian reservation system could not survive in the modern world and that Indians should become American citizens under the full protection of American law. Wheelock was inculcated with Pratt's thinking, namely that Western learning and traditions were far superior and more useful than old Indian ways.

Despite his views that conflicted with those of most Oneidas, Wheelock, who spoke fluent Oneida, helped prevent the tribe's termination in 1910–1911 when the federal government attempted to buy out, in one lump sum payment, its treaty obligations set forth in the Treaty of 1794.[15] He urged making the Oneida Indian Boarding School first a public school and then, when that idea failed, a much-needed health care facility to treat Indian tuberculosis patients. Wheelock believed that all Oneidas were capable people, equal to any people on the face of the earth. He believed, as Pratt did, that all Oneidas could manage their own affairs, that they should be awarded citizenship immediately, since they did not need federal officials to treat them as children. With the help of Isaac Webster (Josephine Hill's husband), he helped organize the Oneida Centennial Celebration in 1921 to show the "progress" in civilization that the Oneidas had made in one hundred years in Wisconsin.

Wheelock returned to his Wisconsin reservation precisely at the time that fee simple patents were being issued to Oneidas under the Burke Act of 1906. He entered the real estate business (and later law focusing on real property) and set up an office in nearby West De Pere, off the reservation proper. He became financially successful as a result of these activities and developed economic, political, and social ties to the non-Indian world of Brown and Outagamie counties. His legal practice, which centered on conversion of trust to fee simple title, questions of heirship and land sales of former tribal lands, combined with his outspoken assimilationist views, put him in disfavor with many of the Oneidas.[16] Eventually in 1923, he went to Washington to practice law, representing more than a dozen tribes until his death in 1927.

A fourth voice in the age of allotment was that of Laura Minnie Cornelius Kellogg (1880–1949?), another brilliant but controversial figure in Oneida history.[17] She was born Laura Cornelius on September 10, 1880, on the Wisconsin Oneida Indian Reservation. Unlike Josephine Hill Webster and Dennison Wheelock as well as many of her contemporary Oneidas, Kellogg managed to avoid attending distant Indian boarding schools. She was educated in the 1890s at Grafton Hall, an Episcopal boarding school largely for non-Indians located at Fond du Lac, Wisconsin. In the first decade of the twentieth century, she studied at Barnard College, Cornell University, the New York School of Philanthropy (later the Columbia University School of Social Work), Stanford University, and the University of Wisconsin; however, she never received degrees from any of these institutions.

One of the best Indian linguists of her generation, with a superior command of Oneida and Mohawk as well as English, Kellogg had gained national attention by 1911 because of her spellbinding oratory before Indian and non-Indian audiences and her writing skills. As a public speaker, she told of the eighteenth-century League of the Iroquois, the lessons and wisdom of Indian elders, and the overriding concerns of Native Americans to win back their lands, which she insisted had been taken fraudulently by New York State and by land speculators. She was equally accomplished with a pen, devoting herself to writing on behalf of Progressive Era reform causes such as women's rights as well as writing political tracts on Indian issues, plays, and short stories.

In 1911 Kellogg was one of the founders of the Society of American Indians (SAI), a national reform-minded organization largely composed of highly educated Indian professionals. Later she served variously as secretary of the organization's executive committee and vice president for education. Kellogg, however, differed from the majority of the SAI in her vehement opposition to the economic and educational policies of the Bureau of Indian Affairs (BIA). She was more confident than other organization members that Native Americans could, without assistance, transform their reservations into self-sustaining communities. After her marriage on April 22, 1912, to Orrin Joseph Kellogg, a non-Indian attorney from Minneapolis, she became more isolated from the SAI. Eventually, she broke with the organization, outlining her views in *Our Democracy and the American Indian* (1920), which drew significant inspiration from the Mormon economic model of community development and survival.[18]

Kellogg and her husband spent much of the time before, during, and after World War I organizing a massive Iroquois land-claims suit. For this legal effort, they made exorbitant promises and collected funds from poor Indians in Iroquois communities throughout the United States and Canada. Their collection methods led to their arrests in Oklahoma (1913) and Montreal (1925), although they were never actually convicted of fraud. In 1927 the U.S. District Court dismissed their Iroquois land-claims suit, *Deere v. St. Lawrence River Power Company,* because of a lack of jurisdiction.

Kellogg continued to exercise influence in Indian affairs into the 1930s, but her insistence on self-sufficiency became less appealing during the New Deal era, when the government provided tribes with economic assistance and promoted Indian languages and cultural traditions. By the 1940s she was a forgotten woman who had outlived her time. According to Oneida tribal sources, she died in obscurity sometime in the late 1940s.

Acknowledged as a precursor of the contemporary land-claims movement and as a determined advocate of Indian education and economic development, Kellogg, nevertheless, has been accused by some Indian elders of fomenting divisions within Iroquois communities and swindling Indians of hundreds of thousands of dollars in her abortive efforts to litigate their land claims.[19] Unlike other portraits of this controversial Oneida woman, Patricia Stovey (see Part III) focuses on Kellogg's involvement in tribal politics, her ideas on tribal economic development (which she labeled "Lolomi"), and her efforts to save the Oneida Boarding School and its grounds for this Indian nation.

Notes

1. Hauptman and McLester, *Chief Daniel Bread,* 153–59. For Chief Hill's obituary, see "Onon-gwat-go: A Chief of the Oneidas," *Southern Workman* 36 (March 1907): 133–34.

2. Hauptman and McLester, *Chief Daniel Bread,* 155–59.

3. Ibid.

4. New York State Legislature, *Senate Document 79*, March 24, 1874, p. 18.

5. The heated debate in these tribal meetings can be traced in Petition of Cornelius Hill et al. to J. C. Bridgman, September 24, November 30, 1878, Bridgman to Commissioner, December 18, 1878, OIA, GBAR, micro-copy 234, reel 334; Cornelius Hill to Commissioner of Indian Affairs, January 20, October 25, 27, 1879, Hill et al. to Bridgman, February 19, 1879, E. Stephens [the new federal Indian agent] to Commissioner of Indian Affairs, July 31, 1879, Notice of E. Stephens of General Council Meeting to be held October 20, 1879, Cornelius Doxtator and Oneida Council of Chiefs to Secretary of the Interior Carl Schurz, September 8, 1879, George and Cornelius Doxtator to E. Stephens, October 6, 1879, Petition of supporters of Oneida Council of Chiefs, July 17, 1879, in ibid., reel 335; Cornelius Doxtator to Schurz, January 14, 1880, Sachem [Cornelius Hill], Councellors [sic] and Headmen Petition to Commissioner of Indian Affairs, March 30, 1880, in ibid., reel 336; all in RG75, NA.

6. Cornelius Hill et al. to Bridgman, February 19, 1879, ibid., reel 335, RG75, NA.

7. Bloomfield, *The Oneidas*, 334.

8. Bonnie Sue Lewis, *Creating Christian Indians: Native Clergy in the Presbyterian Church* (Norman: University of Oklahoma Press, 2003), xi–xiii, 181–82. See also James Treat, *Native and Christian: Indigenous Voices on Religious Identity in the United States and Canada* (New York: Routledge, 1995).

9. Thelma McLester, "Josephine Hill Webster, 1883–1978: Supervisor of Oneida Lace Industry and First Woman Postmaster," in, Campisi and Hauptman, *Oneida Indian Experience,* 116–18. For her husband, Isaac, see "Indian Notes," *Southern Workman* 50 (October 1921): 478–79.

10. Kate L. Duncan, "American Indian Lace Making," *American Indian Art* 5 (Summer 1980): 28–35, 80. The annual reports of the Sybil Carter Indian Lace Association can be found in the textile archives of the Smith-sonian's Cooper-Hewitt Museum in New York City. The editors would like to acknowledge the assistance of Barbara Duggan of that fine museum for helping us locate this important file. See also the annual reports of the Lake Mohonk Conferences of Friends of the Indian for the years 1889, 46, 114; 1892, 117; 1893, 40; 1894, 23, 26, 63; 1896, 43–44; 1897, 56;

1898, 27, 53, 1899, 22, 24; 1901, 75; 1903, 64; 1906, 35 (published proceedings found in research libraries).

11. Oneida Episcopal Mission, *Oneida: People of the Stone,* 47–55. Interview of Woodrow Webster [Josephine Hill Webster's son], June 4, 2004, Oneida, Wis. (notes in the possession of Lawence M. Hauptman).

12. Annual Report of the Sybill [*sic*] Carter Indian Mission and Lace Industry, 1911, [Smithsonian] Cooper-Hewitt Museum.

13. Ibid., 1912.

14. McLester, "Josephine Webster Hill," 116–18.

15. U.S. Congress, House of Representatives, Document No. 251: *Oneida Indians: Letter from the Secretary of the Interior Transmitting Report of Negotiations with Oneida Indians for Commutation of Their Perpetual Annuities, as Provided for by the Act of March 3, 1911,* 62nd Cong. 2nd sess. (Washington, D.C., 1911), 9–21.

16. See Laurence M. Hauptman, Oneida field notes, June–August, 2003 (in author's possession).

17. For treatments of the life of this controversial Oneida, see Laurence M. Hauptman, "Designing Woman: Minnie Kellogg, Iroquois Leader," in *Indian Lives: Essays on Nineteenth and Twentieth Century Native American Leaders,* ed. L. G. Moses and Raymond Wilson, 159–88 (Albuquerque: University of New Mexico Press, 1985), 159–88; Thelma McLester, "Oneida Women Leaders," in, Campisi and Hauptman, *Oneida Indian Experience,* 109–11. See also Stovey, Part III.

18. Laura Cornelius Kellogg, *Our Democracy and the American Indian: A Comprehensive Presentation of the Indian Situation as It Is Today* (Kansas City: Burton, 1920).

19. Laurence M. Hauptman, Iroquois field notes, 1971–2005 (in author's possession). In every community of Iroquoia, there is a different opinion about Minnie Kellogg and her influence.

10

The Autobiography of Chief Cornelius Hill, September 7, 1899

Editors' Note: The following memoir was found in the Records of the Oneida Indian Historical Society, Oneida, Wisconsin.

I was born in Oneida Res[ervation] in the year 1834. When I was ten years old. I was sent away to Nashotah [Episcopal Mission School]. I could not speak a word of the English language. There were two Indian boys there that I could talk to but being young I soon learned the language. When I was there two or three years I was chosen to be the chief of the Bear clan or band and there was a national forest, and all of the different bands were present and also the principal chiefs from Canada. When I was fifteen years of age I came home to Oneida and I had forgotten my own Indian language[.] My parents, brother and sister could not speak the English language and was hard for us to understand one another[.] [W]e had to make motions when we talked in order to understand one another[.] But I soon learned my own language again when I was about eighteen years old. I commenced to go with the chiefs at the consuls [councils] and I am glad to say that the chiefs gave me honor. In the early days the Oneida agents would come and pay the annuitys to the chiefs, and the chiefs would give him a receipt and then they would give me the bag of money that contained seven or eight hundred dollars, and I would have the money until it [was] paid to the tribe[.] [T]hen the chief would chose me and John W. Cornelius to take the census of the tribes. The number was only one thousand [in the late 1850s] that time but now [1897] we are two thousand. It took us three days to pay each person[,] equally old and young. In the year 1870 or there abouts the chiefs chose me to act as the justice of the piece and [I] held the office for several years. The chiefs acted as jurors to the [re]publican form of government. [T]hen we [held] elections [for those] who shall be officers of the tribes and they were called sachem and consulers [councillors]. Sachem was to hold the office for three years and the consulers two years. I was [the] first one chosen as a sachem and consulers were done away with at the time [late 1880s] of our al[l]otment of our land was made[.] I have been to Albany five or six times as a delegat[e] for the tribe and I have also been to Washington two times. The congregation of our church chose me as a delegate for the consules at Milwaukee [for] the first time in the year 1855 or there abouts, and from that time I have always been chosen as a delegate from our Hobart church until I was ordained deacon, and I was also chosen Senior Warden for a great many years. I have made addresses to my people Oneidas for the advancement of their civilisation. I have upheld and honored them always our good father Bishop Kemper, T. R. Hoff, Omridates Bronen and Bishop Grafton, E. A. Goodnough, S. S. Burleson and Merrill. In the early days father Goodnough was at times abused very shamefully by some of the old chiefs for the reason he would not favor their wishes. They had a desire to sell a part or a whole of our land and some of the Indian agents that we had would always favor the old chiefs as they were called. We were always divided into two parties[.] [O]ne party was called Young Chiefs. The young chiefs were always against us selling our land and Father Goodnough was always on their side. And the Indian agents and the old chiefs threatened that they would get Father Goodnough out of the Res[ervation]. I had always defended him for the interest of our people. One of the old chiefs went so

far as to say that he would kick him of[f] the Res[ervation]. This
was in general consul. When he spoke the word[s], and I got up
and made [a] few remarks for what he had said. . . . [I]f he [Rev.
Goodnough] had not been with us we would not be living in this
Res[ervation]. [W]e would have been proba[b]ly in the state of
Indian Territory. There was a time when three men came to my
house about midnight and woke me up. They urged me to sign
a treaty to sell a portion of our land and they said that if I sign
the treaty[,] they would give me a thousand dollars. I told them
that if they gave me ten thousand dollars[,] I would not sign the
treaty. Our [God]mother Mrs. Ellen Goodnough was the first one
that spoke to me about building a stone church just as well as
not for we have a good quarry. I said at the time it would be very
good to have a stone church but I did not think we would be able
to build a new church. She told me to see what the opinion of
our people in building a stone church[.] I said nothing to any of
our people about it. Two months afterwards Mother [Goodnough]
asked me if I had asked the people['s] opinion and I said I had
not but I will call a consul and lay the question before them and
a majority thought it would be a very good work for our heavenly
father but there was [a] few that very strongly opposed. They
thought we would not be able to build a new church and said
that the old wooden church [Hobart Church] was good enough
for us. And the very ones that opposed ought to have encouraged us to build a stone church[.] [T]hey were the old chiefs. [W]e
agreed upon to work in the quarry one day every week during
the summer time and there would be from sixty to one hundred
men working[.] [S]ome would be geting a stone out and others
loading the waggons. [W]e worked several years and we had
enough stone to build with. The last week before the layers of
stone came we worked every day[.] The Indian[s] were mostly
all poor and had large familys and wished they worked at thier
own homes. [W]hile they were working for the church I was glad
that the good Christian people of the east helped us in building. I
have been [the] organist of our church for thirty seven years and
I also have acted as interpreter for fifteen years[.] [. . .] the vestry

men[.] [O]ne of the men name[d] was Cornelius John laid the question before them[.] He said that the organest ought to be paid for what he [had] done for the church and the vestry men agreed to pay him even for the [. . .] fifty dollars a year for about eight years.

11

Three Oneida WPA Stories about Chief Cornelius Hill

Editors' Note: The following three WPA stories illustrate the life of the first major Oneida leader born in Wisconsin.

Two Stories about Chief Cornelius Hill

Chauncey Baird

We Oneidas had a relative whose name was Onuhgwatgó or Big Medicine. This kind of a name by what he was called did not correspond with the meaning of saying Big Medicine. This name was given him in resemblance to their wisdom at that time of which he was more intelligent then they were. Some of the old people at that time when Onuhgwatgó or Big Medicine grew up, they said that there is another pine came up where we live. This they [said] resembled a princess pine. This they said because [he was] the leader for the Oneidas[.] [H]e also was the overseer of what belongings they had at that time. Most of the people agreed with him that therefore they did not sell their land for sometime. He was their leader for a long time.

My uncle Cornelius Hill was born November 13th, 1834. When he was ten years old [, a] white man came there and took him along. He sent him to get schooling. He was thirteen years old when they sent for him[;] they showed respect. He went to school five years then he came back[.] [H]e was then fifteen years old and Chiefs showed more respect for him[.] [T]hats when he started working for the Oneidas. And they got him to do the interpreting for the Oneidas. And he worked with the priest. And it came in time when they made a priest of him. He died on January 26, 1907 [, when] he was seventy three.

Chief Cornelius Hill

Albert Hill

A man by the name of Big Medicine was born in the year of 1834. When he was 10 years old, he was sent to Nashotah to school. It was not surprising that he could not speak a word of English as neither of his parents knew how to speak the English language. Being interested and having the idea to become useful in something very important, he was long in learning to read and write. He was very young when he was chosen to be one of the Chiefs in the Bear Clan. When he was elected to be a Chief all the different clans of the old Chiefs were present[.] [A]lso the Great Chiefs from Canada were present as there was a great feast given at that time. It was not long after the Great Chiefs would take him along at their Councils. The Great Chiefs knew that he would be very useful to their land. At the age of 18 he was of great honor to the Great Chiefs. He was well liked by the people that he was chosen to issue the small amount of money that was given them which is called annuity money. This money was issued equally to young and old[.] [S]ometimes it would take three days to issue out the money. He was also one of the men to take census of the Oneida Indians and at that time there were about one thousand of Oneidas. At that time he was so well liked by his people that they were not afraid to choose him as a delegator [delegate] which they did[.] [H]e had been sent to Albany several times as a delegate for the tribe[.] [H]e also made trips as a delegate to Washington D.C. The Chiefs were divided into two groups. The old Chiefs were separated from the young

Chiefs as they were called. As the old Chiefs were planning to sell a portion of their reservation[,] Big Medicine as he was called was or had more authority over the old Chiefs[.] [H]e [was] opposed to the question [of] selling any part of their land[.] [H]e often lectured to the tribe for them to keep their land so that the Oneidas would always have a home. Being religious [he] supported the Episcopal Church, of which he was a member from boyhood on. He had the priest Father Goodnough to support him in opposing to the question of selling any part of the Indian land. The old Chiefs were not friendly with the young Chiefs for that reason at that time. He also was chosen to be one of the delegates to go to Milwaukee for the conference for the benefit of the Church[.] [A]t that time the Episcopalians had all their conferences there. In time he was elected to be a Senior Warden of his church, and retained that privilege many years[.] [H]e also was organist at the church for sometime. At that time not many Oneidas could understand the English language so Big Medicine was chosen to become an interpreter in Church. In time he had been ordained as deacon, had preached sermons with Father E A Goodnaugh also S S Burleson. Many a time he had preached to the Oneidas on the subject of loving one another. Although some of the Indians disliked the two white priests[,] they [the priests were] still opposed to the question of selling any part of the Indian land. At some time a council was held by the Indians[.] [A]gain the old Chiefs had the same question for the tribe to decide[.] Father Goodnaugh being present and told them he disliked their ideas of selling any of their land. One of the old Chiefs stood up and said, it would be better for us to kick that white man out of our reservation, this meaning the priest Goodnough. Big Medicine stood up and said, not until I am lying here dead, when you can proceed with your idea. The old Chiefs continually planned on selling their land as Big Medicine had control of the tribe. They couldn't succeed without his signature. Another time there were three Indian men [who] came to Big Medicine's house and got him out of bed[.] [T]hey offered him one thousand dollars in cash if he would sign his name to the treaty so as they could have their wishes in selling portions of the tribal land. But his answer was "No[,] I will not sign even though you would offer me three thousand dollars not to those wishes." With the support of some of the Indians[,] he had been fighting hard for their rights. But in time the Indians finally had the privilege of selling their land[.] I suppose it is alright now. He also was the one to ask the people to help him in building a new church. The people he mostly depended on for help objected to his wishes in building a new church. But when the work was started again he received help mostly from the poorer Oneidas. The work was donated by the men in number of one hundred at times. But mostly sixty men were working one day each week while they quarried the stone[.] [T]his work continued for several years before the building of the church was completed. Many thanks was expressed to the white people living far away for the donation of money, which was used in buying windows and necessary needs on the Church. And when Big Medicine died he was buried by the Church. From that time on there has never been another Chief appointed[.] I suppose it is because the Oneidas have changed to the ways of the white people. There is a doubt as to whether there will ever be an Oneida Indian to become a priest at anytime.

12

Lacework

Josephine Hill Webster

Editors' Note: The following two items, both produced by Josephine Hill Webster—her WPA story and her sales brochure promoting the Oneida laceworkers—show her remarkable entrepreneurial abilities as well as the great artistic achievements of Oneida women in the period.

In the fall of 1898 Miss Sybil Carter who lives in New York City introduced the lace work to the Oneida women. The sisters [Sisters of Charity] had charge[.] [T]hey taught the Oneida women until 1909 [when] they gave up, [since] the sisters had too much church work to do. So Sybil Carter wanted the work to go on so the Association from New York City sent Miss Hemingway to Oneida to find somebody to teach us how to make lace[.] [S]he taught us the cut work and bobbin pillow laces. So having learned the lace work where I went to school [Hampton Institute], So I worked with her[.] [S]he taught me how to make cut work. And she asked me to take charge. In the fall 1909 they sent her to another Indian Reservation to teach lace making[.] [S]he put me in charge of the lace makers[.] I used to have about sixty women[.] I used to give out the work for them to sew. The Association used to furnish the supplies in making lace. And they had an office in New York City[.] I always sent the finished work every two weeks, sometimes one to three hundred dollars worth finished work in one sending. There was a time when I had charge of one hundred women. The Oneida women so made lot of lace. They made a bed spread. And they made lot of altar lace. I had charge of the lace workers until 1926. The organization in New York City gave up the work so the Oneida women living here were without work. But I am still doing lace work [. . .] independent of any Association. I still have some old customers and some new customers. I am quite busy at Christmas time to fill the orders. I have to have several women making lace in their spare time. They make a lot of table cloth and handkerchiefs cases and also make a lot of different kinds of bags.

Excerpt from pamphlet written by Josephine Hill Webster (Mrs. Isaac Webster), *The Oneida Indian Lace Makers of Oneida Wisconsin* (Oneida Indian Reservation, Oneida, Wisconsin, 1943).

Cut Work and Lace Industry

The Italian cut work and lace industry carried on among and by the Oneida Indian Women at Oneida, Wis., was formerly under the management of a group of philanthropic women in the East who had associated themselves into an organization called "The Sybil Carter Indian Lace Association," and had its headquarters in New York City, for the sole purpose of helping the Indian women to help themselves. For many years this work was carried on, all materials being furnished by the Association to the Indian Women. Beautiful and expensive laces were all made by hand, such as bed spreads, cushions and doilies. An altar lace used in the Cathedral of St. John the Divine, New York City, was made at Oneida. All work produced and finished were consigned to the office in New York City every two weeks. In the fall of 1926 the organization discontinued as an organization, and the lace industry was about to become a thing of the past. But there was so much demand for fancy laces by people who appreciate an article made by hand, that it remained for Mrs. I. N. Webster, the manager for the branch in Wisconsin, to continue with the art independently, and this has been a great boon to the Indian women who in many cases have to support the whole family on the fruits of their industry. It has been proved that the Indian women can compete successfully with workers in countries where lace-making has been an industry for generations. Laces, made by Indian women, were awarded the Gold Medal in open competition at the Paris Exposition, 1900; the Pan-American at Buffalo, 1901; at Liege, 1905; at Milan, 1906; at the Australian Exposition, 1908; and at the Louisiana Purchase Exposition in 1904, they were awarded the Grand Prize, which is the highest recognition possible. Formerly all work was consigned to the New York office, but since the work has been carried on independently, the people of the Mid-West, who are lovers of an artistic needle work, are now able to secure these high-class articles of lace and cut work direct from one who was formerly connected with the association for sixteen years. Many of the designs and patterns used in the work were secured by special permission from the Metropolitan Museum in New York City. Information cheerfully given, and orders taken by

MRS. I. N. WEBSTER
Oneida, Wis.

13

From Carlisle to Carnegie Hall

The Musical Career of Dennison Wheelock

Laurence M. Hauptman

Today, on the grounds of the U.S. Army War College in Carlisle, Pennsylvania, a majestic bandstand named after Dennison Wheelock occupies a place of prominence. Reconstructed in 1979–1980 on the very site of the original, which dated back to the days of the Carlisle Indian Industrial School, the new bandstand seems out of place in its present location, among buildings where the nation's strategic military thinking is studied and formulated. Yet, music and music education at this federal Indian boarding school founded in 1879 was a reflection of the military thinking as well as the personality of one regular army officer, Captain Richard Henry Pratt, the founder and longtime superintendent of this institution.[1]

The story of Pratt's prized pupil Dennison Wheelock and his extraordinary music career throws light on one aspect of the Indian educational experience at federal boarding schools that has previously been ignored by scholars. Wheelock was the most accomplished American Indian composer, conductor, and cornet soloist of the late nineteenth and early twentieth centuries.[2] His early life illustrates the significant—but often contradictory—role that music played at federal Indian boarding schools. Wheelock, an Oneida Indian from Wisconsin, spent twenty years of his life at Carlisle, Flandreau, and Haskell Institute as a student, clerk, disciplinarian, bandmaster, and professor of music.

Scholars have written extensively about the federal Indian boarding school system. The subject matter of many of these writings fits into three major categories: (1) the ideas of Superintendent Pratt; (2) certain aspects of the acculturation process that shaped Indian education at Carlisle and other boarding schools; and (3) the school's sports teams, especially the 1911–1912 football team coached by Glenn Pop Warner and starring the legendary Jim Thorpe. Yet, long before Thorpe and sports, the musical talents of Dennison Wheelock and other American Indian students at Carlisle were receiving attention from the national press.[3] In the best full-length study of Carlisle, Genevieve Bell writes about this famous Oneida musician:

> Wheelock represents a transition in the positioning of Carlisle students. His was the first generation of students who did not return immediately to their homes, but rather worked in the Indian Service, lived in non-Native communities, assimilated in no small part in a certain kind of American lifestyle. These students, like the interpreters they replaced, were also engaged in a form of cultural brokering. But rather than operating primarily out of a traditional life, they found themselves with multiple locations and many agendas. These were individuals whose lives were to be examples to their own people of how to assimilate, and to non-Native peoples, as to how assimilation was achievable.[4]

Unfortunately, Bell never analyzes Wheelock in depth nor explores how band music served the acculturation process.

Federal school administrators such as Captain Pratt consciously tried to emphasize the European music classics at the expense of Native musical traditions. American Indian music was often brushed aside as "noise" and marginalized by being classified as "primitive" or as a lower art form. Yet, despite these efforts to transform the Indian, Native music was never completely eliminated from these schools, their assemblies, or from "down time" in the students' dormitory rooms. On June 20, 1890, the *Indian Helper,* the Carlisle School publication, noted that an assembly was "enlivened by music. We had piano duets, singing duets, choir singing, quartettes and sextet's [*sic*], operatic and plain, by babies and old men, music on horns and music without, red music and white music, and all kinds of music."[5] Moreover, Pratt's emphasis on regimentation and drill based on his extensive military career actually at times furthered Indian values. The precision regimen of marching bands at the schools brought Indians from diverse tribal communities together working in harmony for a common goal. While being told to play the European classics, these ensembles actually promoted a sense of group achievement and fostered Pan-Indianism.

The feelings of camaraderie and accomplishment gained from musical teamwork were carried back to Indian communities. Soon Indian reservation bands became the rage. By the early years of the twentieth century, Indian bands competed with each other at agricultural and county fairs much like the federal Indian school bands had done in the last two decades of the nineteenth century. Locally, at Oneida, Wisconsin, the Oneida Union Band and the Oneida National Band were prominent in Indian community events and off the reservation throughout the Midwest. Nationally and even internationally, Dennison's brother James conducted the famous U.S. Indian Band well into the 1920s. Hence, music at the federal Indian boarding schools, first popularized by Dennison Wheelock, was to have far-reaching consequences on Native America.[6]

Dennison Wheelock was born at Oneida, Wisconsin, on June 14, 1871, the second child of James A. Wheelock and Sophia Doxtator. Dennison grew up in the 1870s and early 1880s in a poor Indian farm community that was faced with increased pressures—timber stripping, the push for allotment of tribal lands, social disintegration caused by rampant alcohol consumption, and tribal in-fighting following the death of Daniel Bread, the Oneida's longtime principal chief. Dennison was baptized in the Hobart Episcopal Church and attended the Methodist Episcopal school taught by the Reverend E. A. Goodnough.[7]

In 1885, the precocious Wheelock was sent to the U.S. Indian Industrial School at Carlisle, Pennsylvania, to study under the guidance of Superintendent Pratt. Even before his trip east to Pennsylvania, Wheelock had been encouraged to take up the cornet since he had heard his older brother, Charles, playing it. He had also been affected by the visit of an Iroquois musician from the East to the Wisconsin Oneida reservation. Indeed, the accomplishments of Seneca and Tuscarora musicians from western New York was widely known in the period of Wheelock's youth. At least four Indian major cornet bands, highly acclaimed by professional musicians, were winning medals for their excellence at agricultural fairs, as reported by the federal Indian agent in New York State in 1879. Therefore, Wheelock's choice of the cornet appears to be an intentional one.[8]

In a letter to the Pratt family in January 1894, he wrote quite modestly of the "limited musical education I now possess." He described his musical awakening:

When I was a small boy I used to delight in listening to the playing of my oldest brother, who had an old brass cornet given him by a brass band, of which he was a member. I used to wonder also if I could ever be able to play as well as he. My curiosity led me, on several occasions to take the cornet without his permission, and attempt to play on it, which, of course, brought the usual consequences, a thrashing by my mother. That settled my curiosity for the time being, but I became determined to know more about music and play the cornet better than my brother. Just at that time a Tuscarora Indian came to Oneida, who possessed some musical education, and I immediately took advantage of it and learned as much from him as possible. He was with us only two or three months, but in that time I learned a great deal in music-reading and simple composition. When my Indian teacher left I went to a government Indian school [Carlisle] where they were organizing a small brass band. I was given the cornet to practice, and when I say that I practiced hard I mean just that. That dates my beginning of the cornet.[9]

Wheelock's music education was derived from other influences as well. Martial band music, with its zest and gusto, was a byproduct of the patriotism that followed the American Civil War. John Philip Sousa was very popular, and his music clearly had an influence on the Oneida musician. By the late 1870s, European musical instrument makers, especially German artisans, had stores in nearby Green Bay. Around 1880, a German cornet band was organized in the city, one that subsequently gave rise to the Green Bay Concert Band just prior to World War I.[10] In a feature story about Wheelock and his music in 1903, the Oneida musician also indicated that his cornet playing was inspired as a child by his attendance at Wisconsin country fairs where he was exposed to the band music of the times.[11]

At Carlisle, Wheelock discovered the rich cultural diversity of Native America. Indian students from Alaska to New York brought elements of their musical traditions to Carlisle. While generally not encouraged during the Pratt years, from 1879 to 1904, students found a way to remind themselves of home and tribal music by singing and drumming in the school's dormitories. At other times, Pratt reluctantly permitted the inclusions of small samplings of American Indian music in assembly programs at the school.[12]

For many Indians, going off to Carlisle was like dropping off the face of the earth, but for Wheelock the experience was quite different. For over one hundred years since the time of the missionary Eleazer Wheelock and his Moor's Charity School (later Dartmouth College) and Samuel Kirkland's Hamilton-Oneida Academy, (now Hamilton College), Iroquois Indians including Oneidas had been sent away from home for Christian instruction.[13] Dennison's last name itself was a tribute to Wheelock. Hence, it is no coincidence that the Oneidas from Wisconsin and New York were one of the largest contingents of Indians in the Carlisle student body, totaling approximately five hundred tribal members. Only the Sioux, Chippewas, and Senecas had more students at Carlisle (the school's total student body numbered more than eighty-five hundred from 1885 to 1917).[14]

Wheelock arrived at Carlisle with five other Oneidas in 1885. The next year he was joined by his closest personal friend, Josiah Powless, an Oneida who became a prominent physician and who was later killed on the Western front in World War I. By 1890, 103 Oneidas were in attendance.[15] Of Wheelock's nine brothers, half-brothers, sisters, and half-sisters, only two—his oldest brother, Charles, and his youngest half-brother, Harrison—did not attend the school. In addition, several of his first and second cousins were enrolled in the school. Wheelock met his wife, Louise La Chap-pelle, a Chippewa from White Earth Reservation in Minnesota, at Carlisle. They were married and had two children while Dennison worked at the school. Their infant son Paul died at the school in 1900 and is buried at the relocated Indian cemetery at today's U.S. Army War College.[16] Thus, one can conclude that for Dennison Wheelock, Carlisle was more than just another federal boarding school—it was his second home. His extensive correspondence to Pratt written over a thirty-five-year period reflects Wheelock's affection for the superintendent, his wife, his school, and his values. Pratt's affection for Wheelock was time after time revealed in rec-ommendations or in glowing reports about the Oneida's progress. They confided in each other throughout their lives. Indeed, Pratt attempted to push Wheelock ahead, even suggesting in 1920–1921 that President Harding nominate Wheelock to be commissioner of Indian affairs.[17]

In 1901, employing high-sounding words, the official curriculum prepared by the Office of Indian Affairs stated:

Music is an uplifting element in life and its power is felt. Teachers must not forget that amid the drill of daily work we are nourishing the souls of the children. In most of our school work we deal with the mind, while singing is the means by which we can reach the heart of the child, and so develop the good within him. We train the eye and hand and brain, and we should not neglect to cultivate the affections. Teach children the best songs. Be sure they understand the meaning of the words. Too often in singing in the schools the children repeat

meaningless words which convey no idea to their minds. Help
the children to erect for themselves high ideals, and this will
aid them to choose the good in life.

Music as a moral factor makes the pupil feel the charms of
harmony and beauty, thus softening and enriching his nature.
There is no other study which so freely unites the physical,
mental, and spiritual.[18]

Yet, the music program at Carlisle developed rather slowly in a
piecemeal fashion and largely because of private philanthropy
rather than because of federal government financial support.
Indeed, the Indian band members themselves had to contribute
moneys they made to support the travels to major venues,
including the Columbian Exposition in Chicago.[19]

After the founding of Carlisle in 1879, at the urging of Superintendent Pratt, Mrs. Walter Baker, a philanthropist from Boston,
donated a set of musical instruments: cornets, clarinets, and
pianos. Pratt requested this donation for a specific purpose after
a visit by Baker to the school:

Since you [Mrs. Baker] have been here you have heard the
"tom tom" and Indian singing down in those quarters? . . . Well,
I want to stop that, but feel it wouldn't be fair to do unless I can
give them something else as good, or better, on the same line.
If you will give me a set of brass band instruments, I will give
them to the "tom tom" boys and they can toot on them and
this will stop the "tom tom."[20]

Pratt was no fan of Indian traditional music, and with his major
Indian disciple, Dr. Carlos Montezuma, he crusaded against
federal educational policies that promoted tribal Indian cultural
expressions, including music. In their opinions, all education
had to be geared to prepare boys and girls "in the affairs of civilized life." Both Pratt and Montezuma later chastised federal
officials for implementing a new policy based on recognizing
the great worth of preserving and teaching Native music to
Indian schoolchildren.[21]

To Pratt, the Carlisle musical program had several distinct purposes. The first was to acculturate Indian schoolchildren to Western values, including the emphasis on what he felt were the superior achievements of Western civilization. The second was to use music to promote discipline, hence the emphasis on marching bands with their clockwork military drill and precision. The third was to generate favorable public attention, in order to win political and financial support for his Carlisle experiment in Indian transformation.[22]

Wheelock's great talents give Pratt the opportunity to carry out these three objectives. Wheelock became Pratt's surrogate son, one of his special Carlisle boys, along with Dr. Carlos Montezuma, who "made it big" in the white world, a near perfect model of what the superintendent had envisioned when he founded the school. While a student at Carlisle, Wheelock was inculcated with Pratt's and his teachers' ideas about the American Indians' future.

In one of Pratt's clearest expressions of his educational philosophy, the superintendent compared educating the Indians to the past experiences of various immigrants, suggesting: "Mingling with and meeting us on the common ground of the language of our country, and being subjected to the same laws of education and good order, they [immigrants] generally are evolved into full and useful American citizens in one generation." Pratt added:

> Justice demands that we start the Indian child with a knowledge of our language, and then he should be compelled to enter the public schools and industries of our country. Given this start, there should be no Indian reservations to return to, nor continued Indian-school nurseries to dwarf the growth. The school might and should be the ship to bear him from his ignorant home hindrances into the widest opportunities for development. What a misfortune, then, to turn the school into a force for holding the children to the slavery of the old, wild life.[23]

Pratt's influence on Wheelock was pervasive. They both believed that American Indians were fully capable of taking their "rightful place" as productive, tax-paying Americans. Much like his mentor, Wheelock objected to the overbearing control of the federal Indian bureaucracy in Washington and in the field as well as the paternalistic hand of the reformers of the time who were pushing the Dawes General Allotment Act as a panacea. Like Pratt, he saw the need for the immediate release of the Indians from federal control and the extension of U.S. citizenship to the Indians. To him, the Dawes Act delayed full integration of Indians into American society. Later, as an employee at the school in 1893, he indicated that he could not see much in the Dawes Act that was helpful for his Oneida people.[24] Although Wheelock spoke the Oneida language and used it to converse with elders on the reservation, in 1887 he won the school prize for his paper entitled "Is It Right for the Government to Stop the Teaching of Indian Languages in Reservation Schools?" The sixteen-year-old argued that it was right to stop teaching these languages since they had "no use in the world, and should not be kept any longer." Parroting Pratt, Wheelock wrote:

> You can't express a wise idea, with the Indian language in any way that would be wise and you can't make a law with it, and you can never make a speech as well and as good, as you would with the English language. Why? Because the Indians never made laws, never saw so many things to talk about as the white men see, and do not do much thinking for the future, and talk mostly by signs, and thus they have, only a few words in their language. It has only the words of everyday use, and does not have any, I call "hard words." The Indian language is not only a disgrace to the Government for being in it, but it is also the cord that pulls down the race, who have been bound by the same cord to ignorance and barbarism for centuries.[25]

One cannot determine if Wheelock meant all the words expressed or if he was simply trying to please Pratt and his teachers much like a trained bird seeking a cracker. Instead of a food reward, he was to earn a first prize medal. Historians have long suggested that the Indian children at these schools were experts at survival under extreme circumstances; however, Wheelock's later career as an ambitious attorney clearly shows that he was also motivated by self-interest and personal achievement, always seeking, as Pratt taught, the opportunity to push himself forward.

To Wheelock, Pratt's firm hand made the Oneida what he, his wife, brothers, half-brothers, sisters, and half-sisters became in life. Sounding like his mentor, the twenty-year-old Wheelock, serving as Carlisle's "ambassador of goodwill," dazzled the reformers at the Lake Mohonk Conference of Friends of the Indian in 1891 with his Pratt-like speech:

The United States government claims to have facilities for educating all its people, that it has a wide door through which its subjects can pass, to become citizens of this republic. Then I ask, Why does it not let the Indian come in at that door? Why does it close that, and make a smaller hole and expect the Indian to squeeze through that? That is what we are doing when we establish Indian schools. That is what we are doing when we try to educate the Indian by putting him aside and treating him as a special being. That method will never succeed. If the Indian is squeezed through that little hole, some of his limbs will be left out. If we want the Indian to be a good citizen, we want him to have the use of all his limbs. The United States government does not want educated Indians, but it wants educated citizens. If the Indian boy starts out and stops at the day-school, the benefit that the United States gets from that Indian does not amount to much. But if he goes through the day-school, through the boarding-school, through Carlisle or Hampton, and then becomes a citizen of the United States, the solution of the Indian question, so far as that man is concerned, has been effected. That is what we want,—to have the Indian become an individual. We must teach him to have a conscience which will respond to the voice of duty and responsibility. We must teach him the first principles of this free government. We must teach him that, in order to be a good citizen of this republic, he must know the power that lies in the elective franchise, he must know how to think, he must know how to make his ballot

think. In order to do that, the Indian must be taught beside the
white man who knows what it is, who has patriotism and
devotion to his country, and who knows how to act in a free
republic. We must put him by the side of the white school-boy.
We must put him into the public school. You find the solution
of the Indian problem only when you condescend to have your
children with the children of the red man, educated together,
and trying their metal together.[26]

Both Wheelock and Pratt saw the federal Indian boarding school
as a temporary educational formula to "uplift" the Indian so that
he or she would be ready for full participation in American society,
as citizens, as families with children in the public schools of the
nation. Wheelock clearly agreed with Pratt's frequent calls for the
abolition of the BIA, the full integration of Indians into the American
body politic with equal rights as U.S. citizens, and the end of the
reservation system, which he judged as "retarding" Indian progress.

The achievements of Wheelock and his Carlisle musicians could
not have been realized without the omnipresent Pratt and the
military discipline he imposed. Wheelock as a conductor modeled
himself on the old military man's style. The Oneida also relished
his commanding presence as a conductor and the martial music of
John Philip Sousa. At Carlisle in the 1880s and 1890s, Wheelock
grew up on Sousa's band music and later participated as a guest
conductor at Willow Grove Park, the famous venue for concert
and marching bands outside of Philadelphia, in the early years of
the twentieth century. The Oneida was compared to Sousa, and
Wheelock was even nominated to be his successor as bandmaster
of the U.S. Marine Band.[27]

Superintendent Pratt was to permit the establishment of the
Carlisle Indian School Band in 1880. The band, composed of
members of numerous Indian communities, "progressed from
the simplest terms." By the time Wheelock entered the school
in the mid-1880s and demonstrated his great ability on the
cornet, musical programs were a common, albeit rudimentary,
feature of the school. Soon band members mastered what Pratt
valued: Grieg, Mozart, Rossini, Schubert, and Wagner. They fre-

quently performed at school assemblies, holiday festivities, and at the Carlisle Opera House, delighting the students, teachers, and administrators at the school and gaining favorable attention among the local white townspeople.[28]

After having graduated from Carlisle in June 1890, Wheelock went back to Oneida to teach and serve as a justice of the peace, but within less than a year, he returned to Carlisle.[29] Because of Wheelock's excellent work at Carlisle from 1885 to 1890, in the classroom, as a champion debater, as a fine tenor in the choir, and as cornetist extraordinaire in the band, Pratt recommended that his prize pupil attend the prestigious and academically superior Dickinson Preparatory School in Carlisle, Pennsylvania, less than three miles from the Indian school. Only a handful of Carlisle Indian School students, such as Wheelock and Powless, were sent to this institution, one separate but affiliated with Dickinson College. (Wheelock spent one full school year there, 1891–1892). They were sent there to refine their skills, since Carlisle offered them only a rudimentary education during these early years.[30]

Wheelock was not to disappoint Pratt's faith in him. While spending the academic year at Dickinson Preparatory School, he was appointed assistant clerk at Carlisle, working for Pratt directly. He was soon appointed bandmaster at the school, a position he held for over eight years. Taking over the reins of the Carlisle Indian School Band, he recruited new members. His original band of twenty-three members in 1891 included at least six Oneidas. He continued to perform as a solo cornetist and his younger brother James, a student at the school, became a fixture on the "E♭ Clarinet."[31]

Ironically, the Carlisle Indian Band's "coming out" performances occurred at the four-hundred-year anniversary of Columbus's landing in the New World. On October 10, 1892, in New York, over three hundred Carlisle boys and girls, including Wheelock's thirty-one-piece band, marched down Fifth Avenue from Fifty-first Street past Washington Square. As the boys passed the reviewing stand, they uncovered their heads and executed a "double-quick" move opposite the Fifth Avenue Hotel. The boys were followed by "a company of Indian maidens, dressed in dark-blue tennis gowns and blue hats."[32] Both in New York City's and Chicago's commemorations, the Carlisle School contingent was led by Richard Davis, a Cheyenne boy, and two others who carried the banner "United States Indian Industrial School, Carlisle, Pa." followed by the motto "Into civilization and citizenship."[33]

The nation's newspapers praised the boys and girls for their "intelligent faces and dignified bearing," which showed "the result of Indian education" and "justified the wish that the work of Indian education" be "more extended than it now is." The *New York Mail and Express* saw the children as examples of "unmatched proof of our [American] progress," showing "that what Columbus hoped— the conversion of Christianity of the natives of the continents—is now in a fairway of accomplishment, under better and happier auspices than Columbus or his contemporaries could bring to bear." The *New York Recorder* claimed that the boys could pass for West Pointers. The male contingent was divided into four companies and "clad in neat uniform of blue, with fatigue caps of the regular army pattern, each man bearing an American flag and wearing the national colors pinned on the left breast."[34] Special praise was heaped on Dennison Wheelock and his fine band:

> But the one that caught the crowd was the Indian band that headed the delegation from Carlisle. With the smoothest harmony and in the most perfect time, this band . . . played a marching anthem as it swept past the reviewing stand. Both the melody and spectacle were so unusual that the people rose to their feet and cheered again and again. . . . The Indian boys marched with perfect step, and as they came opposite the President's [Benjamin Harrison's] stand every head of stiff black hair was bared in respectful salute and with a military precision that no pale-faced organization equaled.[35]

Thus, it seemed Pratt had succeeded. Music helped sell the Carlisle experiment and Pratt's military discipline, and his surrogate son helped him achieve it. The "unmatched proof of progress" was seen in Native boys and girls' giving allegiance to the United States at the four hundredth anniversary of the Italian discoverer-invader of the New World![36]

By the time the Carlisle contingent reached Chicago for the beginning of that city's own year-long Columbian festivities, newspapers nationwide were hailing Pratt and his Carlisle Indian students. Chicago newspapers praised the students and their decorum, as well as their military drills, marching "like veterans" and exemplifying "what civilization can do and has done for the savage denizens of the far West." The *Chicago Journal* had special praise for the band, calling it "probably the most unique in all the musical features of the parade." The Indian musicians, led by "Dennison Wheelock, a full-blooded Oneida, performed some excellent work on their instruments and were warmly cheered as they passed the crowds on the streets."[37]

Upon his return to Carlisle, Wheelock began a nationwide effort to recruit for Carlisle the most promising young Indian musicians from the reservations. He even "raided" other boarding schools for the best talent. He also started to teach music, being now referred to as "professor." His commitment to music extended beyond the classroom and the bandstand at Carlisle. Throughout the 1890s, he was also composing songs, popular "fluff," band music, as well as a symphony, which he finally completed in 1900.

Now Wheelock and his band were known well beyond Carlisle. By 1894 they, along with the Carlisle women's choir, performed throughout the East. On April 15, 1894, the *New York Times* did a feature on Wheelock (with his portrait included) and his band, reviewing their performance at the city's Lenox Lyceum. The reporter insisted that "few metropolitan bands can boast of greater care and accuracy in the execution of their music." Among other offerings, the band played Mozart and Wagner as well as two selections composed by Wheelock himself: "The Carlisle Indian School March" and a piece entitled "American Medley." The concert's patrons read as a Who's Who of New York's elite families: Mrs. J. Pierpont Morgan, Mrs. Russell Sage, Mrs. James Harriman, Mrs. Elihu Root, and so forth. While describing the program as excellent, the *New York Times* reviewer, in backhanded praise, insisted: "In this concert the Carlisle School has fully demonstrated that Indian youths, when under the influences of favorable environment, may acquire very refined musical qualities." Pratt's ideas had once again taken hold in the public's mind: "civilization" had won out over "savagery."[38]

On Christmas Day in 1894, Wheelock married Louisa La Chappelle, a Chippewa student who had arrived at Carlisle from the White Earth Reservation in Minnesota two years earlier. Her ideas on Indian "progress" largely paralleled those of her husband and were very much influenced by Pratt. The married couple stayed on at and Carlisle, and in 1896 their first child Edmund Richard was born there.[39]

Wheelock continued his role of bandmaster, conducting concerts and composing music. In 1896, he finished a band composition, one revealing Pratt's influence again. It was entitled "From Savagery to Civilization" and had its debut at the seventeenth anniversary celebration of the founding of the school. He performed as a soloist with the band, and the school's newspaper reported that the "sounds produced led up from the wild tom tom, through curious and intricate twists and turns to the sweet and classic strains of civilized horns."[40]

Wheelock continued to hold concerts locally, including at the Carlisle Opera House; however, his goals went far beyond Pennsylvania's capital district.[41] His most ambitious task was preparing for the Paris Exposition of 1900 and the Pan-American Exposition of 1901. For three years prior to the world's fair in Paris, Wheelock traveled around the country recruiting musicians for a seventy-piece all-Indian student band from Carlisle and other federal Indian boarding schools. Influenced by the music of Grieg, he also completed his magnum opus, *Aboriginal Suite,* a full symphony in three parts: "Morning on the Plains," "The Lover's Song," and "Dance of the Red Men."[42] In July 1899, the Carlisle student newspaper reprinted an article that reported favorably on Wheelock's ambitious efforts:

The great United States Indian Band composed of members from several of the Indian training schools of the country is, from all reports, doing excellent work under the able leadership of Professor Dennison Wheelock, at Carlisle. The band now numbers over sixty pieces and we hope will even excel Sousa's and Gilmore's band when they meet across the Atlantic. All the schools feel they have some claim on this band, and will be proud to hear of its accomplishments.[43]

On March 28, 1900, Wheelock and his U.S. Indian Band reached the pinnacle of their success. They played Carnegie Hall. A reviewer for *Metronome* reported that the concert was part of "a series being given by the organization prior to its departure for Paris, where it will demonstrate a new development in Indian civilization." At the Carnegie Hall performance, the band played selections from Gounod's opera *Faust* and from Meyerbeer's *The Huguenots* and featured the world premiere of Wheelock's *Aboriginal Suite*. The response was overwhelmingly positive: "A large and genuinely enthusiastic audience greeted the reservation musicians, forcing them to respond to repeated encores."[44]

The band's triumphant performance at the nation's classical musical capital was the apex of Wheelock's career as a musician. Just at the time of his greatest achievement, Wheelock was to suffer a personal loss that changed the course of his life. A month and a half after the Carnegie Hall performance, his ten-month-old son Paul died at Carlisle. Because Dennison Wheelock's conducting was viewed as irreplaceable, Pratt canceled the planned appearance of the Indian musicians at the Paris Exposition.[45] In tribute to the great Oneida Indian musician, the Republican Guard Band of France played *Aboriginal Suite* at the world's fair in his band's place.[46]

For the next three years, Dennison and Louise Wheelock reeled from the loss. After his son was buried on the grounds of the school, Wheelock resigned his post as bandmaster and tried to restart his career elsewhere. He attempted to get as far away from Carlisle and his son's sad fate as possible. His connections to Carlisle became further weakened in 1904 when Captain Pratt was forced out of his post as superintendent by BIA officials in Washington.

After Wheelock's departure from Carlisle, he attempted to make a go of it as a newspaperman in Green Bay, Wisconsin, and as a disciplinarian at the U.S. Indian Industrial School at Flandreau, South Dakota. Nevertheless, he did not abandon his musical

career and performed as an invited bandmaster at Willow Grove
Park. This premiere venue for bands attracted Sousa, Victor Herbert, Walter Damrosch, and other prominent conductors and composers of the time. On one occasion there, Wheelock drew seventy
thousand people to a concert and was later awarded a gold medal
and a silver cup for his brilliant conducting.[47]

In 1903, Wheelock was appointed bandmaster at Haskell Indian
School, where he helped reconstitute the band. As bandmaster of
the forty-piece ensemble composed of boys from twenty different
Indian tribes, he toured the country in the summer of 1904, making
an especially favorable impression on guests at Colorado's mountain resorts with his own musical compositions and his band's
rendition of European classical music. In a lengthy interview after
the tour ended, the Oneida musician described his education, his
compositions ("Carlisle Indian School March," "Champion Cake
Walk," and *Aboriginal Suite*), and his tastes in music. The interview reveals much about Wheelock and his music. To the Oneida,
ragtime, the current craze, was a "perfectly legitimate" form of
music, labeling it "the humor of music." The interviewer then shifted
his questioning to American Indian music. Wheelock responded
in revealing terms:

> The original Indian music is a strange thing. It is devoid of
> harmony, but the melody and time are there, and it is easily
> harmonized. Some great critics say that our aboriginal music
> is the same as played by all primitive people world over. Chinese
> music itself is built on the same principle and I am planning now
> a composition called the evolution of music. I hope to show
> the growth of harmony. First, some of the musicians will come
> out in Indian costume, playing some primitive melody. Others
> will follow playing something more advanced, and so on until
> the whole band is on stage and we are rendering the best
> grand opera.[48]

Although Wheelock was apparently open-minded when it came
to ragtime, the Oneida simply saw American Indian music as
"primitive," at a lower stage of musical creativity. The Darwinian

model of society, common at that time and one espoused by Pratt and other "reformers," had become deeply rooted in his mind, from his education at Carlisle.

Wheelock's efforts at Haskell were recognized nationally. *Metronome* reviewed the band's artistry in March 1904, calling it an "up-to-date aggregation of capable musicians trained in every respect for high class concert work." Besides performing "their own quaint Indian songs," the impressed reviewer stated, they played Gounod, Mendelssohn, Mozart, and Wagner, led by "Dennison Wheelock, an Oneida Indian from Wisconsin," a well-trained musician comparable to the leading bandmasters of the day. The reviewer predicted a bright future for Wheelock and his musicians in that their "high class music and high class instruments should prove stepping stones to fame and fortune for these original bandsmen."[49]

Metronome's reviewer was well off base about Wheelock's future. The Oneida was unable to survive financially without the efforts of Pratt and the superintendent's now shrinking base of financial supporters. Once Pratt left Carlisle in 1904, his access to major philanthropy dried up. Wheelock was supporting an aging father, numerous siblings, a wife, and a son and could no longer survive as a musician without this support. The Oneida's financial pinch eventually led to his resignation from Haskell.[50]

Thus, without steady employment, angered by the BIA's dismissal of Pratt, and in a financial pinch, Wheelock turned to the people he had known for fifteen years, the town leaders of Carlisle, Pennsylvania, who had marveled at his musical precociousness. He returned to the Town of Carlisle. Soon he began to read law at the Baltimore branch office of John Miller, a leading citizen of Carlisle and head of the Cumberland County Bar Association. After this training, Wheelock returned to Oneida, Wisconsin, where he dabbled in real estate and prepared to take the state bar examination. In 1910, he passed the test and set up his practice, establishing his residence in West De Pere, just off the Oneida Indian Reservation.[51]

In 1911, Wheelock was one of the founders of the first national Indian organization, the Society of American Indians (SAI).[52] The

Oneida attorney remained active in the organization through 1916, heading its law and legislation committees and hosting the organization's 1914 annual convention, which was held at Madison, Wisconsin. In December 1914, Wheelock, as an SAI representative, went to the White House and presented President Wilson with a petition for a specific legislative program. The Oneida urged the appointment of a three-member committee to clarify the ambiguous legal status of American Indians under American law and asked the president to push for the passage of legislation giving the U.S. Court of Claims jurisdiction over all Indian claims against the United States.[53]

Pratt had taught Wheelock that the reservation system would inevitably come to an end and that all Indians would fully integrate into American society. Wheelock took these views with him all his life, including into his role as an SAI member. Wheelock wrote to his mentor in December 1912: "I am in thorough accord with you as to the true solution of the Indian problem. It can never be for the benefit of any race to isolate them, away from the competitive drills and strife with other races of mankind, whether they are superior or inferior than those so isolated." Both Wheelock and Pratt had little faith in the efficacy of the SAI to make real changes, since they both believed the organization had too many BIA bureaucrats and naive reformers of the "Indian Rights Association, Lake Mohonk, and such other paper shooters." Wheelock, like Pratt, saw the ultimate end of Indian reservations. Wheelock insisted: "All the Indian wants is a white man's chance, no more and no less." He added: "If it is a good thing for an Indian to be on a Reservation, given special schools, and to be limited in his environments, then why doesn't the Government do the same thing for the white man?" Wheelock concluded in a Pratt-like way:

If it is a good thing for the white man to be permitted to attend Harvard, Yale and such institutions of learning, it ought to be a good thing for the Indian to do the same thing. If it is a good thing for the white man to be able to do what he pleased with his property, there is no reason on earth why it should not be equally beneficial for an Indian to do so. If it is a good thing for the white man, and God knows he would not submit to any restraint without cause, to have the privilege to go any where he pleases, lived the way he pleased, it ought to be equally beneficial for the Indian to do likewise, and this is all the Indians want. We need no special schools, we are not crying to be protected nor are we desirous of being isolated. Nor are we going to throw our property away, but we do demand that we have the white man's chance to have life, liberty and to work out our own salvation. A simply, clearly worded statute, without any jokers concealed in its verbiage, drawn by one familiar with the situation and in sympathy with the desires of the Indians, eliminating all the present machinery of Indian management, would do it. A few thousand dollars to pay the expenses of two or three persons to study the legal status of every tribe and to draft legislation to emancipate every tribe in the United States, give them their property and to educate every Congressman and Senator as to the merits and aim of such legislation, would be all that is necessary.[54]

By this time, Wheelock had become one of the most successful attorneys in Brown and Outagamie counties, achieving great wealth. He owned a large house in West De Pere, as well as hundreds of acres of property in the two-county area. He represented both Indian and non-Indian clients, at a time when anti-Indian hatred was virulent in north central Wisconsin.[55] By 1915, he headed the Green Bay Concert Band comprised largely of non-Indian musicians. His fame as a world-class musician had allowed him to enter the closed white world of the Green Bay elite.[56]

His relationship with reservation Oneidas was an uneasy one, because of his education, his ideas, his wealth, and his actions. He later insisted: "I have never attempted to do very great things for my people or even to do anything in particular there [on the Oneida Reservation in Wisconsin] than to point out their opportunities." He added: "I try to set a good business example for them and although they all fall into the ditch with me once in a while, yet we manage to get along fairly well."[57] Wheelock served as tribal attorney in 1911 and again served the council in the early 1920s.[58]

In 1921, Wheelock served as general manager of the Oneida Indian Centennial Celebration, commemorating the one-hundredth anniversary of the tribe's migration from New York State. Chosen by his Indian nation to commemorate its century in Wisconsin, Wheelock, nevertheless, was still a captive of his Carlisle training. The elaborate festivities included performances of his symphony, *Aboriginal Suite,* and the "Carlisle Indian School March," as well as a selection from Bizet's *Carmen* and other Western classics. All American Indian nations of Wisconsin were represented in an Indian village where they sold their traditional baskets and other crafts as well as Indian foods. The souvenir program stated that the Menominees and Oneidas would be performing their dances "on a special stand in front of the grand-stand across the track, far away from the audience not to annoy the timid and children." The program insisted that the celebration was "intended to illustrate the progress the Oneida Indians have made in civilization since their coming to Wisconsin," adding that the festivities were aimed "to show again the unquestionable capacity of the Indians to adopt civilized habits of living and to follow professional avocations."[59]

Wheelock was anathema to the Oneidas. Besides his inner conflicts caused by his Carlisle training, he married outside of his tribe and his son was enrolled as a Chippewa at White Earth. To the majority of his tribesmen, Wheelock's views—that reservations were a bad thing for Indians, that tribal lands should give way to Indian fee simple title, that Indians should fully integrate into American society—went against their thinking. Today, rightly or wrongly, some Oneidas picture him as an "apple," red on the outside and white on the inside. Even more critical, other Oneidas suggest that he sold out to the white man; that he acquired his great wealth by conspiring with Joseph Hart, the Indian agent, to profit from the Oneidas' poverty at the time; that he helped to trick Indians out of their land patents after tribal lands were allotted; and that he colluded with outside interests in Green Bay to dispose of the building and the extensive grounds of the federal Indian boarding school at Oneida after it was closed in 1918.[60] Because of increasing criticism from his own Oneidas and his growing legal work for at least twelve separate Indian communities from Washington State to New York, Wheelock moved his prosperous law practice to Washington, D.C., joining the firm of Victor Evans in 1923. Until his death from a heart attack in 1927, he worked in the nation's capital and argued as an attorney before the U.S. Supreme Court and the U.S. Court of Claims in Indian depredation cases.[61]

Wheelock was buried in a Masonic funeral rite at Woodlawn Cemetery, the last resting place of the white power structure in Green Bay, not in the graveyard of the Oneidas' Church of the Holy Apostles, formerly the Hobart Church, where he had been baptized.[62] His alienation from his own people was the great tragedy of his life, one faced by many other Indians who went to federal boarding schools at that time. To Pratt and most Americans of that day, his was the example of American Indian success and progress. Nevertheless, despite his outstanding musical career and national and international achievements, he could not fit back into his own community even in death.

Notes

1. For Pratt, see his autobiography, *Battlefield and Classroom.*

2. For biographical sketches of Wheelock, see "Masons Hold Funeral Rites of D. Wheelock," *De Pere Journal-Democrat,* March 17, 1927, 1; "Famous Indian Lawyer Is Dead," *Milwaukee Sentinel,* March 12, 1927; "Dennison Wheelock Funeral Held Today," *Green Bay Press-Gazette,* March 12, 1927, 2; "Dennison Wheelock, Carlisle Indian, Dead," *Evening Sentinel* (Cumberland County, Pa.), March 16, 1927; Paul L. Stevens, "Wheelock, Dennison," in *The Heritage Encyclopedia of Band Music Composers and Their Music,* ed. Paul E. Bierly (Westerville, Ohio: Integrity Press, 1991), 3 (supplement): 837; Wisconsin State Bar Association, *Proceedings of Annual Conference for 1927* (Madison: Wisconsin State Bar Association, 1927), 331–32.

3. The scholarly literature on Carlisle is too extensive to cite in its entirety. The best treatment is Bell, "Telling Stories out of School." For an analysis of the federal Indian boarding school system, see Adams, *Education for Extinction.*

4. Bell, "Telling Stories out of School," 375.

5. *Indian Helper,* June 20, 1890. See also "A History of the [Carlisle Indian Industrial School] Band," *Red Man* 13 (Feb. 1896): 6; "Carlisle Indian Band," in A. Laura Pratt Scrapbook, 1898–1929, box 29, Pratt Papers, YU.

6. Tom Elm, "The Oneida Band," and Chauncey Baird, "Oneida National Band," both in OLFP.ONIW.

7. U.S. Department of the Interior, *Oneida Census, 1885,* OIA reels 1544–50, RG75, NA; U.S. Bureau of the Census, *Census of 1900, Outagamie County, Wisconsin* (Household 363, p. 339B). For the pressures on the Oneidas after the Civil War, see Hauptman and McLester, *Chief Daniel Bread.* The author would like to acknowledge Susan G. Daniels and her Web site "Oneida People, Places, Dates and Events," in which she provides a full genealogy of the Wheelock family name: http://www.angelfire.com/on3/oneida/page77.html.

8. ARCIA 1879, 124.

9. Dennison Wheelock to Mrs. Richard Henry Pratt, January 9, 1894, folder 567, box 17, Pratt Papers, YU.

10. "Many Organizations Have Promoted [the] Study of Music Here since the Civil War," *Green Bay Press-Gazette,* July 18, 1934, tercentennial edition, "Civil and Social Section," 43.

11. "The Most Famous Band in the U.S. [Haskell Indian Band]—They Really Make Music," unidentified newspaper clipping, Lawrence, Kansas, August 25, 1903, in the file "Jeanette Senseney [Vocal Instructor, Carlisle Indian Industrial School, 1899–1904]," box 29, Pratt Papers, YU.

12. *Indian Helper,* June 20, 1890.

13. James Dow McCallum, ed., *Letters of Eleazer Wheelock's Indians* (Hanover, N.H.: Dartmouth College, 1932); Pilkington, *Journals of Samuel Kirkland.*

14. Although perhaps somewhat low, I have used Genevieve Bell's estimate of Carlisle students, in "Telling Stories out of School," iv.

15. ARCIA 1890, 312.

16. A list of Oneidas at Carlisle was provided by Barbara Landis, specialist in Carlisle Indian School Records, CCHS. I examined the files of Wheelock's numerous siblings, wife, and two sons in the Records of the Carlisle Indian Industrial School, RG75, NA, and Records of Oneidas buried at Carlisle, CCHS.

17. Pratt to Wheelock, Nov. 29, 1890, Wheelock to Mrs. Pratt, Nov. 28, 1895, folder 567, box 17, Wheelock to Pratt, June 14, 1905, folder 323,

box 9, all in Pratt Papers, YU; Wheelock to Pratt, Nov. 27, 1920, in folder "R. H. Pratt, Dickinson College, Carlisle, Pa." in James Henry Morgan Papers, Dickinson College Archives.

18. Estelle Reel, *Course of Study for the Indian Schools of the United States* (Washington, D.C.: GPO, 1901), 160–61.

19. Pratt, *Battlefield and Classroom,* 294–98; "History of the Band," 6.

20. "History of the Band," 6.

21. Montezuma to Pratt, Nov. 23, 1906, folder 214, box 6, and Montezuma, "Carlisle Indian School Drifting from Its Moorings," *Philadelphia Public Ledger,* July 22, 1907, in A. Laura Pratt Scrapbook, box 29, both in Pratt Papers, YU. Pratt was annoyed at certain Smithsonian ethnologists for their encouragement of certain American Indian traditional practices. He was embarrassed that some of his Carlisle students "returned to the blanket" and performed traditional Indian music and dance, which he viewed as "savage orgies" not fit for civilized life. Pratt to James R. Garfield [secretary of the interior], March 7, 1907, folder 350, box 10, Pratt Papers, YU.

22. Federal appropriations for Carlisle decreased from $128,000 in 1891 to $110,000 in 1899, while the average student attendance rose from 754 to 878. Hence, in order to manage the daily operations at the school, Pratt needed funding from outside sources, such as philanthropy, sales of student crafts, manufactures, and agricultural produce from the school, or concerts and sports events. R. L. Brunhouse, "A History of the Carlisle Indian School: A Phase of Government Indian Policy: 1879 to 1918" (M.A. thesis, University of Pennsylvania, Philadelphia, 1935), table 3. One attempt to attract money was to have the Carlisle Band tour under Wheelock's direction, which brought favorable publicity for the school and Pratt's "experiment" as well as financial support from philanthropists.

23. ARCIA 1898, 389.

24. *Indian Helper,* Feb. 14, 1890, Feb. 10, 1893; Dennison Wheelock, "The Dawes Severalty Act," *Red Man,* May 1890, 6.

25. Dennison Wheelock, "Is It Right for the Government to Stop the Teaching of Indian Languages in Reservation Schools?" prize paper, reprinted in *Indian Helper,* Nov. 18, 1887, 1.

26. Proceedings of the Ninth Annual Meeting of the Lake Mohonk Conference of the Friends of the Indian, 1891 (Lake Mohonk, N.Y., 1891), 15.

27. Stevens, "Wheelock, Dennison"; 837; "Masons Hold Funeral Rites of D. Wheelock," *De Pere Journal-Democrat,* March 17, 1927, 1.

28. See note 5 above.

29. *Indian Helper,* Oct. 17, 1890.

30. "List of Indian Students Who Attended Dickinson College, Its Preparatory School, or Law School, with Years They Attended," CCHS; *One Hundred Ninth Catalogue, Dickinson College, Academic Year 1891–1892* (Carlisle, Pa., 1892), 77.

31. *Indian Helper,* Nov. 14, 1890, Oct. 23, 1891.

32. *New York Evening Post,* quoted in ARCIA 1893, 452.

33. *New York Recorder,* quoted in Pratt, *Battlefield and Classroom,* 293–94; ARCIA 1893, 453.

34. *Boston Advertiser, New York Mail and Express,* and *New York Recorder,* all quoted in ARCIA 1893, 452.

35. *New York Tribune,* quoted in ibid. See also "Real Americans These: The Carlisle Indians Fairly Won the Honors of the Day," *New York Sun,* Oct. 11, 1892, 8; and "Good Showing of Indian Pupils," *New York Herald,* Oct. 11, 1892, 11.

36. Pratt, *Battlefield and Classroom,* esp. 293.

37. Chicago Inter-Ocean, and *Chicago Journal,* both quoted in ARCIA 1893, 453. See also "The Parade," *Chicago Tribune,* Oct. 21, 1892, 1.

38. "Concert by Young Indians," *New York Times,* April 15, 1894, 9.

39. Louise La Chappelle student file; for her views, see her letter to *Red Man,* March 3, 1916 in her file; Edmund Richard Wheelock student file; all in Records of the Carlisle Indian School, RG94, NA.

40. *Indian Helper,* Oct. 19, 1896. See also "A Brass Band of Indians," *Baltimore Sun,* July 23, 1898, in A. Laura Pratt Scrapbook, Pratt Papers, YU.

41. Wheelock's Carlisle Band frequently gave holiday concerts in the Carlisle-Harrisburg area. See *Indian Helper,* Dec. 24, 1897.

42. Over one hundred years later, on August 14, 2003, the Green Bay Concert Band played this symphony at the Wisconsin Oneida Indian Reservation. This symphony had not been performed in over three-quarters of a century and clearly revealed the influence of Grieg. I recovered Wheelock's lost symphony from the Music Library at UCLA, whose collections should be acknowledged for contributing directly to this concert and to my article. For Wheelock's recruitment of the finest Indian student musicians from other boarding schools, see *Indian Helper,* June 24, Sept. 9, 1898, July 14, 21, 1899.

43. *Indian Helper,* July 21, 1899.

44. "Greater New York," *Metronome* 16 (April 1900): 15.

45. Dennison and Louise Wheelock's infant son is buried at the Carlisle Indian School grounds, now the U.S. Army War College, Carlisle, Pa.

46. See note 11 above.

47. Stevens, "Wheelock, Dennison.".

48. See note 11 above.

49. *Metronome* featured Wheelock's Haskell Band on its cover for March 1904. For the glowing review of the band, see "The Haskell Indian Band," *Metronome* 20 (March 1904): 8.

50. For his financial juggling, see Wheelock to Pratt, June 14, 1905, folder 323, box 9, Pratt Papers, YU. Dennison Wheelock had two brothers (James and Charles), two sisters (Celicia and Ida), three half-brothers (Joel, Hugh, and Harrison Earl), two half-sisters (Celicia and Martha), and two children with Louise La Chappelle (Edmund Richard and Paul). Please note that Dennison had both a sister and a half-sister named Celicia.

51. "Masons Hold Funeral Rites of D. Wheelock," *De Pere Journal-Democrat,* March 27, 1927, 1. For John R. Miller, see *Cumberland Justice: Legal Practice in Cumberland County, 1750–2000* (Carlisle, Pa.: Cumberland County Bar Foundation, 2001), 60, 68, 223. Alumni questionnaire in Dennison Wheelock student file, Records of the Carlisle Indian School, RG94, NA; Martin, *History of Brown County,* 2:364–65.

52. Society of American Indians, *Report of the Executive Council on the Proceedings of the First Annual Conference, October 12–17, 1911* (Washington, D.C.: SAI, 1912), 210.

53. *Quarterly Journal of the Society of American Indians* 2 (Oct.–Dec. 1914): 269–72. The caption of the photograph opposite p. 272 reads, "Dennison Wheelock (Oneida) Chairman Memorial Committee of the Society. A successful attorney living at West De Pere, Wis."

54. Wheelock to Pratt, Dec. 20, 1912, folder 323, box 9, Pratt Papers, YU.

55. Carlisle educators frequently printed articles about Dennison Wheelock's success and even reproduced photographs of his impressive home in West De Pere, attempting to use him as a role model for Carlisle's Indian students. See *Red Man* 4 (April 1912): 352–54; *The Invincible Yearbook,* 1915–1916 (Carlisle, Pa., 1916), CCHS; *Red Man* 7 (Feb. 1915): 220.

56. Advertisement for Wheelock's band concert in *Brown County* [Wisconsin] *Democrat,* Dec. 27, 1907, 4; "Band Concert Is Postponed until Tomorrow Night," *Green Bay Press-Gazette,* July 31, 1918, 5; "Many

Organizations Have Promoted Study of Music Here since the Civil War,"
Green Bay Press-Gazette, special tercentennial issue, July 18, 1934, "Civil
and Social Section," 43; *Metronome* 36 (Oct. 1915): 56. Wheelock was
involved in conducting the music for charity balls for the elite of Green Bay.
Don Poh, "History of Orchestra Music in Green Bay Covers 50 Years," *Green
Bay Press-Gazette,* Dec. 16, 1950, found in Newspaper Files, 1913–1914, in
the Local History Room, Brown County Library, Green Bay, Wis.

   57. Dennison Wheelock, Carlisle alumni questionnaire, in Wheelock student file, Records of the Carlisle Indian School, RG94, NA.

   58. See U.S., Congress, House of Representatives, Document No. 251.

   59. *Souvenir Program—Oneida Indian Centennial, August 5–7,* 1921,
Pamphlet Collection, SHSW.

   60. Hauptman field notes, May 14–20, 2003, Oneida Indian Reservation,
Oneida, Wis. For Wheelock's own views, see his letter to the Commissioner
of Indian Affairs, January 15, 1909, #8499-09-312 (Oneida), CCF
1907–1939, BIA, RG75, NA. Although BIA officials saw Wheelock as acting
perfectly legitimately, some Oneidas questioned his integrity, and there was
"a great deal of criticism" directed at him for his involvement in promoting
the conversion of trust lands to fee simple patents. Charles L. Davis Inspection
Report to Commissioner of Indian Affairs, October 16, 1909, #86325-09-
312, CCF 1907–1939, BIA, RG75, NA.

   61. He represented many Native American clients—Menominees, Mohawks,
Nisquallys, Stockbridge-Munsee Band of Mohicans, and many others. His
work for the Stockbridge-Munsee Band of Mohicans is documented by
James W. Oberly, in *A Nation of Statesmen: The Political Culture of the Stock-
bridge-Munsee Mohicans, 1815–1974* (Norman: University of Oklahoma
Press, 2005).

   62. Woodlawn Cemetery Brochure, Green Bay, Wisconsin.

14

Three Oneida WPA Stories about Reservation Bands, Musicians, and Performances

Editors' Note: The following three WPA stories illustrate the cultural and social importance of band music at Oneida and in other Indian communities after the Civil War and throughout the age of allotment.

Oneida National Band

Chauncey Baird

The people's band. It is the oldest band. And we still have a band at this time. Only the bandsmen are so scattered. They live here and there in different towns and cities. I would say the Oneida National Band is about eighty years old. They called [it the] Oneida National Band because the band use to belong to the people. Some bandsmen left the Oneida National Band and organized another band and called it the American Band. Some more men left and organized another band and called it the Union Band. There was still another band. They used to call themselves the Bear Band. The people's band has helped our stone [Episcopal] church so much. Every time any church doings, dinners picnics, the people's band always played for them, and they always played free for the church. There are two of us left, that joined the band about the same time[.] [O]nly Jonas left ten years ago and lives in another town. I have been a member of the Oneida National Band about forty-five years. There is still another man [and] his name is Tom [Elm]. He used to be a member of the American Band and when that broke up he joined our band. Tom and I are the oldest men in our band at this time. We still get together some times when we get a job. There was [an] Oneida National Band already here when two Tuscarora men came from New York [around 1880]. Their names were Zanhósgwa and Zagosw^dót. They were the ones that taught the Oneidas how to play music. We used to get quite a few jobs long ago. We would [go to] different towns[.] [S]ome times we would be gone a few days at [a time]. [We] used to play at the different fairs and always on the Fourth [of July]. Those days they used to pay ten [dollars?] to each man [a]t that time. We don't get any more jobs because there are so many High School [students] learning to play in the bands. At this time, Oneida Nation Band sure could play. You could give them any classical music and they could play it.

The Oneida Band

Thomas Elm

It has been a long time already, that the Oneidas had a band here on the reservation. The first band that the Oneidas organized was called the Nation Band. The way the first got the instruments, was donated by the people. The money that they got from the U.S. government at that time was one dollar per head, and they used that to buy the band instruments. Its about seventy years ago [post–Civil War] since the first band was organized. When the instrument got worn out, then they re-organized the band, and they changed the name to [the] National Band. So they been changing the name of the band, and the players. I finally joined the Band myself. James Wheelock [Dennison's brother] organized a traveling band and I went along. We went all over the country[.] [W]e went through about fourteen states. When we was coming back towards their [this] way, we had bad luck. Wilson Skenandore died, and we sent his body home. The band paid all the expenses. One hundred and fifty dollars. About half of the members of that Band are living today and the rest have died. This same band, have played many times at the State Fair Milwaukee. It was the year of 1926 that the Band played there last. From that time on we have been satisfied, just to play here, and the surrounding towns. We took the Seymour bus, and went to Mineral Point to play there. We were there four days. Then we went to Pittsville[. . . .] We were there one day. They were having pawa [a pow-wow] at that place. The Indians sure had a good time. Then from there, we went to Milwaukee and stayed there five days. It was during the Eagles Convention. At the present time they call the Band the Oneida Band. The players [are] getting old[.] [T]hose that are the best players and some of them are poor in health. And the young players are hired by different good bands away from here. So it seems kind of hard to have a band.

Oneida Bands

Mark Powless

Long time ago[,] Nelson Metoxen organized an Oneida Band, and Indian dancers here in Oneida Reservation. It was at Two Rivers where they would go and join a show there, and so they hired out and went there. When they got there, he borrowed a big tent. This was the place, they would put on their show, the Band and the Indian dancers. They were two men, Oneidas, who were the best war dancers. And the way they were dressed up was something like this. They had beaded bands, silver, and different color ribbons around their arm and legs, and also around their neck. Also they had small bells what they used on horses, tied around their legs. And on their heads, they had eagle's feathers war bonnet, and also buffalo's horns they had that too. They were doing very good with their band and dancers, and they drew lots of people to their shows. They were there several days[.] [T]hen one evening, they saw mean looking clouds coming, that looked like [a] strong wind storm and heavy rain with it. And so right away he was anxious and worried, this leader of the show. Nelson, said, by gosh, I think we are going to get that wind storm[.] [W]e might all die now. Hurry up, and tighten those ropes to the stakes. Lets not have the tent go down, because its worth lots of money that tent of ours. Now then they were running around and they all got busy tighting the ropes on the tent to the stakes. These two Oneida men their names were Wilbur Archiquette and Johnston Denny. They were still at it, when the big storm broke loose and struck their big tent. And these two Oneidas had their dancing outfits on[.] [T]hey did'nt have time to change to their civilian clothes so there, they were running around there with the buffalo's horns on their heads. So he encouraged them, he said, do your best my chums[.] [Y]ou see that part of the tent raising up and down over there[.] [Y]ou two grab it, and try to hold it down. And so thats what they done. They were hanging on to the tent[.] [P]retty soon they were off the ground, but still hanging on, their buffalo horns were on back of their heads, but they did'nt let it go, their hold.

15

Opportunities at Home

Laura Cornelius Kellogg and Village Industrialization

Patricia Stovey

In October 1911, Laura Cornelius, a Wisconsin Oneida, stood before an intertribal gathering of educated and "civilized" Indians at the first conference of the Society of American Indians (SAI). She addressed the conference attendees as an already established and important player in the organization of the society and this conference. The sole female founder, she had earlier in the year initiated a meeting of seventeen others at her home in Seymour, Wisconsin, to draft a letter announcing the association's formation and purpose. The October conference held at Ohio State began with a presentation by the commissioner of Indian affairs, Robert G. Valentine, who acknowledged the problems faced by the American Indian in the early years of the twentieth century. He stated that too many Indian children were not receiving an education and concluded that the public did not direct sufficient attention to the problems faced by all Indians. This conference was designed as a first step in changing that.

Many of the attendees believed that the reservation was the source of these problems. In the "Preface" that the SAI published after its first conference, the organization articulated its position on Indian reservations. "A reservation," it stated, "does not afford a normal condition of human environment." It saps Indians of their independence through a condition of "wardship" and leaves them as "neither citizen nor foreigner." SAI members concluded that "thinking" Indians asked for the freedom "to develop normally as an American people in America."[1] To many at the conference, this meant the complete dissolution of the reservation.

Cornelius, however, saw it differently. She was the sole presenter who spoke on the opportunities that life on the reservation afforded the Native American. She made clear her contempt for reservation "paternalism and wardship," and her support for equal opportunity and the importance of a proper environment. But still, she believed, current leaders failed "to calculate upon the possibilities of the Indian reservation," and the "influence of human ties."[2] Besides, she said, "some of the gravest problems in the country to-day are to be found in the industrial world of the white man." She pointed to tenement life in the cities where "hollow-chested" men were forced to toil in shops closed to the wind and sun. She raised the shame of child labor, which robbed children of their childhood and health. "No," she concluded, "I cannot see that everything the white man does is to be copied."[3]

Cornelius proposed a third option, which combined the best aspects of modern industrialization and the environment of the reservation. Her plan attempted to keep the reservations intact, including the concept of communal ownership, but adjusted them to fit the reality of twentieth-century industrial America. In contrast to the push for assimilation, which removed the Indian from the reservation and into private landownership, industrial villages would maintain native communities through incorporation of both capital and labor.[4] Her vision improved upon the Garden City ideal currently in practice in England, Germany, and France by providing purposefully planned communities focused on industry, rather than designed as an escape from it. She envisioned each village as capitalizing on its tribe's expertise, like fishing, herding, or horticulture. The tribe would become an industry in its own right, functioning as a modern business, but without the "middle man's interference."[5] She proposed, she said, that "instead of forsaking what we already have in holdings . . . instead of being fixtures in an industrial world . . . that [we take] the line of least resistance to the greatest possible good under our present circumstances . . . and to reorganize the opportunities of the Indian *at home*" (emphasis in original).[6]

Laura Cornelius did focus her early efforts at home. By the late 1910s, she was deeply involved in issues within the Wisconsin Oneida community, pushing for change and stirring up controversy in the process. In truth, it almost goes without saying, Laura Cornelius is a controversial figure among the Oneida. Her supporters and detractors extend outside of Wisconsin to Oneida communities in New York, Ontario, Canada, and wherever pockets of Iroquois Indians settled throughout the United States. Many members of other tribal groups connected with the Oneida— through tribal confederation within the Iroquois, or emigration, such as the Stockbridges and Brothertowns in Wisconsin—also have decisive opinions on her. She was not one to leave a room, a meeting, or a community without notice. Comments made about her by fellow members of the SAI leadership provide possible insight as to why this might be. Charles Dagenett, for example, called her a "visionary. . . full of great schemes but not practical."[7] Arthur Parker admired her intellect but found the intimation of her rhetoric, "go my way or I will ruin you," unmanageable. Carlos Montezuma described her as a "cyclone," moving from one issue to another, wanting to do everything "without considering the consequences."[8] However, the Reverend Sherman Coolidge remembered her differently. Recalling the first time he heard her speak, Coolidge said, "Tears came to my eyes to realize that we had a woman of her brilliance among us and to think of the great good she could do for the Indian people."[9]

Today Laura Cornelius Kellogg—nee Laura Cornelius—is most remembered for the leadership role she took in the New York land claims of the 1920s. The scars from that period run deep. This essay, however, focuses on Cornelius's work within the Oneida community and Oneida politics prior to the land claims issue. Clearly there is an overlap in time, but her efforts to bring

Indian industrial organization to her home reservation sheds light on an issue she embraced throughout her life. This point is generally lost in the morass left behind from her involvement in the land claims. This is my effort to clear away some of the tangle in order to reveal Cornelius's level of commitment to an issue that she recognized as the answer to the problems Indians faced in the twentieth century.

Cornelius's plan for the reservation grew in part out of her personal history. She was born on September 10, 1880, Laura Miriam (Minnie) Cornelius, on the Wisconsin Oneida reservation. She grew up during a tumultuous period in the tribe's history. After the Dawes General Allotment Act, the entire Wisconsin Oneida reservation was allotted, which, because of the size of the Oneida population and the land area of the reservation, resulted in no land—except for the government-run school—remaining under community ownership.[10] Cornelius was intensely proud of her Oneida heritage. Her bloodline boasted two powerful chiefs—her maternal grandfather, Daniel Bread, a war hero and head chief of the Oneidas, and Elijah Skenandore, a powerful orator and the last of the New York chiefs.[11] Cornelius attributed much of her racial pride and ability to her early years and the fact that she never attended a government-run boarding school. She credited her education to the time she spent at the "soup kettle on the reservation," and at the various public and private institutions she attended. As a result, she considered herself a truly enlightened person, able to appreciate "the real values of truth," whether they came from an Indian or a "Paleface."[12] Cornelius taught briefly at the government school at Oneida, as well as at the Sherman Institute in Riverside, California, but she spent the majority of the years between 1898 and 1910 in pursuit of higher education.[13] She attended Stanford University, Barnard College, the New York School of Philanthropy, Cornell University, and the University of Wisconsin but never finished a program at any one institution.[14] The reason for this is unclear; however, Cornelius's high school diploma already placed her in the ranks of the better educated in American society and among the very best educated Native American women.

Laura Cornelius's formal education ended when she was called home on account of her father's death in October 1910.[15] In the months following, Cornelius drifted between Chicago and her home in Wisconsin in search of a calling that would satisfactorily demonstrate her pride in her Indian heritage. It was during this period that she developed her ideas on transforming reservations into self-sustaining industrial villages and became involved in the Society of American Indians.

The 1910s provided Cornelius with a series of highs and lows. Cornelius married Orrin J. Kellogg, a white man of dubious history and background on April 22, 1912. Kellogg listed his profession as both realtor and lawyer. He gave no address other than his mother's home in Davenport, Iowa, although he claimed to currently work in Seymour, and the couple married more than seventy miles away in Stevens Point, Wisconsin.[16] Throughout their marriage Kellogg supported his wife in her various endeavors but generally remained in the shadows, prompting one newspaper to conclude that the best description of Orin Kellogg would be "as the husband of Mrs. Kellogg."[17]

Less than two years into their marriage, the Kelloggs were arrested in Oklahoma on charges of "Pretense of Indian Agents with intent to invest Indian funds." Although the case was eventually dismissed, the charges prompted scathing articles from the *Tulsa Daily World,* which questioned Laura Cornelius Kellogg's dedication to her race and standing within the Oneida tribe. The paper quoted an unnamed Oneida who called Kellogg a "ready borrower" with "the habit of making little touches wherever she finds any of her people."[18] Throughout her life, Kellogg demonstrated a high level of comfort using other people's money on projects that some would consider highly risky and others would consider self-serving; however, as in this case, Kellogg was never convicted of any financial wrongdoing. Nonetheless, as a result of the arrest, Laura Cornelius Kellogg was kicked out of the SAI, an injustice and humiliation she never forgave.

Local Wisconsin papers reveal very little about Kellogg's activities for the next five years, but by 1919 she was clearly back living in the Oneida area and focused on a project dear to her heart. That year the Indian Service officially closed the Oneida Boarding School. Kellogg recognized the opportunity afforded her by the government's action, to bring the industrial village concept into practice on her home reservation, and so she dived headfirst into the school issue. In June 1919, Kellogg traveled to Washington, D.C., where she tried to meet with the commissioner of Indian affairs, Cato Sells, in order to register her objection to the government's abandoning the students who depended on the school. In a written statement she made for Sells, Kellogg argued that the public schools in and around Oneida could not sufficiently service the students cast off by the government. In Kellogg's typically direct fashion, she reminded Sells of his bureau's shortcomings and responsibility to the Oneida people. Haphazard issuance of patent-in-fee titles had left the reservation without a solid enough tax base for the tribe to build a school of its own once the government facility closed. "Letting the Indian go," she reminded the commissioner, "should not mean a shirking of the responsibility by the Government which should attend this treacherous transition from tutelage to citizenship." She warned him of the lifelong effect made by educational deprivation during one's youth and dismissed out of hand the government's pro-mise of accommodation. She told Sells that the Oneidas had plans to organize the facility as an "industrial and educational center" and assured him that she would not be leaving town until she accomplished her mission of meeting with him concern-ing this issue.[19]

The plans Kellogg referred to concerned the construction of a canning factory and the establishment of an Indian village on the Oneida school property. The school's closing happened to come during the period Kellogg wrote and published her book, *Our Democracy and the American Indian*. In it she further devel-oped her Indian industrial village plan, which she now called "Lolomi."[20] In the book she reemphasized Lolomi's foundation in Indian-run industry set on the reservation, but outside of BIA control. She set it apart from other reformers' plans that called for cutting America's Native population free from all protections and, as she wrote, "leaving the helpless Indian open to every grafter in the land."[21] In contrast, Lolomi provided the Indian with security through federal incorporation. Kellogg contended that federal laws would offer the Indians the security they needed to survive "petty politics" at the state level, where she believed small groups of Native Americans would fare as well as "a lamb would with a hungry lion."[22]

Once incorporated, each Lolomi village would become a self-governing body with pooled assets turned over into fee simple title. Incorporation would end the Indians' current ward system and "semi-citizenship," remove the BIA as middleman skimming off the profits, and allow each community to develop its own industry and equitable system of salaries and wages.[23] Kellogg foresaw Lolomi villages maintaining lifestyles agreeable to the American Indian, through their concentration on the out-of-door pursuits, and training appropriate to each person's ability.[24] Her plan also provided for the social needs of the community through health-care facilities (overseen by the Public Health Service), and educational and recreational centers.[25] She touted homogeneity as an important key that would play into Lolomi's success as well and pointed to Mormon communities as models of this. She wrote: "All successful organization is based on likeness of kind. I believe where white communities have co-operative organizations that have failed, the fact that they were composed of all kinds of race elements has counted largely." Members of Lolomi's single-race communities would triumph over modern societal burdens—such as taxation—because problems would be dealt with in the ancient way of shared responsibility.[26]

At Oneida, Kellogg envisioned a cooperative based on the area's potential for cherry production, and she used her position as a "representative of the Oneidas' interests" to lead the tribal council toward advocating for Lolomi.[27] At one point she exerted her authority to handpick a group of "third party" observers to look at the land and send their conclusions on to Washington. After surveying the property and conferring individually with Kellogg, with Samuel Bell of the Indian Office and E. A. Allen, the federal Indian agent at Keshena, the observers unanimously recommended Kellogg's plan. In a letter they sent to Secretary of the Interior John Barton Payne, they said the facility should remain a school, but that 115 acres of land be appraised with that value used to form a corporation with each Oneida holding equal shares in the stock. They recommended that a canning factory be built to help support the maintenance of the school, but most notably, they believed that the property's location offered an excellent site for an Oneida village. In their closing paragraph they wrote:

> The committee also wishes to state that it has been much interested in learning of the plan of the proposed Lolomi Industrial community for the Oneidas, and feels that if it can be successfully organized and executed, it would provide the Indians with a protection from exploitation which they very much need, and be a stimulus to the social and industrial development of the community.[28]

Kellogg followed their conclusions a month later with a letter she signed along with six other Oneidas, wondering about any forthcoming decision on the property. She reiterated her group's desire for incorporation and industrialization and closed with the assurance that their intentions for the property came "endorsed by reliable public sentiment."[29]

Here the word "reliable" is open to interpretation. Early in the process, the Oneidas divided over the issue of the school property, something Kellogg's own actions certainly contributed to. Kellogg assumed her right to speak for the best interests of the tribe and believed both intellectually and emotionally that her program of Indian industrial villages would solve her tribe's problems. She displayed little care for the decorum of proper channels, especially when they involved the BIA or their "reservation lackeys." She sought action, and so she confidently overstepped or sidestepped anyone who put hurdles in her way. For example, Kellogg organized the group of "third party" observers who looked at the school property almost a full year after her contract to represent the Oneidas had been canceled. In 1919, when a majority at the September council meeting passed a resolution to make the school property available for state or county purchase, Kellogg refused to accept their decision as a true reflection of the tribe's wishes and, in response, called another council where she appointed her own chair and secretary.[30] Actions such as these caused not only confusion but also alarm and precipitated numerous letters between tribal members, state representatives, the local (Keshena) Indian agent, and the commissioner of Indian affairs.

Because of the resulting dissent, the assistant commissioner of Indian affairs, Edgar Meritt, considered the possibility for agreement over the school as "rather hopeless," and the property sat idle.[31] Despite Meritt, however, Kellogg actively continued to pursue the property and her dream of Lolomi. In early 1921, she wrote a letter to Wisconsin senator Irvine Lenroot asking for his help in getting serious consideration from the commissioner on an offer to buy the property. She told him that she had "six of the best Oneida men," who with her were ready to purchase the land and facilities for use as a school, incorporated industry, and eventual model village.[32] Nothing happened, and the property continued to sit.

Then, in March 1922, the De Pere *Journal-Democrat* featured an article on its front page with a headline that read, "Oneidas May Be in Great Luck." It told about the final decision in an eight-year-old land-claims case involving J. H. Boylan and the Oneida Indians of New York. The U.S. Supreme Court refused to hear the case, thereby upholding a federal appeals court ruling that returned a thirty-two-acre parcel of land within the city of Oneida, New York, to the Oneidas. In the case, the federal government represented the Oneidas' right to land currently held by white "owner" Julia Boylan. The decision determined that New York had not followed regulations set by an 1842 state treaty when it allowed the land to slip into white control. It confirmed the U.S. government's right to represent the Indians, as well as the state's limited authority in Indian matters. Boylan's ownership demonstrated that New York State had superseded federal authority in disposing of Oneida land, since no one tribal member could be allowed to sell his or her "interest in the reservation to an outsider." The paper estimated the land to be valued at 4 million dollars and said that the award money would be shared among all the Oneidas, including those who had emigrated from New York to Wisconsin.[33] Coincidentally, one month later, the Oneida school property finally came open for bids, and Kellogg—her name unconnected with any other organization—won with a bid of thirty-five thousand dollars, a full thirteen thousand dollars over the next highest bidder.[34] She paid the 5 percent deposit but never managed to find the money for the remainder.

For the next eight months, numerous letters went back and forth between Commissioner of Indian Affairs Charles Burke, Agent Allen, and Kellogg, as extension after extension on the property's payment was requested, debated, and approved. Certainly the timing of the Boylan case is intriguing, but it is inconclusive in reconciling Kellogg's bid. If Kellogg had depended upon money from New York, she never mentioned it directly in her correspondences. Her reasons for delay varied. She referred to land transactions in the West that failed to reach completion, technicalities in loan applications, illness, and promises unfulfilled. Exactly who she trusted would come through for her is also unclear (she always represented her backers in the vaguest of terms), but what is clear is that she made the bid with nothing more than a hope that the monies necessary for the purchase could and would materialize.[35]

Kellogg did actively pursue loans. In late June 1922 she contacted John Strange, the owner of the John Strange Paper Company in Menasha, Wisconsin, and he wrote a letter to Agent Allen promising to make arrangements for her. By 8 July, Strange again contacted Allen to let him know that the time restriction made it impossible. Strange wrote: "The time required to raise a sum of money of this extent must be made more liberal than [by] a few days. . . Not having any knowledge of the possible value of the property I have not been able to determine the reasonableness in asking friends with ready cash to interest themselves in a loan on the property."[36] Eventually Commissioner Burke and Agent Allen advised Kellogg against asking for additional extensions, so she turned to influential friends—lawyers and congressmen—to do the asking for her. It worked and her final payment date was set at January 1, 1923.

The deal fell through, and Kellogg forfeited the $1,750 deposit. The final letter she sent telling Commissioner Burke of her failure to pay was uncharacteristically conciliatory and polite. In her closing remarks she expressed her "deepest gratitude" to the commissioner for his kindness and declared her regret for the "extreme disappointments I have caused you and myself, and thanking you again and again for your past courtesies." Interestingly, the signature was not hers—"per M. Schulz"—and one wonders just how much the sentiment was as well.[37]

In the spring of 1924 the property was sold to the Murphy Land Company and immediately given to the Catholic Diocese of Green Bay. By summer, Kellogg began to challenge the government's right to sell the property based on past treaty agreements, and although deeply involved in another much larger issue by this date (the New York land claims), she became secretary of a group called the Oneida National Committee (ONC).[38] Through this organization Kellogg maintained an active letter-writing campaign and kept alive the idea of an industrial community based in Oneida.[39]

In late August 1924, the ONC sent Burke a letter protesting the sale of the school. The letter enumerated the committee's concerns pertaining to the Oneidas' lack of input in the sale of the property, and that the property's use—as outlined in the original land agreement—was designated as an educational center. The committee had plans to use the land in just such a matter.[40] They wrote other letters of complaint to U.S. senators, and in late 1924 wrote to the area bishop calling on him to vacate the property. In their letter, Kellogg and the ONC explained to the bishop that, based on agreements made at the time of allotment, the government had no right to sell the property. Therefore, the diocese's ownership was grounded on a "false position," and they advised him against continuing any more building repairs.

The committee apologized for any discomfort their news caused but explained that the letter came as a part of their obligation as "duly authorized representatives of the Oneida Nation."[41]

The sale stood, and eventually, when the government distributed checks for the school, a small contingent of fifteen—including Kellogg's mother, adopted son, and two of her siblings—returned theirs, informing the Indian superintendent that "we will take up the matter of our right to this property through the courts."[42] They never did.

Kellogg's failure to follow up on her threat did not reflect any "giving up" on her part concerning Indian industrial reservations, but rather her deepening involvement in the New York land claims. Although Kellogg later revealed another, more self-serving, side to her interest in the New York claim, her vision of Lolomi never disappeared. For example, early in the land claims movement, she traveled as a part of a committee elected to represent the Wisconsin Oneidas at a gathering of the Six Nations in New York. While there, the leaders met with E. A. Everett, the New York congressman and attorney who initiated the investigation that eventually led to the court case *James Deere v. St. Lawrence River Power Company.*[43] Although the point of the meeting was to determine what preliminary actions the Six Nations tribes would pursue, at some point during the visit Kellogg spoke with Everett about her interest in the Oneida school property, sharing with him her vision of Indian industrial villages. Everett supported this vision and later wrote a letter to the secretary of the interior William Calder that helped to secure Kellogg an extension on the school property payment.[44]

Five years later, and deeply involved in the issue of land claims, Kellogg still spoke of Lolomi's potential. In a 1927 article that appeared in New York's *Syracuse Herald,* she outlined her vision for New York's Onondaga reservation. Lolomi, she contended, would transform it from "shacks and wide uncultivated stretches . . . into a thrifty, industrious [and] self-sustaining settlement." In that same article, she described the potential for model villages on all of New York's reservations offering a full range of educational options, training, and rehabilitation opportunities.[45]

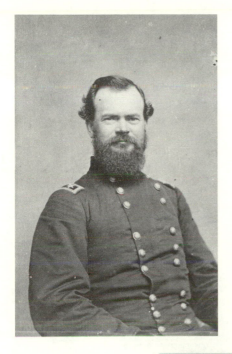

General James Birdseye McPherson (1828–1864), commander of the Union's Army of the Tennessee, whose death near Peachtree Creek during General Sherman's Atlanta Campaign became part of Oneida oral tradition relating to the military service of Private Cornelius Doxtator.
Reproduced from Frederick Meserve, Historical Portraits: A Collection of Photographs.

Richard Henry Pratt, Founder and Superintendent at the United States Indian Industrial School at Carlisle, Pennsylvania from 1879 to 1904. Courtesy of the Cumberland County Historical Society, Carlisle, Pa., image 14-32-3.

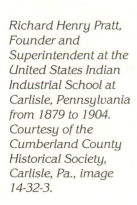

Josiah Powless as a student at Carlisle Indian School, c. 1891. Powless went on to medical school and later served his Oneida community as a physician. He was killed while serving as an army surgeon on the western front during World War I. Courtesy of the Cumberland County Historical Society, Carlisle, Pa., image PA-CH2-019c.

Dennison Wheelock with his cornet in his band uniform as a student at Carlisle Indian School, 1890. Courtesy of Cumberland County Historical Society, Carlisle, Pa., image PA-CH1-V.

James Wheelock as a student at Carlisle Indian School, c. 1890s. James, Dennison Wheelock's brother, was an acclaimed musician in his own right. He was later the bandmaster at several federal Indian boarding schools and headed the United States Indian Band that toured North America and Europe. Courtesy of the Cumberland County Historical Society, Carlisle, Pa., image PA-CH3-044C.

Chester Cornelius, one of the first Oneidas to be graduated from Carlisle Indian School, c. late 1880s. He later taught at several federal Indian boarding schools and practiced law. A brother of Laura Minnie Cornelius, he was raised as an Oneida chief in 1925. Courtesy of the Cumberland County Historical Society, Carlisle, Pa., image PA-CH2-021a.

The Carlisle Indian School Band, 1896. Dennison Wheelock, bandmaster and professor of music, standing in the first row center. Courtesy of the Cumberland County Historical Society, Carlisle, Pa., image 14-20-3.

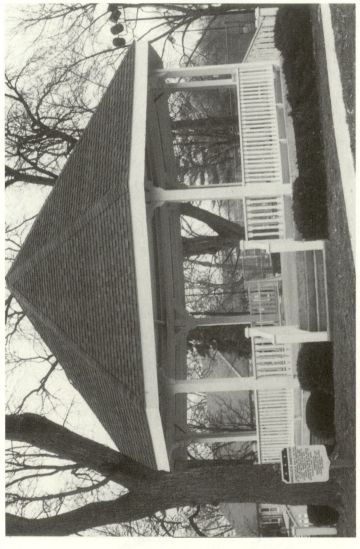

The Wheelock Bandstand at the Army War College, Carlisle, Pennsylvania. Completed in 1980 at the site of the original bandstand at the Carlisle Indian School, it is dedicated to the memory of Dennison Wheelock and his internationally-acclaimed Indian band. Photograph by Laurence M. Hauptman, March 15, 2003.

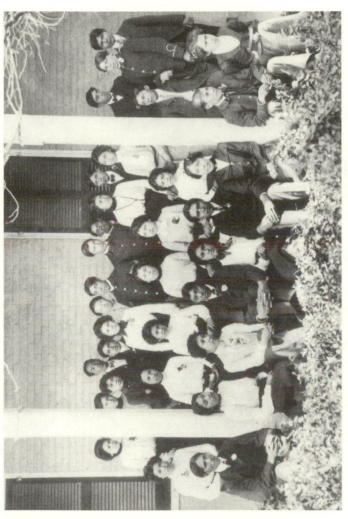

Oneida Boys and Girls at Hampton Institute, c. 1900. Left to right from back: Lucy Coulon, Elsie Powless, Reuben Baird, Solomon Archiquette, William Skenandore, Lena Ludwick, Rose Hill, Albert Webster, Cleveland Hill, Hyson Doxtator, Josephine Hill, Isaac Webster, Nancy Doxtator, Duncan Powless, and four unknown Oneidas (including two from New York). Courtesy of Oneida Nation Museum, Acc. No. 76.81.

Oneida Girls at Hampton Institute, c. 1900. Back row: Lydia Cooper (Webster), Cora Powless (Charles), Minnie Cooper, Rose Hill (House), Josephine Hill (Webster), Marion Skenandore (Williams); second row: Unknown girl, Leah Skenandore (Cornelius), Olive Doxtator (Webster), Lily Silas, Mary Summers, Edna Powless (Webster), Nancy Doxtator (Cornelius), and Lucy Coulon (House). Courtesy of Oneida Nation Museum, Acc. No. 76.80.

The School Buildings of the United States Indian Industrial School at Oneida, Wisconsin, in 1910. Courtesy of the Milwaukee Public Museum, image A-621-D.

Oneida boys in military uniforms with school personnel on the porch of the United States Indian Industrial School at Oneida, Wisconsin. Courtesy of the Milwaukee Public Museum, image A-621-3-C.

Classroom scene at the United States Indian Industrial School at Oneida, Wisconsin. Courtesy of the Milwaukee Public Museum, image A-621-2-J.

Oneida boys posing in front of horse-drawn team while working in the dairy at the United States Indian Industrial School at Oneida, Wisconsin. Courtesy of the Milwaukee Public Museum, image A-621-I.

Oneida girls receiving instruction in sewing class at the United States Indian Industrial School at Oneida, Wisconsin. Courtesy of the Milwaukee Public Museum, image A-621-4-B.

Oneida girls in the school laundry at the United States Indian Industrial School at Oneida, Wisconsin. Courtesy of the Milwaukee Public Museum, image A-621-2-C.

Four Oneida Indian girls baking in the kitchen at the United States Indian Industrial School at Oneida, Wisconsin. Courtesy of the Milwaukee Public Museum, image A-621-2-B.

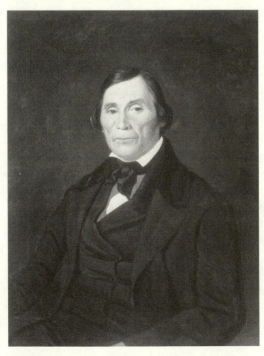

Chief Daniel Bread (1800–1873), painting by Samuel M. Brookes, c. 1860. Chief Bread led the Oneidas to Wisconsin in the 1820s and was the most influential of their leaders until his death nearly a half century later. Courtesy of the Wisconsin Historical Society, image WHi-2550.

Chief Cornelius Hill (1834–1907) in his Episcopal priestly vestments. Reproduced from Julia K. Bloomfield, The Oneidas, *2nd ed., New York: Alden Bros., 1907.*

Dennison Wheelock, c. 1911. Wheelock practiced law from 1907 to 1922 in West DePere, Wisconsin, near the Oneida Indian Reservation. From 1923 to 1927, he represented more than a dozen Indian nations as an attorney in Washington, D.C. Reproduced from Deborah B. Martin, History of Brown County, Wisconsin: Past and Present, *Chicago: S. J. Clarke, 1913, Vol. II.*

Laura Minnie Cornelius Kellogg in 1911. Photograph reproduced from Report of the Executive Council of the Proceedings of the First Annual Conference (1911) of the Society of American Indians, Washington, D.C., 1912.

Oneida women lacemakers, c. 1917. Josephine Hill Webster, third from left. The date was ascertained from a similar photograph in the Oneida Nation Museum. Reproduced from Oneida Lacemakers Sales Brochure, found in Cooper-Hewitt Museum Collections, New York City.

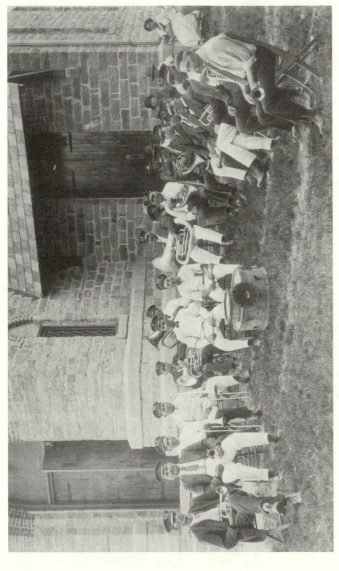

Oneida National Band, left to right: Tom Elm, Herbert Cornelius, Hobart House, Levi Baird, Ainsley Hill, Adam Denny, Fred House, Edgar Skenandore, Chauncey Baird, Alex Webster, Riley Hill, Laban Baird, Martin Archiquette, Peter Danforth, and Eli Hill. The photograph was taken in front of the Oneida's Holy Apostles Episcopal Church during the centennial celebration of the Oneidas' arrival in Wisconsin (Michigan Territory). Oneida Nation Museum.

As late as 1929, when the last real hope had passed for reclaiming Indian lands through her leadership, she again presented her plan for village industrialization. This time before a Senate sub-committee—that convened on her request—she touted Lolomi as not just a solution for New York's native population, but as the solution to "every . . . Indian problem in the land."[46]

In reality, however, Kellogg's 1922 bid for the Oneida school property represented the closest she ever came to the realization of a Lolomi village. But even if she had found backers for a loan, it is doubtful she would have succeeded. First of all, there is no evidence that on the issue of industrial organization Kellogg ever spoke for a majority of the Wisconsin Oneidas. Second, Kellogg had an image of how she wanted an industrial village to look and work, but in reality she had no experience or training to help her transform her vision into practice. Kellogg's poor financial history with a record of borrowing without payment suggested future problems, as did the fact that she had never run a small business—much less an entire factory. She lacked the skills required to bring a product to market, to train workers, deal with the breakdown of machinery, or handle any other facets of business life, and none of the documents suggests that she knew of anyone able to fill that void. Lastly, her headstrong manner, impatience, and inability to accept dissent did not bode well for a community based on cooperation.

Back in 1911, when Laura Cornelius stood before the first (SAI) conference, she knew she championed an approach to the "Indian problem" that fell outside the accepted avenues of most reformers of the day. And to a large degree, she may have considered this one of her plan's strengths. Laura Cornelius Kellogg's efforts at village industrialization demonstrated a pride of race and a deep-felt belief in the innate ability of Native Americans to overcome their problems. To her, the reservation was not the entire cause of the problems faced by twentieth-century Indians. In fact, the reservation could be the answer. Not just another impractical "great scheme," or something she touched upon briefly before whirling on to something else, Lolomi represented a concept that she advocated and sought to bring into practice for at least two decades.

Kellogg's belief in the potential of industrial villages preceded her presentation at the first SAI conference and continued throughout the 1920s, well past the sale of the Oneida property and into her involvement in New York. Never one to shy away from a challenge, Laura Kellogg advanced her program of Indian uplift against great odds. Her greatest effort proved to be on her home reservation at Oneida, Wisconsin.

Notes

1. Society of American Indians (SAI), *Report of the Executive Council on the Proceedings of the First Annual Conference of the Society of American Indians Held at the University of Ohio, Columbus, Ohio, October 12–17, 1911* (Washington D.C.: SAI, 1912), 4–5.

2. Ibid., 44.

3. Ibid., 46–48.

4. Ibid., 52–53.

5. Ibid., 50–52.

6. Ibid., 45.

7. Charles Dagenett to Carlos Montezuma, January 27, 1912, in Carlos Montezuma Papers, 1892–1937, SHSW. It is helpful to know that Dagenett and Cornelius did not care for each other. Dagenett was boarding school trained and the highest-ranking Native American employed by the Indian Bureau. As such, Cornelius considered him a fine example of the government's power over the Indian population through control of Native American education. She considered him a hustler, nothing short of a government lackey. In 1912 she challenged his chair position in the SAI, based on the premise that his role in the government would be a conflict of interest. She managed to bring it to a vote, but Dagenett stayed, and so did Cornelius, for the time being. Dagenett to Cornelius, January 27, 1912, microfilm reel 2, (cited SAI Papers; Ballot 1912, Montezuma Papers.

8. Arthur Parker to Montezuma, undated, 1913, and Montezuma to Parker, April 2, 1913, Montezuma Papers.

9. "'Joan' of Indians Author's Wife?" *Rocky Mountain Times,* October 13, 1913, reel 10, SAI Papers.

10. Arlinda Locklear, "The Allotment of the Oneida Reservation and Its Legal Ramifications," in *Campisi and Hauptman, Oneida Indian Experience,*

85; "Narrative Reports from Agencies, 1910–1938," reel 69, microcopy 1011, Keshena Agency, RG75, NA.

11. "Modern Villages for Indians, Plan of Woman Worker," *Milwaukee Journal,* April 18, 1920; Hauptman, "Designing Woman," 162.

12. "Modern Villages for Indians, Plan of Woman Worker," *Milwaukee Journal,* April 18, 1920; Laura Cornelius Kellogg, "Some Facts and Figures on Indian Education," Quarterly Journal of the Society of American Indians 1 (April 1913): 36.

13. "Oneida," *De Pere (Wisconsin) Journal-Democrat,* December 22, 1927.

14. Hauptman, "Designing Woman," 164.

15. "Oneida," *De Pere (Wisconsin) News,* October 1, 1910.

16. "Laura Cornelius Married to Orin J. Kellogg," *De Pere News,* May 1, 1912.

17. "What Has Become of Investigators," *Tulsa Daily World,* October 5, 1913.

18. Ibid.

19. Laura Kellogg to Cato Sells, June 21, 1919, #806-19-69348 (Oneida), CCF 1907–1939, BIA, RG75, NA.

20. Kellogg took the name Lolomi, meaning "perfect goodness be upon you," from the Hopi language.

21. Kellogg, *Our Democracy and the American Indian,* 58.

22. Ibid., 60–61.

23. Ibid., 63–64, 69–70, 78.

24. Ibid., 76, 79.

25. Ibid., 92–93.

26. Ibid., 63-66.

27. Eli Skenadie to Sells, September 20, 1919, and Samuel Plautz et al. to John Barton Payne, May 21, 1920, in Ernie Stevens Sr. Papers, Division of Land Management (LM), ONIW. Both letters refer to Kellogg as having a contract to represent the interests of the Oneidas. Even Eli Skenadie's letter, although written to complain about Kellogg's behavior, referred to her as an "attorney" for the Oneidas and commented on the council's "contract" with her.

28. Plautz et al. to Payne, May 21, 1920, LM.ONIW.

29. Laura Kellogg et al. to Payne, June 24, 1920, LM.ONI..

30. Skenadie to Sells, September 20, 1919, LM.ONIW.

31. Edgar Meritt to Bishop Weller, June 9, 1921, LM.ONIW.

32. Irvine Lenroot to Sells, January 31, 1921, LM.ONIW.

33. "Oneidas May Be in Great Luck," *De Pere Journal-Democrat,* March 16, 1922; *United States v. Boylan et al.* (see Part V) appeal dismissed 257 U.S. 614 (1921).

34. Edgar Allen to Burke, April 11, 1922, LM.ONIW.

35. Burke to Allen, July 3, 1922, Burke to Kellogg, September 11, 1922, and Thomas F. Konop to Burke, October 11, 1922, all in LM.ONIW.

36. John Strange to Allen, June 27, July 8, 1922, LM.ONIW.

37. Kellogg to Burke, January 1, 1923, LM.ONIW.

38. Oneida National Committee to Burke, August 28, 1924, LM.ONIW. In this letter of protest to Burke, Kellogg introduced the Oneida National Committee (ONC) as "duly authorized to act in behalf of the people." Despite its lofty title and claims of "authorization," the signatures at the bottom of the letter show that its membership was local to Oneida, Wisconsin, and limited to only ten. The ONC, however, did involve itself in issues outside of Wisconsin, in particular, the New York land claim. In this sense, it may have been an offshoot of a fundraising organization called the Six Nations Clubs. For more on this, read Hauptman, "Designing Woman," or the second chapter of my thesis, *Parallel Souls: Studies on Early Twentieth-Century Native American Leaders in Relation to Black Activists W. E. B. Du Bois and Marcus Garvey, 1900–1934.*

39. Burke to Charles W. Curtis, February 19, 1925, LM.ONIW.

40. ONC to Burke, August 28, 1924, LM.ONIW.

41. ONC to Bishop Rhodes, November 18, 1924, LM.ONIW.

42. Oneida Tribal Members to Sam Bell, April 24, 1926, LM.ONIW. The genealogy of Kellogg's son, Robert, is uncertain, although it is commonly believed that Robert was Laura Kellogg's nephew, her brother Frank's son.

43. The case challenged the right of the St. Lawrence Power Company to a one-mile-square plot of land purchased from the St. Regis band of the Mohawks. The purchase stemmed from an 1824 treaty between the St. Regis and New York, which according to Everett violated the 1784 Fort Stanwix Treaty. If won, the case would open the door for other court challenges and possible recovery of millions of acres of land by the Six Nations. Hauptman, "Designing Woman," 176; *Deere v. St. Lawrence River Power Co. et al.,* 32 F.2d 550 (2d Cir. 1929).

44. E. A. Everett to William Calder, August 29, 1922, LM.ONIW.

45. Ramona Herdman, "A New Six Nations," *Syracuse Herald,* November 6, 1927.

46. U.S. Congress, Senate Subcommittee on Indian Affairs, Survey of Conditions of the Indians in the United States, 71st Cong., 2d sess., March 1, 1929, 12:4858.

Editors' Note: After the Civil War, the Wisconsin Oneidas were faced with pressures from all sides—federal efforts to end the reservation system and transform the Indians through education; state, county, and local town efforts to extend jurisdiction and levy taxes on Indian lands to support the expansion of newly formed, mostly white communities; and private efforts by railroad, timber, and real estate companies to acquire Indian lands and resources. Even before the Civil War, the Green Bay region had become the shingle capital of the United States. With the disastrous fires in Chicago and in Wisconsin in 1871, pressures for Wisconsin Indian timber increased. At approximately the same time, the Oneidas had to deal with railroad efforts to secure easements through the reservation. The push for allotment of the reservation soon followed, dividing the nation about what strategy to pursue in dealing with the crisis; however, the ultimate crisis was to occur after 1903, when the "border" towns of Hobart and Oneida were created, which quickly impinged on reservation lands. In 1906 Congress passed the Burke Act, which allowed Oneida allottees (much earlier than allowed under the Dawes Act) to receive fee simple patents to their lands, and thus began the rapid alienation of much of the tribal estate. The final blow to the tribal estate was the work of the Federal Competency Commission, which came to Oneida in 1917.

Part IV

Land Loss in the Age of Allotment

Introduction

Pressures and Legislation

After the Civil War, Morgan L. Martin, a leading Wisconsin politician and entrepreneur heavily involved in land speculation and canal and railroad development, was appointed federal Indian agent. Besides pushing for allotment, Martin was on the board of the Green Bay and Lake Pepin Railway Company, which successfully lobbied for an easement through the Oneida reservation, granted by Congress in 1870. The impact of the railroad on the Oneidas and their lands is described by Carol Cornelius and Loretta Webster (Part IV). Fortunately, as these two Oneida authors show, the lands taken for a railroad easement after the Civil War were returned to Oneida tribal hands in 2005.

Martin was perceived as a longtime enemy dating back to the early 1830s.[1] Some Oneidas saw Martin's appointment as proof positive that the tribe's days in Wisconsin were now numbered. It should be noted that in the three decades preceding Martin's appointment, other Wisconsin Indian nations had faced serious crises—the Brothertowns were made U.S. citizens and lost tribal status in 1839; the Stockbridge-Munsees were relocated within Wisconsin three times between 1822 and 1856; and the Winnebagos (Ho-Chunks) were removed from the state on three separate occasions before the Civil War.[2] Moreover, federal Indian agents frequently urged Oneida allotment and presented it as inevitable.

Oneidas had built their community in Wisconsin from the 1820s onward through the political cooperation of two major leaders— Chief Daniel Bread and Chief Jacob Cornelius. For three decades Episcopal and Methodist Oneidas had put away their past divisions from New York State and had accomplished much.[3] In the years just before the Civil War, and following the conflict, this consensus broke down. To some of the so-called Old Chiefs such as Daniel Bread, who had been born in New York and who had previously experienced being uprooted to Wisconsin, allotment became an alternative to once again going through the trauma of removal and adjustment to new lands. Unable to stop individual Indians from cutting reservation trees, what the Old Chiefs viewed as the tribal estate, and selling lumber to local white-operated mills for shingles, railroad ties, and other uses, the council of chiefs found themselves being attacked by a new generation of Oneidas who had been born in Wisconsin, and being accused of not caring enough about the economic survival of individual families.[4]

In the U.S. Supreme Court case *United States v. Cook*, decided in October 1873, the court declared that the forests of reservations were federal property, off-limits to cutting by individual Indians.[5] The implications of this decision were clear (see Oberly, Part IV). Only by individual Oneidas' acceptance of allotment and fee simple patents would they be able to harvest these timber resources. It should be noted that white pressures from outside to exploit Oneida timber had intensified in 1871 after two of the most devastating fires in American history: the Great Chicago Fire and the Great Peshtigo Fire.[6]

In his annual report to the commissioner of Indian affairs in 1874, Thomas N. Chase, the federal Indian agent suggested that the Oneida "government by hereditary chiefs should be super-seded by some simple but strong system, and their lands should be allotted to individuals of the tribe." He hoped that the Cook decision would check the extensive illegal cutting of timber by Oneidas whom he claimed were being "extensively swindled by purchasers." Chase insisted that a "division of lands will correct this evil."[7]

In 1868 Senator Timothy Howe had proposed a congressional bill to divide the Oneida reservation into allotments. In 1875, a crew led by Henry Esperson of La Crosse, Wisconsin, and hired by the Interior Department, surveyed the Oneida lands and laid out forty-acre parcels in preparation for the formal allotment of the reservation. In 1884, the federal Indian agent wrote the commissioner: "I approve of a division of the whole reserve, and thus put out of existence as far as possible tribal property."[8] Nevertheless, because of bitter divisions within the Oneida Nation, allotment efforts were delayed until the Dawes General Allotment Act was passed in 1887. By that year, there were 1,732 Oneidas living on their reservation. The tribal vote on allotment at Oneida indicated that 656 favored allotment out of a total voting population of 1,064.[9]

Until the Dawes General Allotment Act, the Oneida lands were protected under federal treaty law, most specifically Article 2 of the amended Buffalo Creek Treaty of February 3, 1838. In the same year as the Dawes General Allotment Act, the Office of Indian Affairs (OIA) concluded that 1,537 Oneidas were eligible to receive allotments. Two years later, the Interior Department sent a special agent to administer the allotment policy at Oneida. Unlike in most other Indian reservations allotted under act, there was no surplus land available that was opened up to non-Indians. By 1892, 1,517 allottees were issued patents, which were to be held in trust for twenty-five years. Only a parcel of one-sixteenth of a mile was excluded from allotment.[10]

On May 8, 1906, Congress passed the Burke Act, which authorized the secretary of the interior to issue a fee patent to any Indian deemed "competent and capable of managing his or her affairs" before the end of the twenty-five-year trust period as required by the Dawes General Allotment Act of 1887.[11] According to historian Francis Paul Prucha, the Burke Act "opened the door to early alienation of allotments." Prucha claims that "the intention of the legislators" was "that great care should be taken by the secretary of the interior in determining competency"; however, "in practice the safeguards were often neglected."[12]

In 1907, Congress authorized the sale of restricted lands of "noncompetent" Indians under rules set by the secretary of the interior.[13] Moneys from the sales of these lands were supposed to benefit the "noncompetent" Indian; however, as Prucha brings out, it "became an effective instrument in the dissipation of Indian landholdings."[14] As a result, specifically named individual Oneidas were deemed ready to receive fee simple patents without trust restrictions. By 1908, the OIA had converted more than half of the Oneida allotments to fee simple patents (see Oberly, Part IV).

A third modification of the Dawes General Allotment Act was passed on June 25, 1910. This multifaceted piece of legislation was an omnibus bill that was "to provide for determining the heirs of deceased Indians, for the disposition and sale of allotments of deceased Indians, for the leasing of allotments, and for other purposes." Now any Indian allottee with a trust patent, twenty-one years of age or older, could obtain a patent in fee, as well as will or sell his land.[15]

The issuance of fee patents to "competent" Indians continued unabated from 1913 to 1920. In 1917, a federal Indian competency commission under the chairmanship of James McLaughlin came to Oneida, Wisconsin. By that time, most of the 65,400 acres of tribal lands had left Oneida hands. McLaughlin's efforts were a clear attempt by the Interior Department to speed up the integration process, a plan strongly supported by both Wisconsin state politicians and Washington officials. By 1920, when the federal competency commissions nationwide were disbanded by the new commissioner of Indian affairs, there was hardly any Oneida reservation left.

The work of the federal competency commission at Oneida was the culmination of federal and state Indian policies in the age of allotment. Although it came under the guise of an investigatory committee, its agenda—ending the reservation system—had been set years before. McLaughlin's commission was an early version of what would later (after World War II) be labeled "termination" policy (see Hauptman, Part IV).

Notes

1. Hauptman and McLester, *Chief Daniel Bread,* 44, 57, 104, 147–154; Jack Campisi, "Ethnic Identity and Boundary Maintenance in Three Oneida Communities" (Ph.D. dissertation, Albany, SUNY, 1974),. 146–48.

2. Robert E. Bieder, *Native American Communities in Wisconsin, 1600–1960: A Study of Tradition and Change* (Madison: University of Wisconsin Press, 1995), 151–207; Nancy Oestreich Lurie, *Wisconsin Indians,* rev. and expanded edition (Madison: SHSW, 2002), 5–33.

3. Hauptman and McLester, *Chief Daniel Bread,* 99–126.

4. Ibid., 127–62.

5. 86 U.S. 591 (1873).

6. Bloomfield, *The Oneidas,* 252–53; Peter Pernin, "The Great Peshtigo Fire: An Eyewitness Account," *Wisconsin Magazine of History* 54 (Sept. 1971): 246–72; Anthony Godfrey, *A Forestry History of Ten Wisconsin Indian Reservations under the Great Lakes Agency* (Salt Lake City: U.S. West Research, Inc. for BIA Branch of Forestry, 1996).

7. ARCIA, 1874: 186.

8. D. P. Andrews to Commissioner of Indian Affairs, December 11, 1883, found in Records of the Oneida Indian Historical Society.

9. Reginald Horsman, "The Wisconsin Oneidas in the Preallotment Years," in Campisi and Hauptman, *Oneida Indian Experience,* 77.

10. Arlinda Locklear, "The Allotment of the Oneida Reservation and Its Legal Ramifications," 83–93. For the Dawes General Allotment Act, see 24 *Stat.,* 388–91. To follow its development at Oneida, see ARCIA, 1884, 177–78; 1885, 206–207; 1886, 251; 1887, 228; 1888, 240; 1889, 296–300; 1890, 41; 1892, 512–14; 1893, 341–45.

11. 34 *Stat.,* 182–83.

12. Prucha, *The Great Father,* 2: 876.

13. 34 *Stat.,* 1018.

14. Prucha, *The Great Father,* 2:876–77.

15. 36 *Stat.,* 855–63.

16

The Dawes Act and the Oneida Indian Reservation of Wisconsin

James W. Oberly

The National Center for History in the Schools, after much debate and controversy, published in 1996 its *National Standards for History*. This work set forth for middle school and high school students the task of acquiring "historical knowledge," which the authors defined as "what students should know about families, their communities, states, nation, and world." Students who learn "historical knowledge" and who become skilled at "historical thinking" can then proceed to become fully informed members of the American polity, able to place themselves in the "stream of time."[1] The compilers of the *National Standards for History* did not overlook the teaching and learning of American Indian history. One element of historical knowledge that the authors of the *National Standards* expected middle and high school students to learn was termed "Federal Indian policy and United States foreign policy after the Civil War." One substandard calls for students to "[e]xplain the provisions of the Dawes Severalty act [Dawes General Allotment Act] of 1887 and evaluate its effects on tribal identity, land ownership, and assimilation."[2]

It is only fair to ask educators to demonstrate for their students what will be expected of the learners, and what may be expected on the assignment. In the spirit of the *National Standards*, this essay will offer some historical knowledge about the provisions of the Dawes General Allotment Act of 1887. In addition, it will try to answer the questions about the particular effects of the Dawes Act on the Oneida Nation of Wisconsin, including effects on "tribal identity, land ownership, and assimilation." This essay will conclude with some thoughts about the legacy of the allotment of the Oneida Indian Reservation on families, communities, the state of Wisconsin, the United States, and the world.

The Dawes General Allotment Act was signed into law by President Cleveland on February 8, 1887. The title was "An act to provide for the allotment of lands in severalty to Indians on the various reservations and to extend the protection of the laws of the United States and the Territories over the Indians, and for other purposes."[3] The reference to "other purposes" is mysterious, but Congress otherwise had a clear twofold intent. The first stated goal was to divide up tribally owned reservation land into plots for individual Indians ("allotment of lands in severalty to Indians"). The second goal was to extend U.S. law over what was known as "Indian Country." Each policy goal was a radical departure from the understanding of federal Indian policy of a century earlier, as codified in the 1787 Northwest Ordinance. The ideas of Indian reservations and the extension of federal law over Indian Country were unimagined at the Philadelphia convention of 1787 that scrapped the Articles of Confederation and drafted the Constitution.[4]

History textbooks also refer to the Dawes Act as the "General Allotment Act," because its provisions were to apply generally to Indian reservations across the United States. Some, but not all of the provisions of the Dawes Act applied to the Oneida Indian Reservation. A review of the relevant provisions of the legislation shows that sections 2, 3, 5, 6, 9 and 10 applied to the Oneida Indian Reservation. Section 2 of the statute called for individual Indians to select their own allotment parcels. Section 3 required the appointment of special agents appointed by the president of the United States to look after the allotment of orphans and to resolve disputes. Section 5 was the longest part of the legislation. It mandated a twenty-five-year period during which the United

States would hold the patent—legal title—to individual allotments. This meant that the Indian who made his allotment selection could not sell his land or lease it or use it to secure credit. And if the president of the United States did not think twenty-five years was sufficient, he could extend the period that the United States acted as a trustee of the allotment. Section 5 also stated that any lands not needed to accommodate all the lands required for allot- ment could be purchased by act of Congress. Section 6 provided that state criminal and civil law applied to the lands of allottees at the end of the twenty-five-year trust period. Also, Indian allottees would become U.S. citizens at the same time. For the Oneidas, this meant that Wisconsin state law would come to the reservation in 1912 and that the Indians' exclusion from U.S. citizenship under the Fourteenth Amendment to the Constitution would also end in 1912.[5] Section 9 appropriated one hundred thousand dollars for the purpose of surveying or re-surveying reservations so as to make clear the boundaries of individual allotment parcels. Finally, section 10 of the act stated that the process of allotment did not affect the power of Congress to make railroad rights-of-way across Indian reservations.

The text of the Dawes General Allotment Act lists an extended number of tribes to which the law did not apply, because of pre- existing policies about land in severalty. The Lake Superior Chippewa bands of Wisconsin and the Stockbridge-Munsee Tribe of Wisconsin appear on that list. By process of elimination, therefore, it is apparent that in Wisconsin in 1887 the Dawes Act could apply only to the Oneida Indian Nation and the Menominee Nation.[6] The Menominees never did have their reservation allotted, despite various attempts to do so. As far as the history of all the Wisconsin Indian nations is concerned, it may be concluded that the historical impact of the Dawes Act upon Indian tribes within the borders of the state of Wisconsin was limited to the Oneida Nation.

Here it is appropriate how the Oneida Nation of Wisconsin compares and contrasts with the other Wisconsin Indian nations. Why was it different? The answer lies in the specific allotment histories of each Indian reservation in the state. The treaty of September 30, 1854, created four reservations within the state of Wisconsin for bands of the Lake Superior Chippewas. That treaty also called for the president of the United States to carry out allotments on those reservations. Similarly, an 1856 treaty between the Stockbridge-Munsees and the United States laid out in detail an allotment procedure. The Oneida treaty with the United States of February 3, 1838, contained no provision for allotment. Instead, the lands of the reservation were to be held in common.

It would be a mistake, however, to assume that federal Indian policy toward the Oneida Nation was inactive between the signing of the treaty of 1838 that established the reservation and the Dawes Act forty-nine years later. Instead, Congress and the Executive Branch took an active interest in enacting and implementing an allotment policy on the Oneida Indian Reservation almost two decades before the Dawes General Allotment Act. In the first session of the Forty-first Congress (1868), Senator Timothy Howe, a Green Bay Republican, introduced a bill to allot the Oneida Indian Reservation. Howe's action indicated that he did not believe the allotment policy could be affected by a new treaty between the United States and the Oneida Nation. Instead, Howe was quite prepared to assert congressional plenary power over the lands of the reservation and to override the 1838 treaty agreement that placed Oneida lands in common occupancy. Howe's bill failed that session, but he returned to the task during the second session and this time secured the support of the commissioner of Indian affairs and the secretary of the interior and reintroduced Senate Bill 894 in May 1870.

The policy move in Washington was certainly favored by white business and political leaders in Green Bay. The *Green Bay Gazette* and *Green Bay Advocate* engaged in a running editorial debate in December 1869 and January 1870 about changing the status of the Oneida Indian Reservation. The *Advocate,* a Democratic newspaper, favored allotment in severalty of the reservation to the Oneidas. The *Gazette,* a Republican newspaper usually allied with Senator Howe, advocated the complete termination of the Oneidas as a nation and the disestablishment of their reservation. The *Gazette* editor in his editorial columns called the Oneida reservation an "eyesore" and a "large, unproductive and non-taxpaying property located in our midst."[7] Privately, the editor of the *Gazette* voiced similar sentiments, as when he wrote to the secretary of the interior: "We are agitating here through the local press the best plan of getting rid of the Oneidas, a dreadful eye-sore, and a big dead-weight to this county."[8] Local public opinion of whites, as measured by editorials in the newspapers, occupied a narrow range of thought, calling for allotment and ultimate detribalization on the one hand, and immediate termination and removal on the other.

Correspondence in 1869 and 1870 from tribal members shows that there was a split between two parties on the reservation itself, one in favor of allotment and the other opposed. The pro-allotment group was led by the old Oneida leader Daniel Bread, who had helped negotiate the 1838 treaty with the United States. Bread was repudiated on March 7, 1870, by Cornelius Hill, Paul Powless, and other Oneidas, who wrote the commissioner claiming that Bread had been removed as a chief of the Oneida Nation and that the Office of Indian Affairs (OIA) should have no further dealings with Bread. In a follow-up letter on March 24, 1870, Hill and Powless repeated their opposition to allotment and to Bread's leadership. The dissidents reminded the commissioner of their right under the Treaty of 1838 to keep their lands in common. The commissioner of Indian affairs would have none of this rebellion. He instructed the U.S. Indian agent at Green Bay, W. R. Bourne on April 5, 1870: "Daniel Bread will be regarded by this Office as a chief of the Oneidas, until he is properly superseded according to their laws and customs."[9]

The allotment issue in the late 1860s was closely tied to a parallel policy issue that occupied the attention of the Oneidas, the OIA, and the federal judiciary, namely, the cutting of timber on the three Indian reservations in the Green Bay Agency. All three— Oneida, Menominee, and Stockbridge-Munsee—had extensive pine holdings that were much coveted by white lumbermen. The OIA in the Grant administration tried to prohibit logging on the reservations on the theory that the cutting of timber on Indian common lands would reduce the value of future individual Indian allotments. The OIA convinced the U.S. attorney in Milwaukee to initiate lawsuits against white lumbermen engaged in lumbering at all three reservations. Although unsuccessful at the federal district court level, the OIA's view eventually prevailed at the U.S. Supreme Court in the *United States v. Cook* case. The Supreme Court reviewed the principle established by the Marshall Court in the 1823 case of *M'Intosh v. Johnson* that Indians enjoyed only a right of occupancy of their lands but not fee ownership. The fee, contended the Court in *United States v. Cook*, belonged to the United States. The Court reasoned from this that the Oneidas could do one of two things with the trees on their reservation. The Oneidas could either gaze upon the trees "in the state of nature," or they could cut down trees strictly to clear land for agricultural purposes. But they could no longer fell trees to sell for sawlogs or pulpwood or firewood. Such an action would reduce the value of the U.S. ownership in fee of the reservation lands. The Court's logic was clear: the Oneidas could only realize the economic value of their standing timber by accepting allotment and converting the 65,400 acres of commonly occupied land into individual Indian parcels.[10]

The other capitalist economic-development project on the Oneida Indian Reservation in the late 1860s and early 1870s was the extension of a railroad and its right-of-way across the reservation. The Green Bay and Lake Pepin Railway Company (later the Green Bay and Western, and today known as the Fox Valley and Western) lobbied Senator Howe and Congressman Philetus Sawyer to enact legislation granting the railroad the right to build and operate a line across the lands protected by the 1838 treaty. After much confusion in 1869 and 1870, Congress did pass legislation granting the Green Bay and Lake Pepin Railway Company its right-of-way. The railway did not pay a fixed sum of money to the Oneida Nation for the right-of-way, nor did the company pay an annual rental for use of the right-of-way. The railway did pay a modest sum to individual Oneidas for damages done to their fences and livestock during the construction of the railway.[11]

After the Supreme Court issued its decision in *U.S. v. Cook*, the OIA moved quickly to implement allotment of the Oneida

Indian Reservation, even without any congressional authorization. The first step was to perform a land survey of the 65,400-acre reservation and to divide it into forty-acre parcels. In 1875, the commissioner of Indian affairs appointed a La Crosse surveyor named Henry Esperson to survey the Oneida Indian Reservation into forty-acre parcels preparatory to a contemplated allotment. Esperson's work was troubling to the anti-allotment Oneidas, but his survey work did not result immediately in implementation of the allotment policy. That did not happen until after the Dawes General Allotment Act in the next decade. Still, the Esperson survey of 1875 is used today as the basic document of allotment parcels by the Oneida Office of Land Management.

The Congress in the years after the formal end of treaty-making in 1871 did not always exercise its full plenary powers to dispose of Indian lands, especially those protected by treaty. Congress did tend to respect and require Indian consent to legislation in the 1870s. With the replacement of the Oneidas' council of chiefs by the Hill and Powless party in the late 1870s, the Wisconsin congressional delegation and the OIA realized that the protests of Oneidas against the Esperson survey meant that the Oneida Nation's leadership would not consent to allotment. For another decade, until passage of the Dawes General Allotment Act, the Oneida Nation managed to forestall allotment of the reservation.[12]

Democratic president Grover Cleveland did not use his new power under the Dawes General Allotment Act to order the Oneida Indian Reservation to be divided in severalty during the remainder of his term in office. By contrast, newly elected Republican president Benjamin Harrison moved quickly in 1889 to appoint special agent Dana Lamb from the OIA to implement allotment on the Oneida Indian Reservation. U.S. Indian Agent for the Green Bay Agency, Charles Kelsey, assisted Lamb. Agents Kelsey and Lamb took a census of the Oneida Nation and then worked with the Esperson survey to match individual Oneida Indians with specific parcels. On November 3, 1890, they reported back to the OIA that there were 1,503 allotment parcels on the 65,400-acre-reservation.

The original allotment book that agents Lamb and Kelsey created is preserved in the National Archives and is a rich historical source for the history of the Oneidas in the late nineteenth and early twentieth centuries. It lists the name, gender, age, land-parcel acreage, public lands survey coordinates, and genealogical information of each allottee. The book was kept at the OIA headquarters in Washington and was subsequently annotated after Lamb and Kelsey did their work as the status of each allotment changed. For example, when a trust patent was converted to fee, the OIA clerks noted the date, patent number, and office letter file number. The information in the allotment book is organized by allotment number, so it is necessary to work backward from the allotment number to a map of the reservation prepared by the OIA in 1890, and maintained today for legal purposes at the Oneida Office of Land Management, and in the Office of the Register of Deeds for both Outagamie County and Brown County.

The commissioner of Indian affairs told agents Kelsey and Lamb in 1889 that no new survey would be needed of the Oneida Indian Reservation because of the previous work done by Henry Esperson in 1875; however, the commissioner did not know that more than two hundred Oneida Indians had claims on specific parcels that Esperson had ignored in his earlier work. Known as "private claims," these would-be landholdings resulted from settlements along Duck Creek that individual Oneidas had made in the years after the great relocation from New York State in the 1820s and 1830s. The OIA hired a new surveyor in 1889, N. S. Boardman, to make a survey of the "private claims" on the reservation and to work with agents Lamb and Kelsey to make sure that the private claimants were satisfied with the allotments.

Nearly 100 percent of the land at Oneida was allotted by Kelsey and Lamb to 1,503 tribal members. A parcel of slightly more than one-sixteenth of a square mile was excluded from allotment for use by the Episcopal Church and its school. The right-of-way used by the Green Bay and Western Railway was also excluded from allotment. For the first three decades of its operation, the state railroad commission levied taxes on railroad companies based on the size of their operations and their track mileage. For example, in 1900, the railway commission had four classes of railways with different tax rates. The Green Bay and Western was a "Class One" railway taxed at 4 percent of gross earnings, or about $294 per track mile. The legislature abolished the practice of taxation by class in 1905 and set a flat corporate tax on railroads of 1.1 percent of the road's value. The Green Bay and Western was estimated to be worth $2.15 million in 1909, and consequently it paid taxes of $24,500 that year.[13] In return for state railroad tax payments, the railways of Wisconsin did not pay local property taxes.

The allotment history of the Oneida Indian Reservation should be put into comparative context. A few other Wisconsin Indian nations such as the Stockbridge-Munsees, the Red Cliff Chippewas, and the Lac Courte Oreilles Chippewas had 100 percent, or nearly so, of their reservations allotted. Other tribes such as the Bad River Chippewas and the Lac du Flambeau Chippewas experienced allotment but had more than enough land to accommodate all tribal members. The remainder was declared surplus land and transferred to the public domain where non-Indians could purchase it. This history of "surplus land" acts by Congress and executive orders by the president was far more common among tribes on the Great Plains with bigger preallotment land bases than the Oneida Nation of Wisconsin. In fact, the bigger the land base before allotment, usually the bigger the surplus land that was opened to non-Indian acquisition. As many as 100 million acres disappeared from tribal ownership and opened occupancy to non-Indians as "surplus lands." Such was not the case at the Oneida Indian Reservation. Land certainly passed into non-Indian ownership as a result of the Dawes General Allotment Act, but not as a consequence of the work done by Kelsey and Lamb.[14]

The secretary of the interior approved the allotments on September 25, 1891. And on June 13, 1892, the Interior Department granted trust patents to the 1,503 Oneida allottees, under the provisions of the Dawes Act. This action set into motion the twenty-five-year trust period during which the United States would act as guardian of the allotments on behalf of individual

Oneidas. However, in the 1906 Appropriations Act for the OIA, eleven years before the scheduled expiration of the trust period, Congress specifically converted some of the Oneida Indian Reservation trust patents to fee simple patents. The obscure term "fee simple patent" meant a legal status where the owner had full control of his or her property, including the power to sell it, mortgage it, or transfer it to another. With that power the owner also bore responsibility for property taxes on the land, levied by the civil power. The language of the act (34 *Stat.*, 380) read: "That the Secretary of the Interior be, and is hereby authorized in his discretion, to issue fee-simple patents to the following parties for the lands heretofore allotted to them." [15] What followed in the statute were two pages of the names and allotment numbers of Oneida tribal members. The statute added:

> The Secretary of Interior be, and he is hereby, authorized, in his discretion, to issue a patent in fee to any Indian of the Oneida Reservation in Wisconsin for the lands heretofore allotted him, and the issuance of such patent shall operate as a removal of all restrictions as to the sale, taxation, and alienation of the lands so patented. [16]

This was also comparable to the language of the 1906 Burke Act, which Congress had just passed barely a month earlier. The special language about Oneida gave the secretary the power to find individual Oneidas who were competent to manage their own affairs any time after 1906, and therefore well before 1917, in addition to those mentioned by name in the Appropriations Act.

The conversion of trust patents to fee simple patents meant that the local government bodies in Outagamie and Brown counties had to register title to the land parcels among their local records. [17] When the trust allotments of the Oneida Indians were converted to fee simple ownership status, as so many were after 1906, the parcels became subject to local taxation. Even before the widespread conversion from trust to fee status, the Wisconsin state legislature authorized the creation of the Town of Oneida in Outagamie County, and the Town of Hobart in Brown

County. Those two towns soon had assessors estimating property values on fee parcels and preparing tax rolls. The first surviving tax roll from the Town of Oneida dates back to 1910. As early as that year, many of the Oneida Indian allottees in the Town of Oneida no longer owned their parcels.

A handful of trust patents were delayed in conversion to fee status by executive order in the Wilson and Coolidge administrations. Mary Stevens's trust patent for forty acres on the SW ¼ of the SW ¼ in Section 33 Township 24 North Range 19 East was one such parcel. The trust status on her allotment was extended indefinitely in 1927 so that she and her heirs never did become fee simple owners.[18] The 1930 and 1935 tax rolls acknowledged the continuing trust status of the forty-acre parcel.

During the Indian New Deal of the 1930s, Commissioner of Indian Affairs John Collier viewed the history of allotment on the Oneida Indian Reservation as the leading example of a flawed and failed policy. Collier noted that more than 95 percent of Oneida Indian allottees were landless. A contemporary estimate by J. P. Kinney put the figure of lost allotments even higher, at about 99 percent.[19]

How did the reservation go from almost 100 percent owned in fee simple by Oneida Indians in 1906 to as much as 99 percent non-Indian owned within three decades? A complete answer calls for research into the land and property history of the 1,503 allotments, work that is in progress, yet incomplete, by this author and the Oneida law office. A preliminary answer points to three forms of land loss by the allottees of their fee simple parcels. First, some Oneida Indians took the opportunity to sell their parcels for cash in the Brown County and Outagamie County land markets. Second, some Oneida Indians mortgaged their property and then were unable to repay their loans and lost their land to their creditors. Third, some Oneida Indians failed to pay their property taxes and had their lands first declared delinquent and then forfeited to the town government.

Those who sold for cash were not necessarily swindled in the exchange. Many made sale agreements at fair prices. For example, in November 1908, Oneida tribal member John Reed sold his ninety-three-acre allotment parcel in Section 33 of Township 24 North, Range 19 East, in the Town of Oneida for $1,000 in cash to Ira Martin of Green Bay. In February of that same year, Curtis and Lucy Denny sold their forty-eight-acre parcel in Section 36 of the same township and range for $715 to M. Bender of Seymour, Wisconsin.

Those Oneida Indians who borrowed money on their real property holdings were undertaking a risky transaction. Mortgages made in 1908 and subsequent years were typically for one year's term and the lender charged between 8–10 percent interest. For example, in 1912, Miller Denny borrowed $165 with his twenty-six-acre parcel as collateral. In addition, Denny pledged to pay taxes and assessments on the property. In a sense, the lending practice was similar to a home equity loan common today where a borrower with some equity borrows on the strength of that equity. If Denny did not repay the principal and 8 percent interest, he would forfeit his property, worth likely more than $300. The Oneida Indian attorney Dennison Wheelock was active in brokering mortgages between Oneida Indian landowners and Green Bay investors in the years after the conversion to fee simple ownership of the reservation allotments.

The third way that Oneidas could lose their land was if they failed to pay property taxes. The new towns of Oneida and Hobart collected taxes to support schools, roads, local law enforcement, and other township government operations. In 1910, for example, the Town of Oneida had a levy rate of $2.07 for every $100 worth of real property. An Oneida Indian who owned an unimproved forty-acre parcel, assessed at $600 ($15 an acre), would have to pay more than $12 in cash in taxes each year. A landowner who fell behind owed the taxes and a penalty and had his property tax declared delinquent.

This essay began with a consideration of what the *National Standards for History* asks of schoolchildren in their knowledge of the history of allotment. For the Oneida Indian Nation of Wisconsin, it is clear that the allotment of the reservation into parcels held in trust did not result in any land loss. For more than fifteen years after the awarding of trust patents, the Oneida Indian Reservation was effectively closed to non-Indians. However, the critical action taken by the United States was the act of Congress in 1906 that began to convert some Oneida trust patents to fee simple status. This opened the way to sales, mortgages, and tax delinquencies. The precise history of how many Oneida Indians realized full value for their parcels, and how many received less than full value or even no value at all, is a matter that awaits further empirical investigation. The timing of the land loss between 1906 and 1934 also needs further study, although the preliminary work reported here suggests that there was a dramatic turnover of land on the Oneida Indian Reservation to non-Indian ownership in the first five years after Congress approved the conversion to fee simple ownership of allotments.

The other two historical challenges determining the effects of the Dawes General Allotment Act on "tribal identity" and on "assimilation" have received some scrutiny from scholars but are worthy of more research. Historian Laurence Hauptman has written about the politics of the Oneida Nation in the years after allotment but before the Indian New Deal. He identifies several different factions, or parties, within the Nation, based on a mix of family, clan identity, and issues. One of the issues that stirred the politics of the Nation was the perceived oppressive level of taxation by the towns of Oneida and Hobart and the land loss due to delinquent taxes and foreclosed properties. William "Willie Fat" Skenadore testified before the Senate Subcommittee on Indian Affairs in July 1929 about the problems of land loss due to excessive township taxation. Skenadore found particularly obnoxious the case of the Henry Doxtator family who in 1928 were "forcibly removed from their home by the sheriff because they could not pay their taxes." The use of "fire, gas, and ax" to evict the Doxtators was a violation of the 1794 and 1838 treaties that the United States signed with the Oneidas, Skenadore insisted. He also estimated that "out of 2,700 Indians who had allotments all but 21 have been put on the tax roll and most of the Indians have lost their land." Oneida Indians who recalled their nation's history to WPA interviewers in the early 1940s frequently mentioned the land loss and their bitter feelings about the unfairness of taxation by the towns.[20]

The collective experience of the Oneida Nation with land loss did have an impact on tribal identity. Many, if not most tribal families had to find wage labor to support themselves. Such labor was not widely available in the Town of Oneida or the Town of Hobart, and many had to leave the reservation in search of work. In a peculiar way, however, the largely negative experience that the Oneida Indians had with the Dawes General Allotment Act confirmed them in their tribal identity, particularly in the power and continuing relevance of their treaty rights.

The final remaining question is what impact did the Dawes General Allotment Act have on the assimilation of the Oneidas, presumably into the larger non-Indian culture. The act contemplated some sort of assimilation at the end of the trust period on the assumption that the individual Indian allottee could manage and defend his or her own property. The tools of citizenship, such as access to the courts to defend property, and access to the ballot to support like-minded viewpoints, lay at the end of the twenty-five-year trust period outlined in the 1887 statute. The act of 1906 sped up this dual establishment of the property-owning Oneida Indian and the citizen Oneida Indian. According to Willie Fat Skenadore, the "issuance of fee simple patents to the allotments of the Oneidas severs the relation of guardian and ward."[21] From the state of Wisconsin's viewpoint, the United States ceased to have jurisdiction over the Oneidas, except for the small eighty-acre parcel containing the building and grounds of the Episcopal church and boarding school. Similarly, the annual reports of the U.S. Indian agent at Keshena regularly reflected a viewpoint that there was little to supervise among the Oneidas.

Certainly the assimilationist intent of the Dawes General Allotment Act on the Oneida Indians and their reservation must be judged a failure more than a century later. The fact that between 95 and 99 percent of the nation's members lost their land parcels indicates that the intent of the Dawes Act to make

Oneidas and other Indians into small-scale farmers was unsuccessful. The Oneida Indians took to the federal courts for defense of their property, not against individual trespassers but against the state of Wisconsin and its creatures the towns of Hobart and Oneida. The effect of the Dawes General Allotment Act on the Oneida Indians was profound, but not in the way that Congress expected in 1887.

Notes

1. National Center for History in the Schools, *National Standards for History* (Los Angeles: UCLA, 1996), 1–2.

2. Ibid., Standard 6-4, substandard 4a-3.

3. "An Act to Provide for the Allotment of Lands in Severalty to Indians on the Various Reservations," 24 *Stat.*, 388 (Feb. 8, 1887).

4. Vine Deloria, Jr., and David E. Wilkins, *Tribes, Treaties and Constitutional Tribulations* (Austin: University of Texas Press, 1999), 17–31.

5. Ibid., 141–48.

6. The Chippewa treaty of September 30, 1854, called for allotment, as did the Stockbridge-Munsee treaty of February 5, 1856. See Charles J. Kappler comp., *Indian Affairs: Laws and Treaties*, (Washington, D.C.: GPO, 1903–1941, 2:648, 742.

7. *Green Bay Gazette,* Dec. 11, 1869, Jan. 29, 1870.

8. George E. Hoskins to Secretary of the Interior, January 27, 1870, reel 327, microcopy 234, GBAR. OIA, RG75, NA.

9. Commissioner of Indian Affairs to Agent Bourne, April 5, 1870, ibid.

10. *United States v. Cook*, 86 *U.S.*, 591 (1873).

11. "An Act granting the Right of Way to the Green Bay and Lake Pepin Railway Company for its Road across the Oneida Reservation, in the State of Wisconsin." 16 *Stat.*, 588 (March 3, 1871).

12. Hauptman and McLester, *Chief Daniel Bread,* 151–57.

13. *Annual Report of the Wisconsin Railroad Commission, 1901* (Madison: Wisconsin Public Documents, 1901), 176–87; *Laws of Wisconsin, 1905,* chap. 216.

14. McDonnell, *The Dispossession of the American Indian, 1887–1934*; Kirke Kickingbird and Karen Ducheneaux, *One Hundred Million Acres* (New York: Macmillan, 1973).

15. Indian Affairs Appropriations Act of 1906, at 34 *Stat.*, 380–81. For comparative purposes, see the Burke Act at 34 *Stat.*, 182–83, which is silent on the question of rights-of-way after trust patents become fee.

16. Indian Affairs Appropriations Act of 1906, at 34 *Stat.*, 380–81.

17. I have examined the deed records in Outagamie County for the twenty-three allotments in that county that were bisected by the railroad's right-of-way. The Outagamie County Register of Deeds possesses deed, probate, or mortgage records on all but four of the allottees. Quite a few sold their lands immediately upon receiving a patent in fee simple in 1907, or as soon as they could after the Appropriations Act of 1906.

18. Kappler, *Indian Affairs*, 4:1056.

19. Hauptman, *The Iroquois and the New Deal*.

20. "Survey of the Conditions of the Indians in the United States," Senate Subcommittee on Indian Affairs, 71st Cong., 1st sess. (March 1, 1929), 12:1918–1921. See also "Skenadore Organization," OLFP, ONIW.

21. See note 20.

17

The Wisconsin Oneidas and the Federal Competency Commission of 1917

Laurence M. Hauptman

The coming of the Federal Competency Commission to Oneida in 1917 was the final crisis over the tribal estate faced by these Wisconsin Indians in the age of allotment.[1] By the time the three-member commission arrived at Oneida, Wisconsin, over 50,000 acres of the 65,400-acre reservation had already been alienated; nevertheless, the commission's work nearly ended Oneida landed existence. By studying the origins and impact of this commission, one can clearly understand how federal policies were formed and how Wisconsin state policies shaped American Indian policies in the first two decades of the twentieth century. The ten-year process leading up to the commission and the fight over its recommendations throw light on the heroic but unsuccessful efforts of a determined group of Oneida community activists, the so-called Indian Party, to save the remaining lands and stave off dispossession.

In the years after the Burke Act, the Indian Party was most vocal in opposing conversion of trust lands to fee patents. The leader was Paul Doxtator, the third child of Cornelius and Susan Doxtator. Paul, his brother George, and his father, Cornelius, were Civil War veterans. Along with a younger brother, Henry, Paul until his death in 1921 was the most vocal critic of patenting trust lands. The Doxtators were often joined in their efforts by John Archiquette, the official Oneida government translator and peace officer.[2]

The push for conversion of trust patents occurred well before the Burke Act and its two modifications in 1907 and 1910. In 1903, the Wisconsin legislature's formal establishment of the Town of Oneida in Outagamie County and the Town of Hobart in Brown County set in motion events that created a major crisis for the Oneida Indians. These new municipalities, which quickly established town governments and came under county and state rules and regulations, were carved out of the original Oneida reservation.[3] Initially, Oneidas controlled the governments of the two towns: Dr. Josiah Powless was town supervisor of Hobart, Chauncey Baird was treasurer, Eli Skenandore was town clerk, Moses Elm was assessor, and Solomon Webster and Anderson Skenandore were on the town council. Nelson Metoxen was the Town supervisor of Oneida, while Josiah Charles was clerk and Richard Powless was assessor.[4]

Once trust patents were converted to fee simple patents, the Oneida lands became subject to taxation, and numerous allotments were lost to the two towns for nonpayment. Land speculators moved in and promoted rapid white settlement on these lands formally held by the Oneidas. Within a short time, because of this land rush by whites, the Oneidas began to lose political control of both town governments, as they were now outnumbered by the new white residents. Other Oneidas, using their new fee simple patents as collateral, were encouraged to take out cash loans or to mortgage their property, ideas promoted by local real estate brokers and land jobbers in collusion with the Indian agent, local politicians in the Green Bay area, and even a few Oneida tribal members themselves. When they could not repay the loan or mortgage, their lands were foreclosed.[5] One Oneida WPA story described that others were cheated out of their lands "by not being able to read." They thought that "they were mortgaging only a small portion of their land," but they found "out too late that they had mortgaged the whole place." This Oneida added: "The people started to lose their home one way or another, and white people bought them from the real estate men. White farmers started to settle on the reservation land, and they bought Oneida land as cheap as they could."[6]

Historian James W. Oberly has brought out that not all of the land loss was the result of whites or their Indian allies swindling Indians.[7] At least some Oneidas themselves made sales agreements at fair market value. This fact should not be surprising since Oneidas who had been sent off to federal boarding schools often came back with the views of the teachers and administrators at those institutions. They had been taught that reservations were not suitable for modern Indians, and that private property—and with it, American citizenship—were the requisites for success.

The split between some Indians, not all, who had been sent off to a federal boarding school and those who remained on the reservation clearly shaped the debate over accepting or pushing for fee simple title. Approximately half of the Oneidas had been to federal boarding schools by 1917.[8] Although some, not most, were involved in land speculation and getting ahead at the expense of their neighbors, the vast majority chose to convert their trust patents into fee simple patents quickly from the time of the Burke Act onward. Rapid white settlement led to rising land values. The Oneidas' desperate need for cash to overcome impoverishment and to support themselves and their extended families resulted in the conversion of trust lands to fee simple patents, and then to the sale of these same lands. Moreover, some Oneidas jumped at money as well as at the chance of controlling their property and escaping the oppressive colonial administration of Washington's bureaucracy and the tyrannical federal Indian agents.

As early as 1909, the Indian Party had filed formal protests with the commission of Indian affairs and sought an investigation of the situation at Oneida. Members argued that the towns of Oneida and Hobart were illegally created, that both town governments and the county governments of Outagamie and Brown counties had no jurisdiction over federally protected Indian treaty lands, namely, the Oneida Reservation, and that local efforts to collect taxes and/or to foreclose on the Oneida patents were illegal.[9] To those pushing conversion, whites and Indians alike, members of the Indian Party were not "modern" Indians looking to the future, and their motives were frequently questioned. They were seen in contrast to the so-called progressive element of the community, which included some of the Oneidas' boarding school graduates.[10]

As a result of the protests by the Indian Party, the commissioner of Indian affairs sent Charles L. Davis, superintendent of Indian schools, to investigate the complaints. In a letter to the commissioner dated October 16, 1909, Davis concluded that the actions by the towns, counties, and the state of Wisconsin relative to Oneida lands had the overwhelming support of the majority of whites, and that the whites also had the right to assess and levy taxes on lands and personal property that had been converted to fee patents. Although Davis specifically sidestepped the legality of the state laws of 1903, he said that it would be an "easy matter for the legislature [of Wisconsin] to correct it by a legalizing act." Davis concluded that the "only thing left for the Office [BIA] is to cooperate [with the state of Wisconsin] to the end of pacifying the Indians as far as possible, that they will accept the action of the State [of Wisconsin] in organizing the township[s] and collecting the taxes."[11] Two days earlier, Davis had sent a letter to all Oneida tribal members. In it, he maintained that the Oneidas could challenge the 1903 state acts in court if they so desired, but he advised the Indians to pay their taxes or else they would be subject to court actions and foreclosure proceedings. In an attempt to stem an open rebellion, Davis assured the Oneidas that by accepting fee simple patents, they were not forfeiting federal annuity payments set forth in treaties, and that Wisconsin had no right to interfere internally in the operations of the existing "old Indian Council."[12]

Declaring Indians "competent" did not begin with the Federal Indian Competency Commission that met at Oneida in 1917. The BIA had sent commissioners out to Indian reservations as early as 1910 to determine competency. In the years before Wilson took office, the commissioner of Indian affairs reported that 30 percent of the Indians who received unrestricted title to their land failed to make good. Agents in the field were describing the failure of the policy because the Indians were losing out to local whites who lusted after these newly designated unrestricted lands. Despite the signs that the policy was devastating to Indian communities, President Wilson's two administrations continued to pursue it. Between 1915 and 1917, Washington officials released 17,241 acres from trust patents.[13]

One might then ask why the Indians who objected to this policy—including a sizable number of Oneidas—did not simply refuse to have their trust patents converted. President Wilson's Indian policies from 1913 to 1921 were largely set by Secretary of the Interior Franklin K. Lane, a Progressive Democrat from California, who was unbending in his resolve.[14] Historian Janet McDonnell described the secretary as insisting that if "any Indian refused to accept his patent, the superintendent was to send it registered mail and to inform the tax collector that it had been issued." She stated: "Lane would not let a qualified Indian avoid the responsibilities of citizenship simply by refusing to accept his fee patent." McDonnell added: "If the Interior Department mailed the fee patents, the Indians had to take them, and the department did not have the burden of holding the patents until the allottees acquiesced."[15] It should be noted that approximately two out of every three Oneidas who later testified before the Federal Indian Competency Commission in August 1917 voiced strong objections to the conversion of trust patents.

President Wilson's Indian policies were set against the backdrop of war in Europe. Although there was nothing very efficient in the operations of the Interior Department in the period, both Secretary Lane and Commissioner of Indian Affairs Cato Sells were Progressives enamored with the "Gospel of Efficiency" mentality so typical of the first two decades of the twentieth century. The policy also fit into what has been labeled the "Great Plow Up": U.S. agricultural policies intended to meet the growing demands caused by World War I. Smaller Indian trust patents had to be consolidated into larger, more productive units.[16] To Sells, this policy could be achieved only by quickly ending the trust period and allowing the Indians to have unrestricted title to their lands. Thus, the logical result of Sells's idea of progress was that the Indians would then sell off their smaller, less productive parcels to those individuals who would consolidate and make agriculture more efficient. In other words, the gospel of efficiency combined with the federal goals of assimilating the Indians. In this view, separate Indian reservations were no longer suitable for the modern era and the BIA was directed to phase out "wardship."

In 1915, Commissioner Sells stated that he refused to "permit thousands of acres of fertile land belonging to the Indians and capable of great industrial development to lie in unproductive idleness." Sells further insisted: "Former widespread negligency and mismanagement in the cultivation of the soil, the breeding of stock and the handling of grazing land is no excuse for the continuance of such conditions, and they will not be permitted to exist on an Indian reservation during my administration."[17] To Sells, "competent" Indians had to be freed from government dependence by loosening up federal supervision of their lands. With war waging in Europe and the need to export more American foodstuffs and manufactured goods, Washington policy makers pursued Sells's plan.

In 1915, the secretary of the interior appointed James McLaughlin to head a federal competency commission to determine the "qualifications of each Indian who may apply for a severance of tribal relations, or who, in its judgment, has arrived at the degree of business competency that he should assume the duties of citizenship."[18] McLaughlin, who had been born in Canada, was a naturalized citizen of the United States and was married to a Sioux woman. He had worked in the Indian Service for over forty years. He was made U.S. Indian inspector in the mid-1890s, serving in that capacity at Oneida in 1910–1911 and again in 1917.

McLaughlin's long career in the federal Indian service, from 1871 to 1923, has been praised by historians. They have largely interpreted his performance as enlightened for the times, working under most difficult circumstances in a government agency that was often corrupt, filled with patronage, and frequently insensitive to the needs of American Indians. According to the eminent historian Robert M. Utley, the "Indian truly was his friend. The Indian was his friend because, even more important, he was the

Indian's friend." To Utley, he represented the voice of eastern philanthropy and reform within the overly politically charged Bureau of Indian Affairs of the U.S. Department of the Interior. The historian concluded: "He was a rarity too as an experienced, intelligent, dedicated, honest Indian agent seemingly immune from the spoils system." To McLaughlin, as Utley points out, the Indian had to be "individualized" (cut loose from the authority and society of the tribe), settled on his allotment of land, and helped to learn how to support himself and his family by farming. He should be "taught to live and think like his white counterpart on a Midwestern farm, to render patriotic allegiance to flag and country, and ultimately to assume the privileges and obligations of U.S. citizenship."[19]

This praise by Utley and most historians fails to take into account that McLaughlin had changed over the years and by 1917 had become the "company man." What might have appeared to many as a logical government policy in the 1870s and 1880s was a recognizable disaster by 1917. McLaughlin's approach to the Oneidas from 1910 to 1917 and his failure to see what was happening in Indian Country, including on the Wisconsin Oneida Indian Reservation after the passage of the Burke Act of 1906, cannot simply be rationalized away. By not recognizing the disaster that had befallen the Oneidas—the impoverishment and the homelessness since 1906—and by turning a blind eye to the motives of Brown County and Outagamie County real estate interests and Wisconsin politicians, McLaughlin's actions cannot be sloughed off as those of an aging paternalistic reformer.

In the immediate two years prior to his work at Oneida in 1917, Chief Inspector McLaughlin went all over the American West selling the idea of converting trust patents to the Indians. The haste in which the policy was undertaken between 1915 and 1917 contributed to mistakes. Historian McDonnell has pointed out that one federal competency commissioner, John R. Wise, stated before Congress that he did not require Indians to have any education to be judged competent, that he heard as many as twenty to thirty cases a day, and that he spent only fifteen to thirty minutes on each individual case. Compared to Wise and other federal competency commissioners, McLaughlin, who made mistakes as well, stands out as the best of the worst.[20]

Inspector McLaughlin was no stranger to the Oneidas. In 1910 and 1911, he had headed a previous commission that attempted to buy out the federal obligations to the Oneidas set forth in the Treaty of Canandaigua (1794). In an early version of federal termination policies, his commission tried to convince the Oneidas to accept a onetime lump-sum payment in lieu of their small annuity. The Oneidas of different political parties, including Dennison Wheelock and Laura Minnie Cornelius Kellogg, rejected this effort. In 1911, McLaughlin had made it clear that the end of federal trust responsibilities and the end of separate Indian reservations and tribal existence were inevitable. Although he claimed that federal government officials would not act arbitrarily, he cited the U.S. Supreme Court case *Lonewolf v. Hitchcock* (1903), telling the Indians that Congress had the power to legislate for them even without consulting them. He also insisted that Oneida claims against New York State were not a federal matter, and he inaccurately informed them that the Empire State had jurisdiction over all of its Indians.[21] Thus, when McLaughlin showed up once again at Oneida in 1917, few of the Indians expected that he was bringing a panacea to cure all their troubles.

Early in 1917, Commissioner Sells sent McLaughlin and Orlando M. McPherson, a former postal inspector and specially appointed Indian agent, to Oneida to prepare the groundwork for a later visit. McPherson and an assistant compiled a list of 106 Oneidas who held trust patents (exclusive of heirship lands) and recommended that thirty-two of these patents be immediately converted to fee simple title.[22] The next month Commissioner Sells issued a policy directive setting forth more liberal guidelines on declaring Indian competency. Sells insisted that the federal government discontinue guardianship of all competent Indians, "giving even closer attention to the incompetent that they may more speedily achieve competency." The new rules provided:

1. *Patents in fee.*—To all able-bodied adult Indians of less than one-half Indian blood, there will be given as far as may be under

the law full and complete control of all their property. Patents in fee shall be issued to all adult Indians of one-half or more Indian blood who may, after careful investigation, be found competent, provided, that where deemed advisable patents in fee shall be withheld for not to exceed 40 acres as a home.

Indian students, when they are 21 years of age, or over, who complete the full course of instruction in the Government schools, receive diplomas and have demonstrated competency will be so declared.[23]

This latter provision is noteworthy since Wisconsin Oneida students had been among the most represented American Indians nation-wide at boarding schools—Carlisle, Flandreau, Hampton, Haskell, Mt. Pleasant, Oneida, Pipestone, Tomah, and other institutions. Thus, the Oneidas had more of their community eligible for "com-petency" designation than most other Indian communities.[24]

Sells's directive clearly had a racist tinge to it. After all, this was an age of eugenics and the rebirth of the Ku Klux Klan. The Wilson administration was hardly a model for enlightened racial attitudes and was noted for excluding racial minorities from cer-tain governmental agencies, including the U.S. postal service. Now Commissioner Sells insisted that the policy was "calculated to release practically all Indians" who had "one-half or more white blood," although there would "be exceptions in the case of those who are manifestly incompetent." Hence, so-called full-bloods need not apply or at least had to speak fluent English even to be considered "competent." Hence, the more white, it appeared to federal officials, the more competent and the more capable of taking on the rights and responsibilities of American citizenship. Long before McLaughlin's return to Oneida in August, Commissioner Sells had determined what the inspector was to recommend in his final report. Writing to the assistant secretary of the interior, Sells forcefully insisted that the Oneidas had to take fee patents "in harmony with our new declaration of policy." The commissioner opposed extending the trust period for any amount of time. When the chief clerk of the BIA and Wisconsin senator Paul O. Husting worked out a compromise for a one-year extension of trust patents at Oneida, Sells expressed his disappointment.[25]

Wisconsin Oneida society was severely divided by the time McLaughlin's commission arrived. Sharp divisions worked against long-term community interests. Besides educational and class differences created when Oneidas went off to federal Indian boarding schools, other divisions were noticeable. There was clearly a generational gap. The elders—Oneidas over fifty-five years of age who held trust patents—were more resistant to conversion to fee simple title than the younger tribal members.[26]

In 1917, John Archiquette and the Doxtator brothers—Paul and his younger brother, Henry, better known as "Duke"—led the opposition to conversion of trust to fee simple patents, with its new imposition of taxes, fearing further tribal land loss. Many of those who spoke at the Federal Competency Commission hearings in 1917 reflected this position, one that appears to have been held by well-respected Oneida tribal elders at the time. This opposition group also included Isaac Webster, who was married to Josephine Hill Webster. Isaac was a graduate of Hampton Institute, and his involvement in resisting conversion of trust patents shows that not all boarding school "products" supported McLaughlin and his efforts in 1917.[27]

The internal harmony of the Oneida community was also disturbed by the BIA's plan, formulated as early as 1908, to phase out the U.S. Industrial School (the Oneida Government School or Oneida Boarding School), which had been established in 1893 on the reservation. Most of the employees at the school were Oneidas, and the community derived other economic benefits, such as supply contracts, from having this federal presence on the reservation. Some Oneidas favored Wheelock's plans to convert the institution to a public school or to a federal sanitarium to treat Indian tuberculosis patients. Others such as Minnie Kellogg, whose sister Alice taught at the school, were outspoken opponents of Wheelock's proposal and insisted on the continuance of the Oneida Boarding School.[28]

Trying to save the institution was on at least some Oneidas' minds in 1917. This point was reinforced since Joseph Hart, the school's principal and the federal Indian superintendent at Oneida, was a member of McLaughlin's three-man commission. The presence of this highly controversial principal-superintendent suggested to the Oneidas that the work of the Federal Competency Commission and the BIA's plans to close the school were intertwined.

Wisconsin state politics clearly was the driving force behind the Federal Competency Commission's work among the Oneidas in 1917. On April 18, 1917, Wisconsin congressman Joseph Martin wrote to Senator Paul Husting concerning a telephone call he had received from the "chairman of the Town of Oneida" who questioned the possible extension of trust patents on the Oneida reservation for another ten years. Martin, a member of the Democratic Party's National Committee, urged Husting to resist any congressional or Interior Department action extending the trust period until the towns of Oneida and Hobart were given their opportunity to present their views on the matter.[29]

On May 7, 1917, Husting and several representatives of the town and what purported to be a delegation representing the Oneidas met with Chief Clerk C. F. Hauck at BIA headquarters in Washington, D.C. The meeting was largely dominated by P. W. Silverwood, representing the two towns' position, Dennison Wheelock, and Orrin J. Kellogg, a non-Indian and the husband of Laura Minnie Cornelius Kellogg. At the conclusion of that meeting, there was agreement that the trust period should end after a one-year extension, that deceased allottees' land should be put into fee simple patents, and that the problem of so-called duplicate allotments should be investigated in order to convert some of the lands of overlapping trust patents.[30] Ten days after this meeting, the trust period on the remaining Oneida allotments was extended by an executive order for one year.[31]

On May 10, Senator Robert LaFollette, Sr., wrote the commissioner of Indian Affairs about the need to complete the allotment as well as the fee patenting processes on the Wisconsin Oneida Indian Reservation. He indicated that there were still 5,500 undivided acres left of tribal lands, 5,300 allotted lands held by Oneidas in trust, and 825 acres of so-called double allotments, namely, overlapping claims to allotted lands resulting in unclear title. The prominent Wisconsin senator indicated that 110 (actually 106) living Oneidas, who still held allotments in trust, were the "most prosperous members" of the tribe and were intentionally avoiding their civic responsibilities by not paying taxes to the towns of Hobart and Oneida. These lands, the senator insisted, were "the best lands," on "the most favored locations and have the best improvements made by the Oneidas." He pointed out that these two towns had built roads, bridges, and schools and made other improvements where only "very poor roads, just an Indian trail," had existed before. LaFollette strongly recommended that the Oneidas on these lands should, like other individuals, white as well as Indian, pay their fair share of taxes to the two towns. To "insure" that the Indians on these lands were capable of taking on this new responsibility, LaFollette urged a temporary extension of restrictions on issuing fee simple patents but suggested that a federal "competency commission visit the reservation and personally pass upon each of the one hundred ten cases of allottees who have not applied for fee patents" to determine their "competency." In response to Senator LaFollette's letter, a week later, Secretary of the Interior Lane recommended that President Wilson appoint a "Competency Commission with the view of releasing from Government control all of the Oneida Indians who are capable of managing their own affairs."[32]

The Doxtators worked feverishly to stymie the efforts to extend fee patents. As early as March 1916, they were appealing for support from Senator Robert LaFollette, asking for a congressional investigation of the situation.[33] On June 7, 1917, they wrote the senator complaining about a tax warrant filed upon William Danforth's allotment. They indicated that only twenty-two Oneidas (of twenty-five hundred) participated in organizing the two towns, that federal Indian school superintendent Joseph Hart did not protect their interests, and that in fact he helped the whites "beat us out of our property while our young men were preparing to go overseas to fight the Germans." The brothers concluded: "It seems they [town officials, land speculators, federal Indian superintendent] want to kill [the] reservation as soon as possible."[34]

McLaughlin, along with Frank Brandon, a special Indian agent of Shawnee ancestry, arrived at Oneida in early August 1917. Although tribal enrollment was 2,575 members, many Oneida men were now serving in the American Expeditionary Force in the war in Europe. Not only was the community devoid of some of its population, but also the size of the reservation proper had shrunk by more than 75 percent since 1906.[35] McLaughlin and Brandon were joined by Superintendent Hart, who became the third member of the commission. Hart had eighteen years of experience among the Oneidas and played a major role in the commission's work.

McLaughlin had brought questionnaires to seventy homes, even before the first hearing, supposedly to determine Oneida "competency." Only ten of thirty-two Oneidas interviewed by McLaughlin signed applications for fee simple title. Among the holdouts were Willie Fat Skenandore and Melissa Cornelius, two of the more prominent Wisconsin Oneidas of the twentieth century.[36] Among the questions asked by the commissioners at Oneida included (1) degree of blood; (2) educational level; (3) physical condition; (4) marital status; and (5) occupation, full- or part-time. The competency commissioners were also required to certify the following for each potential patentee:

- How is his self-support obtained?
- Is he addicted to the use of intoxicants?
- If the applicant is a married woman, what is the reputation of her husband?
- Is he a man who would be likely to get possession of his wife's property and then desert her?
- Is he a man whom you would recommend as a suitable person?
- Is his name on the roll of honor?
- Have you made a personal investigation with a view of determining what progress or advancement the applicant has made, whether he is in debt and, if so, to what extent, and whether the answers made by the applicant to the questions in his petition are correct?[37]

Chart 6

Wisconsin Oneida Opponents of Conversion of Trust Lands to
Fee Simple Title at the Federal Commission Hearings,
August 7, 14, 1917

Name	Age	Size of Trust Patents Held
1. John Quincy Adams	66	90
2. Isaac Archiquette	62	15
3. John Archiquette	72	90
4. Sampson J. Cornelius	69	60
5. Thomas Cornelius	63	90
6. Chauncey Doxtator	32	26
7. Henry Doxtator	63	89.85
8. Paul Doxtator	75	89.90
9. Nicholas Elm	66	90
10. John K. Powless	66	60
11. Solomon Skenandore	76	40
12. Joseph Smith	94	90
13. Sampson Stevens	51	45
14. William Kelly [Webster]	51	44.69

Source: Compiled from James McLaughlin Papers, box 1, SHSW,
and from CCF 1907–1939, BIA, RG75, NA.

The Federal Competency Commission held its first formal
hearing in the parish hall of the Episcopal church before one hundred mostly Oneida people on August 7, 1917. Superintendent
Hart opened the meeting. He recounted the legislative changes
since the passage of the Burke Act that had resulted in the sale of
many estates after a "great many [Oneida] people have asked
and received fee patents for their land." He mentioned Orlando
McPherson's earlier visit in March 1917 to Oneida and the special
agent's report, which recommended patents in fees to some and
the continuance of the trust period for others. Hart then assured
the Indians assembled that Commissioner Sells had sent "a trusted
employee, who has been long in Indian work, Major McLaughlin,
and Mr. Brandon, who has had much experience in his work." He

assured the Oneidas that the three-member commission's purpose was "to ascertain what should be done for your best interests
and for your protection, if protection is needed."[38]

Inspector McLaughlin then addressed the gathering, reporting
that he had ten signed applications and twenty-two unsigned
applications for fee patents, which had been collected in March.
The inspector indicated that he had visited about seventy homes
of "restricted Indians." He claimed that his role then at Oneida
was to hear the Oneidas express themselves freely on the subject. He added that the purpose of the hearings was to determine
"whether you wish to receive patents in fee for your restricted
lands, which carries with it full citizenship, giving you the same
standing as the white citizen, with a white man's chance, or have
the trust period further extended."[39] It should be noted that both
McLaughlin and Hart tried to dispel personal blame by telling
the Indians assembled at both of the hearings that the commission could recommend but not determine the final outcome on
Indian competency, that the final decision was to be made by
officials in Washington.[40]

The first noncommissioner to speak out at the hearing was
a non-Indian, Orrin J. Kellogg. He asked whether Oneidas over
sixty years of age would be considered for fee patents. McLaughlin
answered that there was now no hard and fast official rule concerning age restrictions. McLaughlin then recognized Dennison
Wheelock, followed by Orrin Kellogg's wife, Minnie. As highly
educated Oneidas who operated on the national level of Indian
politics, they knew that McLaughlin came with a predetermined
agenda. At the hearing, neither Dennison Wheelock nor Minnie
Kellogg openly challenged Washington's policy direction on trust
conversion. Both detested the BIA's colonial control over the
Indians. Their testimony reflected their long-held views that Washington officials should not treat the Indians as children incapable
of making decisions for themselves. Whatever their motivation,
both viewed the federal fee simple patent policy as an inevitable
one. At the conclusion of this first hearing, a motion was passed
recommending that the Interior Department sell off the lands of

deceased allottees without heirs. All moneys collected would be held in trust for the benefit of the Wisconsin Oneidas.[41]

At the two hearings, a minority of Oneidas, only six total, spoke on behalf of extending fee patents. One Indian observed that Oneidas should not be afraid of losing federal protection, since Washington had done so little to help Wisconsin Indians in the past. He then spent his time testifying in defense of the delegation that had gone to Washington in May to speak with BIA officials about converting trust patents. Another Oneida proudly insisted he was capable of managing his fee simple patent as well as take on all the rights and responsibilities of U.S. citizenship: "I have an education; I graduate[d] from Carlisle, from the eighth grade and second grade high school." Critical of those more conservative Oneidas who refused to convert their trust patents, he added: "You take old Indians, the only Indians that are uneducated are the trust holders. I know that they don't really understand the right thing of citizenship; they don't get the idea."[42]

The vast majority of those who testified at both hearings, mostly members of the Indian Party, challenged the end of trust patents. At the first hearing, Joseph M. Smith told the commissioners that these people who "got fee simple patents for their land" have now "gone through it and have no homes today." He added that a "great many of them," including well-educated Oneidas who had been sent off to "Hampton School and different schools" have "left the reservation entirely; they can't make a living here, and worse than all of it some of our best men that have got fee simple patents for their land, what have they did with their lands?" Smith answered his own question: "They dispose of their land and they have no homes today; some of them, I don't know where they are. They are way off; they have left the county entirely, homeless, penniless, beggars, loafers."[43]

At the first hearing, John Archiquette proposed the extension of the trust period since he saw the suffering of those who had received fee simple patents to their lands. Archiquette insisted: "They are not getting along the way they ought to. They are suffering and when I see them suffer, I suffer too because I love my people."[44] At the second meeting, he argued for the extension of the trust period to protect Oneidas for fear that they would become "gypsies, going about from one place to another. Let us remain as we are." He insisted that the Oneidas had always served "to defend the flag of the United States" and "stood by Uncle Sam from the beginning and they have never given any trouble to the United States."[45]

Much like Archiquette, Paul Doxtator described the negative impact of conversion of trust lands to fee simple patents and that the process had created beggars of the Indians. He also recommended an extension of the trust for ten more years. Chauncey Doxtator called for unity in the face of this crisis and suggested that the Oneidas had better unify by getting Superintendent "Hart out of office."[46] Thomas Cornelius, who spoke at both hearings, countered the argument pushed by the three commissioners that the Indians, for their own good, had to accept the inevitability of progress by becoming tax-paying American citizens. Cornelius maintained that those Oneidas who "took patent deed; [sic] they are gone and scattered today. They 'aint got no pillow to lay down to rest. So I don't call it improvement." He noted that the Oneidas had "about 65,000 acres before allotment made, and since that we got not more than 5,000" (actually more like 10,000 acres in 1917). Cornelius in part blamed Indian officeholders in the towns of Hobart and Oneida for the continued move to extend fee simple patents.[47]

At the second hearing—on August 14, 1917—the Oneidas were even more vocal against conversion of their trust patents. Adding to comments by John Archiquette and Thomas Cornelius made at the first hearing, Sampson J. Cornelius, speaking in Oneida, pointed out the problems caused by fee simple title. He insisted that land speculators had bought up "thousands and thousands of acres of land right here." Cornelius labeled the government policy under the Burke Act as a major mistake that was destroying the Oneidas. Other Indians questioned whether Oneida opinion was represented at the May BIA meeting in Washington. Nicholas Elm, speaking in Oneida, observed: "The delegation that went from here to Washington seemed to be headed by a white man [Orrin J. Kellogg]. They went before the department and laid the whole thing before them on just one side of the view." Sampson Stevens, speaking in Oneida and having Isaac Webster translate it, suggested that the push for fee simple patents was by the more "educated class of people" among the Oneidas. At the same meeting, Solomon Skenandore, a sovereignty-minded Indian, insisted that the Oneidas had a long-standing treaty relationship with Washington that provided an annuity and protection. He urged the Oneidas to appeal directly to President Wilson to let him know that the Indians wanted to remain as they were.[48]

Two other Indians speaking in Oneida offered intriguing reasons for their opposition. William Kelly [Webster] testified that, despite the temptation for "quick money," he and the tribe's old men were against the change. In a shrewd twist, he said that by turning down conversion to fee simple title, the Oneidas would actually save the two towns money since fewer Indians would end up in the poorhouse. Despite insisting he was not opposed to "white man's laws," John K. Powless stated that these laws should not be imposed upon him. In a self-deprecating way, he maintained that he "don't want to be a full-fledged [U.S.] citizen" because "I am not as smart as I ought to be. I am ignorant." Hence, even competent Oneidas humiliated themselves and questioned their own intelligence to try to avoid fee simple title. At the end of the second hearing, Isaac Webster presented a petition asking the federal officials to recommend the extension of the trust period. The hearing ended when the Oneidas voted twenty to seven, with seven abstentions, to allow the petition to go forward to Washington.[49]

In response to the Oneida criticism expressed at the two hearings, McLaughlin was largely ineffective. He tried flattery, attempting to win over the Indian women at the first hearing by praising their housekeeping and suggesting he needed to speak to them personally. He lauded the Oneida women for maintaining their homes in a tidy fashion, with clean floors and laundry on the line as well as having weedless gardens. In a patronizing manner, the inspector stated: "No white person in the country could have done any better." With Oneidas fearful about the closing of the federal boarding school on the reservation and the talk about shutting down the Carlisle Indian School, the inspector stated that the Indians of one-quarter blood quantum or higher would not be deprived of the "privilege" of sending their children to government schools as long as Congress continued to fund them. McLaughlin, however, indicated to the Oneidas that they would become full-fledged citizens "under the laws of the State in which you reside," a thought that must have sent chills to sovereignty-minded Indians who objected to state jurisdiction. After all, to many Oneidas, it was state politicians who had created the crisis by establishing the towns of Hobart and Oneida. McLaughlin, nevertheless, made it clear that as a member of previous competency commissions, he had recommended "a great many patents in fee going against Indian objections. . . . They are granted arbitrarily upon the report that we have made that they are fully competent and well provided with worldly goods."[50]

In its official report to Washington on August 31, 1917, the commission recommended that the trust period on 125 allotments of deceased Oneidas comprising forty-five hundred acres be ended after June 12, 1918. The commissioners suggested immediate action since the "settlement of these estates becomes more complex from year to year." The commissioners recommended the extension of the trust period on all other Oneida allotments for one year, and that seventy-one in number be converted to fee simple title after that date. McLaughlin and the other two commissioners rationalized the changes, focusing on the acculturation of the Oneidas, claiming that their "close association with white people" had influenced them to the point that they have "adopted white methods and profited thereby, and in some instances prospered equal to their white neighbors." The commissioners further described the community as "intelligent, law abiding, peaceable citizens" who "take their place in the religious, educational, industrial and political activities of the community." The commissioners indicated that one-half of the 2,550 Indians had attended government schools, a further indication to the three commissioners that most, if not all, Oneidas should be released from federal supervision. They concluded that, "while some have outdistanced others," the Oneidas were "further advanced in civilized ways than any other of the northeastern tribes."[51]

In some ways, the language of the commission's report was similar to the post–World War II rhetoric of the federal Indian policy of termination.[52] For their own good, the Indians had to be turned loose from federal restrictions and control, free of the shackles of BIA bureaucracy and inefficiency. The commission report of August 31, 1917, indicated that the vast majority of these lands need not be held in trust since the judges of Brown and Outagamie counties, "in which these lands are situated, are men of high character, who will undoubtedly see that the rights of widows and minor heirs are properly protected."[53] Thus, the commissioners refused to acknowledge the existence of long-standing racial antipathies held by local whites toward the Oneidas. In May 1918, President Wilson, in an executive order, confirmed the work of McLaughlin's commission and extended the remaining thirty-five trust patents for nine more years.[54]

The Doxtator brothers later characterized the shoddy work performed by Inspector McLaughlin and his two colleagues. To the Doxtators, it was the commissioners, not the Oneidas, who had to be judged for competence. Writing to Senator LaFollette in May 1918 and not knowing of the senator's commitment to promote McLaughlin and his work, Paul along with his brother Henry criticized the inspector's work at Oneida. The Doxtators charged that McLaughlin had refused to investigate "charges against certain party [sic] as to how our people were being beat out of their land and defrauded in other ways."[55]

Not getting satisfaction from their appeals to Senator LaFollette, the Doxtators pursued a new course in June 1918. They attempted, but unsuccessfully, to secure support from Wisconsin's newly elected junior senator, Irvine Lenroot. Paul then wrote to President Wilson. He appealed directly to the president's sense of patriotism, by pointing out that Doxtators had fought on the American side at Bunker Hill in the American Revolution, had been killed at the Battle of Chippawa in the War of 1812, had served in the Civil War, and were now overseas fighting in World War I. He indicated that he, his brother George, and his father,

Cornelius Doxtator, had faithfully served the Union in President Lincoln's time, and that Paul's son John was then a doughboy in the American Expeditionary Force. He urged the president to stop fee patenting Oneida allotments since he insisted that his fellow Indians were "not fit to look after their interest" and because "they get beat so much." Despite the poignancy of the protest, Doxtator's appeal was to fall on deaf ears once again.[56]

In February 1920, John Barton Payne replaced Lane as secretary of the interior and officially abolished these federal competency commissions.[57] Later, in a petition to the commissioner of Indian affairs in 1922, twenty Oneidas summarized the frauds that had followed the Burke Act of 1906, criticized the work of the Federal Competency Commission of 1917, and appealed for relief. Much like Paul Doxtator had done earlier, the Oneida petitioners attempted to show that federal Indian agents in the field had "betrayed the trust or were incompetent," that Washington officials had the responsibility to protect the Indians' interests and prevent the Oneidas from losing what little land they had left. The petitioners detailed the method of the frauds under the Burke Act and its later amendments.

> It was used to promote the interests of the land speculators who would and did seduce the ignorant Indians to go with them to the Indian Agent so that there would be an appearance of complying with the law regarding getting the permission of the Secretary of the Interior and the speculator would pay a certain sum so that the Indian may sign his fee patent over to the speculator as soon as the Agent procures it for him. When the fee patent comes, the speculator goes and tells the Indian that his fee patent is at the Agent's Office and takes him over there and has him sign over to the speculator. Much of this signing over to a speculator has been done even without having been done through the Agent. The perpetration of these frauds is evidenced by the fact that probably as much as 95% of the lands sold immediately upon receipt of a fee patent has been sold to speculators who have made it a business to wrest the lands from the Indians through fraudulent means and apparently

aided by the Indian agent as shown by the apparent disregard as to the competency of the Indian.

The petitioners then focused on McLaughlin's commission and the consequences of its work in 1917:

> The Competency Commission [which] visited the reservation reported the Indians as being quite competent to receive fee patents as the Commission traveled through the reservation and saw good houses, barns and stock but they saw the property of white people who live on lands owned by speculators or are paying for such lands on the installment plan and perhaps 90% of such whites are not "making good." Fee patents were issued through the recommendations of the Competency Commission and excessive taxes are levied so that we are not able to pay them and apparently we will lose our holdings entirely through our inability to pay taxes. We [are] assessed for taxes although it appears that Indians who receive annuities are not citizens.[58]

Despite this appeal, Washington officials did nothing to remedy this situation until the establishment of a new Indian Reorganization Act government in 1934.[59]

The inner workings of American politics, with its tradeoffs and paybacks, are often not well understood by historians writing history. Yet many Oneidas revealed in their testimony before the federal competency commission that they understood all too well what was happening around them. Although competency commissioners McLaughlin, Hart, and Brandon can be judged harshly for their actions and for what happened, the decisions were made higher up the line by Wisconsin politicians of both parties in collaboration with Washington insiders.

Notes

1. For the work of the federal competency commissions and Indian lands in the West from 1915 to 1920, see McDonnell, *Dispossession of the*

American Indian, 87–102; also McDonnell's earlier article (although here she excludes the Oneidas from her treatment): "Competency Commissions and Indian Land Policy, 1913–1920," *South Dakota History* 11 (Winter 1980): 21–34; and Hoxie, *A Final Promise,* 175–80.

2. Paul C. Doxtator was born on June 18, 1843, and died on March 17, 1921; Henry "Duke" Doxtator was the sixth child of Cornelius and Susan Doxtator. He was born in February 1853 and died c. 1935. Jordan, "Descendants of Cornelius Dockstader."

3. Charles L. Davis [superintendent of Indian schools], Inspection Report to Commissioner of Indian Affairs, October 16, 1909, #16491-09-312 (Oneida), CCF 1907–1939, BIA, RG75, NA.

4. Ida Blackhawk, "Hard Times at Oneida," OLFP.ONIW.

5. Campisi, "Ethnic Identity and Boundary Maintenance in Three Oneida Communities," 148–51.

6. Blackhawk, "Hard Times at Oneida," WPA.OLFP.

7. See Oberly, Part IV.

8. Federal Competency Commission (Oneida) Report, August 31, 1917, James McLaughlin Papers, box 1, SHSW.

9. Charles L. Davis, Inspection Report to Commissioner of Indian Affairs, October 16, 1909, #16491-09-312 (Oneida), CCF 1907–1939, BIA, RG75, NA.

10. Davis specifically mentioned two Carlisle graduates who "have been bringing a number of individual applications for patents in fee to the Office [of the federal Indian agent]." He added that the two were making "perfectly legitimate" real estate transactions but that Oneidas were questioning their "integrity." Ibid., #86325-09-312.

11. Ibid., #16491-09-312.

12. Charles L. Davis to the Oneida Indians, October 14, 1909, in ibid.

13. See McDonnell, *Dispossession of the American Indian,* 87–102; also McDonnell "Competency Commissions," and Hoxie, *A Final Promise,* 175–80.

14. McDonnell, *Dispossession of the American Indian,* 94–95; Franklin K. Lane, *The Letters of Franklin K. Lane: Personal and Political,* ed. Anne W. Lane and Louise H. Wall (Boston: Houghton Mifflin, 1922), 129–35, 140–41, 208–10; and Franklin K. Lane, "From the Warpath to the Plow," *National Geographic* (January 1915): 73–87.

15. McDonnell, *Dispossession of the American Indian,* 94–95.

16. Thomas A. Britten, *American Indians in World War I: At Home and at War* (Albuquerque: University of New Mexico Press, 1997), 132.

17. Quoted in Prucha, *Great Father* 2:879.

18. ARCIA 1915, 25.

19. Robert M. Utley, "Introduction," in James McLaughlin, *My Friend the Indian* (1910; reprint, Lincoln: University of Nebraska Press, 1989), viii–xiv.

20. McDonnell, "Competency Commissions," 30–32.

21. U.S. Congress, House of Representatives, Document No. 51.

22. For the list compiled, see "Oneida Indian Agency, Oneida Wis. Aug. 1, 1917: List of Indians Holding Trust Patents for Allotments," in James McLaughlin Papers, box 1, SHSW.

23. ARCIA 1917, 3–9.

24. Ibid.

25. Cato Sells to E. C. Bradley [assistant secretary of the interior], May 15, 1917, #48535-1917-313 (Oneida), CCF 1907–1939, BIA, RG75, NA.

26. See Chart 6. Half of the Oneidas were over fifty-five years of age; 70 percent were over fifty. Oneidas started going off to federal boarding school in the mid-1880s, so if you went to school in 1885, your age would be no older than the early fifties.

27. Isaac N. Webster was the translator for the opponents of fee simple patents at the two Federal Competency Commission hearings at Oneida in August 1917. At the second hearing, he also presented the Indian Party's petition to McLaughlin and his commission asking for an extension of the trust period. See "Minutes of the [Second] Hearing of the Federal Competency Commission at Oneida, Wisconsin, Aug. 14, 1917," 21, in James McLaughlin Papers, box 1, SHSW.

28. Minutes of a meeting of the "Oneida Business Committee" (related to the continuance of the Oneida Boarding School, with Peter J. Powless as acting chair, and Orrin J. Kellogg as secretary), November 29, 1916, in the file "Oneida, 1912–1923," in LaFollette Family Papers, series B-29, LC. For more on the school fight, see Cornelius, Part II, Hauptman, Part III, and Stovey, Part III.

29. Joseph Martin to Paul C. Hustings, April 18, 1917, #44594-13-313 (Oneida), CCF 1907–1939, BIA, RG75, NA.

30. Transcript of Hearing before Mr. C. F. Hauck, May 7, 1917, #83738-17-127 Part 2 (Oneida), in ibid. (the transcript can also be found in James McLaughlin Papers, box 1, SHSW).

31. Robert M. LaFollette to Cato Sells, May 10, 1917; Sells to LaFollette, received date May 17, 1917, #44594-17-313 (Oneida), CCF 1907–1939, BIA, RG75, NA.

32. Federal Competency Commission (Oneida) Report, August 31, 1917, in James McLaughlin Papers, box 1, SHSW.

33. LaFollette forwarded the Doxtators' request to Commissioner Sells. Robert LaFollette to Sells, March 17, 1916, #29974-16-313 (Oneida), ibid.

34. Paul C. and Henry Doxtator to Senator Robert LaFFollette [sic], June 7, 1917, in the file: "Oneida, 1912–1923," LaFollette Family Papers, series B.29, LC.

35. Federal Competency Commission (Oneida) Report, August 31, 1917, in James McLaughlin Papers, box 1, SHSW.

36. "List of thirty-two Oneidas," found in McLaughlin Papers.

37. "Application for a Patent in Fee" (Act of May 8, 1906, 34 Stat., 182), in McLaughlin Papers.

38. "Minutes of the [First] Hearing of the Federal Competency Commission, Aug. 7, 1917," 1–2, in McLaughlin Papers.

39. Ibid., 2–5.

40. "Minutes of the [Second] Hearing of the Federal Competency Commission, Aug. 14, 1917," 23–24, in McLaughlin Papers.

41. "[First] Hearing," 6–11, 16–23, 56.

42. Ibid., 24–28, 47–49, 56.

43. Ibid., 28–31.

44. Ibid., 33–35.

45. "[Second] Hearing," 2–7.

46. "[First] Hearing," 40–41 (Paul Doxtater), 42 (Chauncey Doxtater).

47. Ibid., 45–47.

48. "[Second] Hearing," 1–2 (Cornelius), 12–15 (Elm), 11–12 (Stevens), 17–19 (Skenandore).

49. Ibid., 15–16 (Kelly), 20–21 (Powless), 21 (petition).

50. Ibid., 55–56, 21–24.

51. Federal Competency Commission (Oneida) Report, August 31, 1917, in James McLaughlin Papers, SHSW.

52. For the Oneidas in the age of termination, see Laurence M. Hauptman, "Learning the Lessons of History: The Oneidas of Wisconsin Reject Termination," Journal of Ethnic Studies 14 (Fall 1986): 31–52.

53. Federal Competency Commission (Oneida) Report, August 31, 1917, in James McLaughlin Papers, SHSW.

54. Woodrow Wilson, Executive Order No. 2856, May 4, 1918. The extension of the trust period for thirty-five allotments, which was to expire on June 12, 1918, was extended to June 12, 1927. Joseph Tumulty to Woodrow Wilson, May 6, 1918; Cato Sells to Edward E. Brown, June 20, 1918, #83738-17-127, Part 2 (Oneida), CCF 1907–1939, BIA, RG75, NA.

55. Paul C. and Henry Doxtator to Robert M. LaFollette, May 13, 1918, in the file "Indian Affairs—Oneida, 1912–1923," LaFollette Family Papers, LC.

56. Paul C. and Henry Doxtator to Senator Irvine Lenroot, June 22, 1918, #52706-18-312 (Oneida), and Paul C. Doxtator to President Woodrow Wilson, July 23, 1918, #64300-18-312 (Oneida), both in CCF 1907–1939, BIA, RG75, NA.

57. McDonnell, "Competency Commissions," 21–24.

58. Oneida Petition of twenty Oneidas [including Stadler King, James Schuyler, and William Skenandore] to the Secretary of the Interior, March 27, 1922, #30709-08-313 (Oneida), CCF 1907–1939, BIA, RG75, NA.

59. Hauptman, The Iroquois and the New Deal, 70–87.

18

The Railroad and Wisconsin Oneida Lands

A Case Study in Oneida Tribal Sovereignty

Carol Cornelius

The return of 133 acres of original treaty land to the Oneida Nation, from the railroad in 2003, provides an excellent study in how the Oneida Nation can exercise its tribal sovereignty. It is also a fine example of how unified tribal efforts can lead to success, in this case the return of tribal land.

In 1870, the chiefs of the Oneida Nation were Baptist Doxtator, Jacob Cornelius, Daniel Bread, Cornelius Hill, Elijah Scanando (Skenandore) (Turtle Clan), Paul Powless, John Cornelius, Martin King, Abram Scanando, Adam Swamp, Daniel Williams, Daniel Webster, and Henry Powless. On June 3, 1870, these chiefs entered into an agreement with the Green Bay and Lake Pepin Railway Company to allow the railroad to construct a "railway across said Reservation appropriating further uses there of a strip of land one hundred feet wide and extending the whole length of such part of said Railway as will be within the limits of the Reservation." The agreement included provisions for compensation for damages to property of Oneida people living along the railway line. It is clearly stated in the agreement that the land for the railway did not include land for depots or for any other purpose than the "road bed and tracks and usual right of way of such railway."[1] On March 3, 1871, Congress passed an act recognizing this agreement and formally granting the railroad a right-of-way:

> Be it enacted by the Senate and House of Representatives of the United States in Congress Assembled, That the Green Bay and Lake Pepin Railway Company be, and is hereby authorized to build and maintain its railway across the Oneida reservation, in the State of Wisconsin, and to take sufficient land, not more than a strip one hundred feet in width, for the purposes of said railway, in accordance with and subject to the conditions of an agreement made by the chiefs and head men of the Oneida tribe of Indians, on the twenty-third day of May, eighteen hundred and seventy, approved by and on file with the Secretary of the Interior.[2]

It is important to note that these documents—the 1870 agreement and the congressional act—granted a right-of-way but did not sell the land to the railroad.

About five years ago, in the year 2000, the Oneida Nation was notified that the railroad intended to abandon the railroad track. The railroad filed a request to the National Surface Transportation Board (NSTB) to be exempt from doing a Section 106 report, which requires consultation with the tribe on cultural resources. A Section 106 report requires an assessment of the impact of removal of the tracks on any cultural resources within the reservation. In August 2001, the NSTB ruled that the railroad did have to comply with the Section 106 process required by the National Historic Preservation Act. The Oneidas then found out that the railroad, now Fox Valley and Western, was going to negotiate with the Wisconsin Department of Natural Resources (DNR) to transfer the abandoned railroad corridor to the DNR for a federally funded rails-to-trails program. It was at this point that the tribal historian, Loretta Metoxen, brought forward documents, including the original agreement. Cultural Heritage Department staff began researching the railroad's history. Metoxen remembered that an elder, Woody Webster, used to write a column for the Seymour paper and that he had mentioned the railroad. A staff member went to Seymour and found the column from 1970.[3]

The next step was to research the Oneida stories contained in the Works Progress Administration (WPA) papers for any statements about the railroad. In one of these accounts, in 1939, Mrs. Nelson Cornelius told Dennison Hill:

> About sixty years ago there was a picnic among the Oneida. They picked out certain ones to speak. Some had the practice of speaking in public and nothing bothered them. Elijah (His Long House) was the last one to make his speech. He said, you younger people take care of this loan we made with the railway company which will fall due ninety years. And they also said the Oneida will be allowed to ride in this train without charge. Some did ride in this train, mostly the Chief's and soon as they all died, then these free rides were stopped.

Mrs. Cornelius was referring to an Oneida picnic around 1880. In another WPA story, Tom Elm told Stadler King:

> In the year 1870, work was started to build the railroad that goes through Oneida. Two years before this an agreement was made by white men and the Chiefs of the Oneidas. The agreement was that the white men lease the land for a period of ninety nine years, the government was notified of this agreement, they did not buy the land. It is now a long time that they have been using the land but so far they have never paid anything on the lease. At this time they have an idea that it really belongs to them. There is still twenty-two years left after which the lease will expire then we should get the land back or they could buy it from us.[4]

Hence, it was the general belief among the Oneida people that the agreement had been a ninety-nine-year lease.

On January 21, 1871, an appraisal agreement was signed. This agreement listed the Oneida people who lived along the railway line and were awarded damages for the railway's impact on their property:

Mary Ann Beard	$60.00
Henry Powlas	15.00
Adam King	15.00
John Stevens and Henry Stevens	12.00
Atchiquit [Archiquette]	8.00
Henry Beard and George Beard	37.50
Adam Swamp	41.25
Baptist House	40.00
Peter Webster	67.50
Elijah Skenandoah [Scanando or Skenandore]	22.40
Jacob Skenandoah	30.00
Elijah Hill	15.00
Mosy Reed	40.00
Elijah Skenandoah [Scanando or Skenandore]	8.00
Aaron Hill	16.00

Peter Webster, on the list as being owed $67.50, was never paid. The total amount was paid to the Indian agent, Wm. T. Richardson, who was to disburse the above payments. Seven years later, Peter Webster wrote letters to the commissioner of Indian affairs stating that he had not received the payment from the Indian agent.[5]

Another issue that surfaced during this time pertained to Oneida men cutting timber on Oneida land for railroad ties. The U.S. Supreme Court had ruled in *United States v. Cook*, 1873, that timber was owned by the United States and could not be sold. The Indian agent at that time seized the railroad ties that Oneida men had cut.[6] This was quite a controversy up until the time of the allotment of Oneida lands.

In our research, we had collected five important documents: (1) the 1870 original tribal agreement, which granted the railroad right-of-way; (2) the 1871 congressional approval of the right-of-way; (3) the 1871 appraisal agreement for payment of damages; (4) two Oneida WPA stories recalling a ninety-nine-year lease; and finally, (5) a 1970 article by Oneida elder Woody Webster on the expiration of the ninety-nine-year lease. This information was given to the Oneida law office and the opinion was that the land might well belong to Oneida because the documents did not ever say the land was sold to the railroad. The railroad had only a right-of-way for use of the land.

Meanwhile, the tribal historic preservation officer, Corinna Williams, and I were being badgered nearly every day by the railroad to give approval for the tracks to be removed. The NSTB required the railroad to consult with the Oneida Nation on a Section 106 basis because removal of the tracks could affect cultural resources. A letter was sent to the railroad and the NSTB stating that the Oneidas did, in fact, have concerns regarding the removal of the railroad track and the possible impact on cultural resources. The archaeological study on the Duck Creek corridor identified twenty-one sites along the railroad corridor that are cultural resources. The twenty-one archaeological sites predated the 1822 arrival of the Oneida people to the present reservation.

Prior to 1822, the land now known as the Oneida Nation of Wisconsin Reservation had been Menominee and Ho-Chunk (Winnebago) land. Therefore, developing a Memorandum of Agreement (MOA) for the removal of the tracks included the Menominee and Ho-Chunk Nations. Our tribal historic preservation officer contacted both nations, and they agreed to participate in the MOA. Federal law requires that all parties involved must submit a MOA. Negotiations continued with the Oneida, Ho-Chunk, and Menominee nations and the railroad. The Oneida land management attorney, Loretta Webster, conducted a title search. At first, it was thought that real property law would show that the railroad land belonged to the individual property owners along the railroad line; however, her research revealed that real property law did not apply because the railroad right-of-way was never allotted during the 1887 allotment act.

The information gathered by the Oneida planning department, the Office of Land Management, the law office, cultural heritage department, environmental, and transportation department was discussed at a meeting with the Oneida Business Committee, who directed that the law office write a letter to the railroad informing them that the Oneida Nation continued to own the land, and that the railroad could not turn the land over to the

DNR. At this point the law office and the business committee conducted negotiations with the railroad. This case could have become a long court battle; however, the research clearly showed that the Oneida Nation had never sold the land to the railroad. Therefore, it was determined that the abandoned railway continued to belong to the Oneida Nation, and an MOA was drafted.

An Oneida railroad team was officially established to work together on the return of the land, and to take this information to the community. The first community meeting was held on February 4, 2003, in order to provide the information to the community and to begin collecting community input on how to use the land once it is returned to our Nation. The meeting was well attended and the information was shared.

During the fall of 2002 and into the spring of 2003, work continued on two MOAs: (1) for return of the land to the Oneida Nation, and (2) for the removal of the railway tracks. Both MOAs were formally completed and signed by all parties in January 2003. On August 6, 2003, the railroad presented a check for ninety-three thousand dollars to the Oneida business committee. Thus, the process for return of the abandoned railroad land to the Oneida Nation was set in motion.

Notes

1. Railroad agreement between Green Bay and Lake Pepin Railway Company and Oneida Nation, June 3, 1870, oLMd.ONIW.

2. An Act Granting the Right of Way to the Green Bay & Lake Pepin Railway Company for Its Road Across the Oneida Reservation in the State of Wisconsin. U.S. Stat. Chap. 142, March 3, 1871.

3. Woodrow Webster, a respected Oneida elder, is the grandson of Chief Cornelius Hill, one of the signatories to the original railway agreement of 1870.

4. WPA stories on file at Oneida Cultural Heritage Department, Oneida, Wis.

5. Appraisal Agreement, January 21, 1871, oLMd.ONIW.

6. 86 U.S., 591 (1873). For more on timber pressures, see Hauptman and McLester, *Chief Daniel Bread,* 131–59.

19

The Railroad and Wisconsin Oneida Tribal Lands

A Legal Memoir

Loretta R. Webster

The 1800s were a time of unparalleled westward expansion in the United States. Both state and federal governments were anxious to promote and support development of an efficient method of transportation for settlers and their products. Railroads appeared to be the transportation answer, but it was an expensive answer.

Private investors were not readily drawn to the risk of building railroad lines across vast empty spaces of the country. Congress was the first to come through by developing a system whereby public subsidies could be provided to private enterprise. The federal government granted some 130 million acres of public lands to railroads and loaned more than 60 million dollars. By 1850, more than nine thousand miles of track had been laid in the United States, the most extensive being in the Northeast.

In the Midwest, there was a need for a cheap route to transport Minnesota's surplus grain to market, and the Wisconsin timber industry needed rail service to carry in its supplies. Settlers pressed for transportation to carry them to public lands, and then to transport their excess agricultural goods. All these factors combined to motivate the formation of a railway company between the two states. As early as 1846, the Green Bay and Minnesota

Railway Company was organized and was granted a charter by the state of Wisconsin. Railroad land-grant scandals plagued the southern portion of Wisconsin, and the Green Bay and Minnesota Railroad was never built because of lack of funds.

In 1866, the Green Bay and Lake Pepin Railroad Company received a state charter. Four and one-half million dollars had to be raised to build the railroad. Efforts to obtain land grants from Congress had failed and the Wisconsin constitution specifically prohibited state assistance for internal improvements. After substantial effort by the Green Bay and Lake Pepin commissioners, the state passed an act that granted to cities and towns along the proposed railroad route the right to vote aid for its development. Many communities were pledging money if the railroad came their way, and spikes were finally driven in Green Bay on November 3, 1871. By July 17, 1873, the railroad was nearly completed.

Within a year, the control of the railroad passed from those who first promoted it into the hands of the Lackawanna Iron and Coal Company of Pennsylvania. Plans were made to extend the line to Winona, Minnesota, but the actual cost to do this ran about two times what had been originally estimated. The company went through a series of bankruptcy proceedings and eventually went into receivership in 1878. The property was then sold at foreclosure and conveyed for two million dollars to John Blair, a wealthy New Yorker who had already invested heavily and successfully in the Chicago and Northwestern line. The railroad became the Green Bay, Winona and Saint Paul Railway Company and was incorporated in 1881 for the purpose of taking over the Green Bay and Minnesota line.

The Green Bay and Western Company was born in 1896 through a series of complicated financial dealings, which transferred all the property of the Green Bay, Winona and Saint Paul Railway Company to it. The capital structure, indentures, and bylaws of the Green Bay and Western Railroad are unique in the railroad industry. They were set up in 1896 by a New York law firm to prevent the recurring bankruptcies that plagued the railroad. The end result was a business that must pay its bills before any security holder can take a profit.

The Oneida Tribe's initial contact with the railroad dates back to 1869. Oneida Indian agent, John Manley, wrote the U.S. Indian Office on behalf of the Green Bay and Lake Pepin Railroad concerning the right-of-way through the Oneida reservation. Agent Manley informed the Indian Office that he had told the railroad that a right-of-way through the Oneida reservation would be approved by the Indian Office if it was secured by an act of Congress.

In May 23, 1870, the Indian agent for the Oneidas sent a communication to the Indian Office that was signed by thirteen of the fourteen Oneida chiefs giving the consent of the tribe to a right-of-way for the railroad. This agreement allowed the railroad to "construct and operate" their railway across the reservation. It provided that damages to Indian property as a result of the right-of-way would be appraised, determined, and awarded "as if the lands belonged to white persons." In 1870, the land on the Oneida reservation was held communally with the members of the tribe living on assignments of land. The land was not held in "allotments" or individually owned tracts of land. The agreement signed by the chiefs was approved by President Grant in June 1870, and subsequently on March 8, 1871, Congress approved the act granting the right-of-way to the Green Bay and Lake Pepin Railway Company. This act stated that it was passed "in accordance with and subject to the conditions of an agreement made by the chiefs and headmen of the Oneida Tribe of Indians."

The meaning of the simple provisions of the agreement and act of Congress have been an issue with the Oneida tribal government almost from the moment it was signed. During the latter part of the 1800s and throughout the 1900s, the Oneidas have consistently complained that compensation for damages done by the right-of-way was never paid. Railroad officials claimed that compensation was made, and further, that the Wisconsin state statutes placed a limit on seeking further compensation. (The chiefs' agreement states the railway activities were "subject to the laws of the State of Wisconsin"). Joseph Hart, superintendent of the Oneida Indian School, followed through with a 1903 complaint to the Indian Office. After several other documents were passed on to the Indian Office, the acting commissioner for the

Indian Office wrote Superintendent Hart that his report "closes the matter in so far as any unsettled claims against the company are concerned."

In 1937, Mr. Fred Daiker, assistant to the commissioner of Indian affairs requested, on behalf of the Oneida Tribe, the appraisal for the Oneida reservation and a listing of how damages were paid out by the railroad. A Mr. Halladay from the railroad's engineering department returned an itemized list of payments that were made to tribal members. In 1948, Andrew Beechtree, secretary of the Oneida Indian Reorganization Act government (tribal council), again raised the issue of payment of damages by the railroad to the tribe. This correspondence from Mr. Beechtree went to the Tomah Indian agency and then on to the commissioner of Indian affairs. BIA correspondence seems to indicate that to answer Mr. Beechtree's inquiry they sent the itemized list of payments, which they received in 1937, to tribal members of the Oneida Tribe. In addition, there was a hearsay report from one of the Oneida executive committee members saying that his grandfather had told him that consideration for damages was paid to the chiefs. The chiefs then gave the tribal members some benefit from the transaction by issuing permits to individual members that allowed them to remove and sell timber from a stated number of rods in the right-of-way.

The first correspondence found in the Office of Land Management files that questions the title or ownership of the land over which the railroad was built is a letter from Senator Gaylord Nelson dated February 22, 1963. The letter is written to Hon. Philleo Nash, commissioner of Indian affairs, and simply says: "Mr. Norbert S. Hill of Oneida, Wisconsin, has written me asking for information about the 99-year right-of-way lease through Oneida Tribal land by the Green Bay and Western Railroad. He also asks for a copy of the original lease. Is such information available? If so, please send it to me for forwarding to Mr. Hill. Many Thanks." At the time, Norbert S. Hill was on the elected executive and business committee. In less than two months (a blink of an eye for those who wait years for the BIA to answer a query), Deputy Commissioner John O. Crow sent a "copy of an instrument approved by

President Grant on June 3, 1870, whereby the Chiefs of the Oneida Nation of Indians consented to the construction and operation of a railway across the Oneida Reservation by the Green Bay and Lake Pepin Railway Company." No further explanation was given.

In 1972, the BIA area director responded to a query about the railroad ninety-nine-year lease in a memo to the superintendent of the Great Lakes agency. This memo provided a little more clarity to what the status was of the land used by the railroad. In part, it said:

> Documents from your files indicate the Green Bay and Western Railroad Right of Way was acquired by agreement with consent of the Chiefs of the Oneida Nation of Indians which was the basis for an Act of Congress dated March 3, 1871 (16 Stat. 588) granting the land for the purpose of constructing a railway. The original recipient was the Green Bay and Lake Pepin Railway Company and the consent and grant by act of Congress make no reference to a term of years or leasehold condition. The railroad has a right by said Act of Congress to occupy and use the 100-foot wide easement for perpetuity; however, there may be further questions as to ownership of the land upon abandonment. It would appear that the land is still tribal property (or with the landowner of record) since the grant was for construction and maintenance. Considering the fact that an Act of Congress granted use rights, it is doubtful any lease exists and certainly no lease authority applicable to the Oneida Tribe extends any 99 year authority. If you have additional information as to the origin of the belief that a 99 year lease exists, please advise us so a check on it can be made.

This short paragraph answered a query from Billy Bolin for a title status report on the railroad right-of-way easement. Some people in the Oneida community may remember him as the BIA field representative with an office at the first tribal building on the corner of Fish Creek Road and County Road H. His request for information on the railroad right-of-way through the Oneida reservation did not get a clear answer, but it raised the concept of a railroad easement, with use rights in perpetuity. There was plenty of law on this subject, and an easement does not transfer title from the original owner.

The laws of easements and rights-of-way was not researched as to how it related to the railroad through the Oneida reservation until 1998. At this time the Fox Valley and Western (FVW) Railroad was asking for payment from the tribe for running water, sewer, and fiber optic lines under the track and to the Little Bear Development Center. In addition, the Wisconsin DNR had the railroad through the Oneida reservation on certain of their rails-to-trails maps. The rails-to-trails program is federally funded. It allows a state or municipal government the right to convert an abandoned railroad bed into a public trail. Under the federal act, this public trail could be called back into service as a railroad should it be warranted by some public emergency. This federal program was also called rail banking. Both the state and the FVW railroad were acting as if they, not the Oneida Tribe, owned the land, and the Oneida Business Committee asked the Oneida law office to provide an opinion on title to the railroad right-of-way.

Mike Lokensgard, an attorney with the Oneida law office, wrote a lengthy memo on the subject of who owned title to the land over which the railroad ran. It discussed the history of the right-of-way through the Oneida reservation and looked at nineteenth-century laws and cases to understand federal railroad policy at that time. Attorney Lokensgard concluded that the 1871 right-of-way granted to the Green Bay and Lake Pepin Railroad by the Oneida chiefs and Congress did not include a title interest in the lands. He went on to state:

It is questionable whether the Fox Valley and Western (originally the Green Bay and Lake Pepin) is in a position to be able to charge the Oneida Tribe for the privilege of subterranean track crossings (other than for costs associated with insuring that such crossings do not damage the rails and repairing any damage that occurs).

Given the language of the Oneida Agreement, the Fox Valley
and Western's right would appear to be limited to those activities
associated with the operation and maintenance of the track bed
and rails. The Oneida Agreement limited the Green Bay and
Lake Pepin, and the Fox Valley and Western as its successor-in-
interest, to using the right-of-way for those "usual" purposes
associated with such rights-of-way. While the permission of the
Fox Valley and Western would be required for work within their
right-of-way, it would not appear that the Fox Valley and Western
has any rights to the land under the track bed which would allow
them to charge a fee for subterranean track crossings.

Based on Attorney Lokensgard's opinion, the Oneida Tribe did
not pay for going under the railroad tracks to run various service
lines to the Little Bear Development Center as it was being built.

On October 3, 2000, FVW gave notice to the Oneida Tribe that
it was petitioning the NSTB for authority to abandon the railroad
line going from Green Bay to New London. Approximately ten
miles of the railroad goes through the Oneida reservation. FVW's
petition triggered a process for negotiating the use of the railroad
bed for "trail use/rail banking under 49 CFR 1152.29." The NSTB
set the first deadline as December 21, 2000, for local entities to
respond that they were interested in managing the abandoned
railroad right-of-way for "trail use/rail banking" as allowed by
federal law. The Oneida Tribe was not interested in requesting "trail
use/rail banking."

Further, the Oneida Business Committee did not want any
Wisconsin governmental entity authorized to do this on the portion
of the railroad that ran through the reservation. Concerns about
transport of hazardous waste and jurisdictional issues formed
the basis for the official Oneida tribal response to the NSTB. On
January 5, 2001, a letter from the Oneida tribal chairman went
to FVW, the NSTB, and the Wisconsin DNR. This letter indicated
that the Oneida Tribe supported the abandonment of the railroad
but did "not approve of any negotiation between the railroad and
the State to establish a State Trails System through the Oneida
Reservation."

Throughout the year 2001, FVW continued to keep negotiations open with the Wisconsin DNR and DOT for a "Rails-to-Trails Agreement" for the entire railroad right-of-way, including the portion through the reservation. The land management attorney, working with a small team of interested staff people—mainly from the cultural heritage and environmental departments—focused on finding proof that title to the railroad easement remained with the Oneida Tribe of Indians of Wisconsin, and that it was still held in the same status as when the chiefs signed the original agreement in 1871. By August 2001, it was fairly clear that the 1887 allotment act and federal laws regarding railroad rights-of-way had not taken away Oneida Indians' title to the hundred-foot wide railroad easement. Title search further confirmed that the railroad easement had been specifically excluded from the legal descriptions of most allotments when they were surveyed and passed to individuals by patent.

By January 2002, the Oneida Business Committee was ready to approve a legal strategy based on the title information. Direct negotiation with the FVW general attorney was implemented by the Oneida chief counsel and a staff attorney. This was recently successfully concluded with the signing of an agreement by the Oneida Tribe and FVW Railroad. Upon abandonment, FVW will relinquish any interest it may have in the land it has been using for a railroad through the Oneida reservation, and the company acknowledges that the title is retained and owned by the Oneida Tribe, as reserved by the U.S. government in 1838.

The easement given to the railroad in 1871 by the Oneida chiefs will be officially abandoned sometime before July 31, 2005. Thus begins a new era of regulation and planning for the use of the hundred-foot-wide right-of-way through the Oneida reservation. The next era is in the hands of the Oneida people and the Oneida government.

Note

All documents mentioned in this memoir are found in the records of the Oneida Law Office and the Office of Land Management, ONIW.

20

Four Oneida WPA Stories
about Land Loss

Editors' Note: The following four WPA stories told by Oneidas illustrate the pressures that these Indians faced in the age of allotment.
There were federal efforts to push the allotment policy; the newly
created towns of Oneida and Hobart whose officials imposed new tax
burdens on the Indians; and also outright "flim-flam" men, Indian and
non-Indian, who perpetrated frauds to secure Indian fee simple patents.
Two of the stories suggest that Carlisle and Hampton Indians worked
against tribal interests. Yet, one of the same stories takes pride in that
Oneidas were star athletes at the boarding schools.

[Dawes] General Allotment Act

Filmore Cooper

This is what happened when we divided up the land on the
reservation. The Government passed the [Dawes] General Allotment Law, which it tendered to the Oneidas. It was a referendum
law, that is it was up to each tribe to accept it or not. It said, if
we accept it, they will divide up our land. Ninety acres to the
man who is the head of a family. And those of legal age but
can't find a mate, they will receive forty five acres. Those who
are still dependent will be entitled to twenty six acres. And when

they have received their share, an interval of twenty five years shall elapse when they shall be examined to see if it is all right for him to take over the white man['s] laws. But it was not so. It did not agree with the Oneidas because he was not educated[.] [H]e could not understand such law. The Oneida was not used to being harnessed. He was used to being a free man. He himself, would determine when he shall sleep.

Before They Started to Pay Taxes

Rachel Swamp

The way it used to be before they started to tax them for their land, and personal property, such as houses, cows, pigs, chickens and sheep. They had lots of horses, cattle, etc, and they used to be all over in the woods, and also where the land was cleared, and not in cultivation. They got along nicely, and no one bothered them, and everybody got along fine. We used to have lots of horses and cattle, etc, but when they started to make us pay something every year, (what the white people call tax)[.] [T]hen we began to get behind. We finally had only ten acres left, when my husband died.

In Deceit

Levi Baird

We could say we lived in Heaven up to the time a devil came to us Oneidas. He was well paid too. [H]e got two thousand dollars of inducing and urging the Oneidas to become tax payers and this Government Agent worked with him. He got all the people together at the Parish Hall for a meeting. He talked so much and explained that so many white people were coming into Oneida and not being taxed so it is best to establish a town[.] [T]hen all of the people will pay taxes. All the older men disagreed with him so he failed at this meeting and he was so disappointed[.] [T]hen he went around and talked to different people especially those who were against him and he paid them two hundred dollars each to work on his side. So a few days after he called another meeting and all those men who were against him were on his side so the majority of the people voted on his side. So the Township was established and they called it the Town of Hobart. The Oneidas then started to pay taxes and just about five years after this some Oneidas got behind with their taxes and some began to lose what they had, because they were not accustomed to paying taxes. Now days there is hardly an Oneida who have their own home. It has always been so that if anything turns up it always ends in a loss for the Oneidas. This man who worked for this was an Oneida Indian[.] [H]e was hired by white men to bring this on, where the Oneidas live.

Property and Loss of Land

Guy Elm

The Oneida Indians were allotted the land in the years 1888 [actually 1892]. Before that time the land was owned by the tribe as a whole, and held in trust by the United States Government. The Oneidas had their agent or Supt. [Superintendent] as he was called by the Oneidas. His job was to handle all transactions between the Oneida tribe and the United States Government. And also to look after the Oneidas in their well fare in general. . . .

Some time in 1904 [actually 1906] the fee simple patents were issued to the Oneidas, but it was only for inherited, heirship property that the Oneidas could sell, and they sure disposed of it in hurry, some by effecting loans on these heirship property, some by selling at its face value and the rest by crooked land sharks working with the Oneidas called "spotters." These few Oneidas [were] suppose[d] to be well educated [and] were graduates of Carlisle and Haskell Indian schools. They were instrumental in causing their people to loose their land and property. Some years later, I think it was in 1910 [actually 1906–1917], the deeds were issued to the Indians that the agent thought were competent, and they call[ed] themselves citizens. These people also were the victims of the crooked educated Oneidas and the land sharks. But it was worse than what happened to the people before on the heirship land property. Because this time, they lost everything they owned.

The dealings were about the same in some instance[s], [then] what they used [to be] before. Only that it was more streamlined in its effect to [cause the] ruination for the Oneidas. I'll give you an example just how it was done. Usually these Oneidas who were hired by the real estate man to work together were called spotters. Well, these went around the barrooms in the surrounding towns and cities on Saturdays. The Oneidas called this day "Injun day" because it was a day when all the Oneidas went to town to do their trading and drinking sprees. These spotter[s] usually had [a] big roll of money so that they could treat their prospective victims with intoxicating liquors. When they got them drunk, they then told them where they could get a loan on their property, to buy we'll say [a] team of horses, or perhaps [a] few cows and also farm implements, or to buy materials to improve their homes. And still later the automobile caused the Oneida tribe [to become] landless.

On Monday these fellows would go to town and make their report with a list of names to their boss the real-estate man. The next procedure was to bring the Oneida who wanted to get a loan to the real estate man's office to make the deal. He was instructed to bring his deal along with him. The same Oneida that are working with the land sharks acted as their interpreters with the Oneidas and whites. The loans were from $200 dollars to $600 and more, depending on the value of the property.

If the deal was agreed, then the interpreter would tell his fellow tribesman that the only thing to do now was for him to sign the contract for his loan. At this stage of [the] game some times the real estate man would try to slip the deed along with the rest of the papers to get the Indian's signature on it too if possible, and if he didn't sign then he was adviced to leave his deed there in care of [the] land dealer for safe keeping. Usually in time they got his signature on it, signing [over] of his deed to them. Some-times [it occurred] when he had [a] few drinks of liquor, and was short of funds[.] [H]e would go to the office, and demand . . . more loan [money] and[,] at the same time[,] sign his deed on his own free will. It is true that some of the land were sold on fair deals. But I am sure that I wouldn't be exaggerating to give you the figures in percentage basis from my own personal opinion

[of] the result of these land deals between the whites and the Oneidas. I would say that at the present time the whites own about 99 percent of the land that was once the original Oneida Reservation, and the Oneidas still own [only] one percent of it. This 99 percent own[ed] by the whites, 75 percent of it was acquired by means of crooked deals. And the balance . . . was gotten on reasonable deals. Now, who was [to] . . . blame for it. I would say, the Indian department at Washington for keeping an agent here in Oneida, that was doing more harm for the Oneidas then [than] trying to help them because he was also in the ring with the real estate man and the rest. The scheme of the plan to beat these Oneidas were so worked out to perfection that there was no recourse from any angle for them in the courts. Besides I doubt if they did get a case of law . . . in the courts, or if they would get a fair trial, because the majority of the white people in our neighboring cities are prejudice[d] against us Oneida Indians for reasons that I must say, I don't know. Perhaps they haven't forgot the [Mohawk's] Deerfield Massacre in New York State [actually Massachusetts] years ago or it might be that in recent years we have met the white man's football teams on the field of battle. It was our only chance to get a revenge on them from all the cheating they have committed against the Indian through out the United States. And usually the Indians gave them [a] good beating at football. Just look back at the records of Carlisle, Haskell and some other Indian school, and the prove [proof] is right there.

Editors' Note: The Oneidas in the age of allotment did not simply react to efforts by the towns, counties, and the state of Wisconsin to acquire lands and resources or to extend their jurisdiction by taxing the Indians. The Wisconsin Oneidas and Oneida communities in central New York and Ontario were also focused on dealing with long-standing grievances that dated back to the 1780s. Memories of being defrauded of their lands in central New York did not fade with time, even in their new settings in Wisconsin and Canada. By the mid-nineteenth century, only thirty-two acres of six million acres of the Oneida homeland remained in New York.

The three Oneida communities were never isolated from each other. Oneidas from Wisconsin and Canada visited the homeland or appealed for justice in Albany. Agricultural fairs brought Canadian Oneidas to Wisconsin, and Oneida singers traveled back and forth. Lacrosse matches brought healthy competition among communities. Moreover, on occasion, Oneidas from one reservation found their future spouses in the other communities. The large presence of Wisconsin Oneidas at Indian boarding schools, especially at Carlisle and Hampton, brought them in contact with New York Oneidas and helped them reestablish bonds between these two communities. One of those youngsters at Carlisle was William Hanyost Rockwell, whose family member Abraham Elm was to file the first important civil rights case involving an Oneida (see Part V). Oneida legal struggles that occurred from 1876 to 1920 have had a long-term impact on the three communities. Indeed, the roots of the contemporary Oneida land claims case in the federal courts began with the case *United States v. Boylan* in 1920 (see Part V).

Fighting Back in Federal Courts, 1876–1920

Introduction

Overview

The Oneidas' legal struggles are a major focus of tribal history. Three major federal cases shaped Oneida Indian history from 1877 to 1920. These were *United States v. Elm* (1877), the Kansas Claims (1838–1905), and *United States v. Boylan* (1920).[1]

Abraham Elm, an Oneida Indian, attempted to vote in a congressional election. In 1876, he was arrested, indicted for illegally voting, tried, and convicted. Elm, born at Oneida, New York, in 1842, was a Civil War veteran, having been a member of Company B of the Fifth Vermont Volunteer Infantry. In 1877, upon appeal, the U.S. District Court heard Elm's arguments and concluded he was a U.S. citizen and consequently had the right to vote in the election. Despite winning his freedom, Elm and his Oneida people actually lost the case. The federal court held that the New York state legislature had allotted the Oneida Indian Reservation in 1843 after the main body of the tribe migrated to Wisconsin. Blinded by racism and ignorance about the Oneidas, federal Judge Wallace insisted that these Indians were no longer culturally, linguistically, or socially set apart from the surrounding non-Indian population, and that a distinct Oneida community no longer existed in New York. As a result, Elm, although born an Oneida Indian, no longer had a tribal affiliation.[2]

In order to reach judgment in the case, Judge Wallace had to answer the question of whether the Oneida Indians were citizens of the United States and were therefore entitled to vote. According to the judge, this question depended on the viability of the tribe. The judge went on to argue that had the Oneidas maintained their "tribal integrity" and had Elm continued to recognize his tribal relations, not attempting to vote in an American election, he would not have been a citizen under the Fourteenth Amendment. The judge found the facts to be otherwise; the Oneidas of New York had not maintained their tribal identity and Elm had "abandoned his tribal relations." The judge found the Oneidas of New York to be citizens of the United States and the state of New York, "entitled to the corresponding rights which spring from that relation." In deciding that the Oneidas were citizens, the judge applied a principle that U.S. citizenship was inimical to the existence of a viable tribal relationship.[3]

The second federal case, the Kansas Claims, dated from 1838. In that year, the Iroquois and allied Indian nations entered into an agreement at Buffalo Creek to move to lands set aside for them west of the Mississippi River. The federal government allotted 1,824,000 acres to the parties of the 1838 treaty; nevertheless, few Indians emigrated west, and of those who went out, most returned.[4] The U.S. government opened these lands to white settlement, thus depriving the Indian tribes of their title. As a result, the U.S. Supreme Court subsequently rendered a judgment of $1,967,056 in favor of these Indians; however, the Court did not decide to whom moneys were to be awarded or on what basis they were to be allocated. The Court left these matters to the U.S. Court of Claims to decide.[5]

In 1905, the U.S. Court of Claims recognized that tribal communities had undergone major changes since 1838. Oneida society had significantly been altered, thus presenting problems in determining eligibility.[6] As the court noted, it would be impossible to determine "who were the communal owners in different groups and scattered homes of more than five thousand Indians on a given day forty-five or sixty-seven years ago."[7] The court held that the only equitable way was to treat the three Oneida bands as a single community, basing eligibility on the membership requirements of each of the three groups. Consequently, the Court of Claims found that, as far as the Canadian Oneidas were concerned, their migration to Southwold, Ontario, did not sever their ties to the United States and that they were a recognized party to the Buffalo Creek Treaty of 1838. For the Oneidas of New York, the decision meant that they were considered a federally recognized tribe with the right to enter into litigation against the United States and to secure compensation derived from such suits.[8]

The Kansas Claims case had a major impact on the Oneidas. The Court of Claims findings modified the Elm decision by recognizing the continued existence of an Oneida tribal unit, irrespective of the citizenship status of its membership. The court indicated that the three separate Oneida communities—each with its own membership and qualifications, and differences in organization and location—represented a single community recognized by Washington. In essence, the Court of Claims held that the changes in these three communities since 1838 did nothing to alter their tribal status or end the obligations of the United States to the three bands.[9] This favorable decision also prompted the Oneidas to pursue other legal remedies.

The third case, *United States v. Boylan et al.* (1920), involved the attempt of a non-Indian family to gain control of the remaining thirty-two acres of the original Oneida reservation by foreclosing and evicting the Oneida residents from lands these Indians had lived on since aboriginal times. By 1885 these lands had accrued a mortgage of $1,250. The Indian occupants of the land—Mary George, Isaac and Nicholas Hanyost, and Mary Shenandoah— "lost" the property through a foreclosure sale and soon faced eviction. In 1905 the land was sold off to a Michael and Kathryn Burke who, the following year, resold the land to Julia Boylan. In 1906 Boylan then took legal action that resulted in the evictions of the four Oneidas three years later.[10]

As a result of effective Oneida lobbying, the federal government intervened on the side of the Indians in an attempt to overturn these evictions. In 1920, the U.S. Circuit Court of Appeals held that the New York Oneidas continued to be a tribe under the protection of the federal government, that the evictions were not sanctioned by federal law or even pursuant to state statutes, and that federal guardianship was rooted in the special status of Indians in the American polity. The court held that the determination of tribal viability did not hinge on the preservation of past Indian customs and forms. Consequently, the decision basically overturned *United States v. Elm* and justified the right of the U.S. government to intervene in the Boylan case to carry out its federal trust responsibilities to these Indians. In effect, the judges insisted that the control over and determination of policy for federally recognized Indian tribes was the particular responsibility of Congress when there was an absence of specific legislation abolishing federal tribal status. Hence, the Court of Appeals restored the thirty-two acres of the approximately six million acres that the Oneidas had held in 1784 to this Indian nation. This landmark Boylan decision further stimulated Oneida efforts to seek legal redress against New York State, which continue down to the present day.[11]

Notes

1. *United States v. Elm*. U.S. District Court, Northern District of New York—Albany, case no. 15,048, 25 Fed. Cas. 1006–1008, December 24, 1877 (See Appendix C); *New York Indians v. United States,* U.S. Court of Claims doc. no. 17861 (1905); *United States v. Boylan et al.* 265 F. 165 (2d Cir. 1920), appeal dismissed 257 U.S. 614 (1921).

2. *United States v. Elm* (1877).

3. Ibid.

4. For the Treaty of Buffalo Creek (Jan. 15, 1838) and its Amended Treaty with the Oneidas at Washington (Feb. 3, 1838), see Kappler, *Indian Affairs,* vol. 2, reprinted as *Indian Treaties, 1778–1883* (Mattituck, N.Y.: Amereon House, 1972), 502–18.

5. *New York Indians v. United States* (1905).

6. Campisi, "Ethnic Identity," 432–35.

7. *New York Indians v. United States* (1905).

8. Ibid. See also Campisi, "Ethnic Identity," 435–36.

9. Campisi, "Ethnic Identity," 437–40.

10. *United States v. Boylan* (1920). For more on this landmark case, see Campisi, "Ethnic Identity," 437–40; Philip Otto Geier, "A Peculiar Status: A History of the Oneida Indian Treaties and Claims: Jurisdictional Conflict within the American Government, 1775–1920." (Ph.D. diss., Syracuse: Syracuse University, 1980); Anthony Wonderley, *Oneida Iroquois Folklore, Myth, and History: New York Oral Narrative from the Notes of H. E. Allen and Others* (Syracuse: Syracuse University Press, 2004), 196–219; George Shattuck, *The Oneida Land Claims: A Legal History* (Syracuse: Syracuse University Press, 1991), 44–46.

11. *United States v. Boylan* (1920). Hauptman, *The Iroquois Struggle for Survival: World War II to Red Power* (Syracuse, N.Y.: Syracuse University Press, 1986), 179–204.

21

United States v. Elm
25 Fed. Cas. 1006
Case No. 15,048.
[December 24, 1877]

WALLACE, District Judge. The defendant, an Oneida Indian, who was born and had always resided within the town of Lenox, Madison county, voted for representative in congress at the election of 1876, claiming to be a citizen of the United States. He was indicted for illegal voting, tried, and convicted in this court. Sentence was suspended by the court in order that the questions presented on the trial, and which were then formally ruled against the defendant, might be deliberately considered and decided upon a motion for a new trial. That motion has been made, and the question is now presented whether or not the Oneida Indians are citizens of the United States, and, as such, entitled to vote.

If the defendant was a citizen of the United States, he was entitled to exercise the right of suffrage. The right to vote is conferred by the state, not by the United States, and it has been conferred in New York upon "every male citizen of the age of twenty-one years who shall have been a citizen for ten days and an inhabitant of this state one year next preceding an election, and for the last four months a resident of the county, and for the last twenty days a resident of the election district in which he may offer his vote." By the fourteenth amendment to the constitution it is declared that "all persons born or naturalized in the

United States and subject to the jurisdiction thereof are citizens of the United States and of the state wherein they reside," and by force of this language every citizen of the United States is a citizen of the state wherein he resides. It is not enough to confer citizenship on the defendant that he was born in the United States. It must also appear that he was "subject to the jurisdiction thereof," within the meaning of the fourteenth amendment.

In a general sense every person born in the United States is within the jurisdiction thereof while he remains in the country. Aliens, while residing here, owe a local allegiance, and are equally bound with citizens to obey all general laws for the maintenance of peace and order which do not relate specially to our own citizens, and they are amenable to the ordinary tribunals of the country. But there are classes of residents who, though they may be born here, are not subject to the exercise of those prerogatives of sovereignty which a government has the right to enforce over its own citizens, and over them alone, and it is to these that the language of the amendment applies. Within this sense, those persons who, though born here, are born within the allegiance of a foreign sovereign, or of another government, are not subject to the jurisdiction of the United States. The children of ambassadors, though in fact born here, are, in the theory of the law, born within the allegiance of the foreign power the parent represents.

Indians who maintain their tribal relations are the subjects of independent governments, and, as such, not in the jurisdiction of the United States, within the meaning of the amendment, because the Indian nations have always been regarded as distinct political communities, between which and our government certain international relations were to be maintained. These relations are established by treaties to the same extent as with foreign powers. They are treated as sovereign communities, possessing and exercising the right of free deliberation and action, but, in consideration of protection, owing a qualified subjection to the United States.

If defendant's tribe continued to maintain its tribal integrity, and he continued to recognize his tribal relations, his status as a citizen would not be affected by the fourteenth amendment; but such is not his case. His tribe has ceased to maintain its tribal integrity, and he has abandoned his tribal relations, as will here-after appear; and because of these facts, and because Indians in this state are subject to taxation, he is a citizen, within the meaning of the fourteenth amendment. This conclusion is sanctioned not only by the language of the fourteenth amendment, but is fortified by other legislation by congress concerning citizenship.

By Act Cong. 1866, c. 31 [14 Stat 27], commonly known as the "Civil Rights Bill," all persons born in the United States and not subject to any foreign power, excluding Indians not taxed, are declared to be citizens of the United States. Native Indians in this state are taxed. By an act of the legislature passed in 1843, native Indians are authorized to purchase, take, hold, and convey real estate, and, when they become freeholders to the value of $100, "are subject to taxation and to the civil jurisdiction of courts of law and equity in the same manner and to the same extent as citizens." When by the civil rights bill Indians not taxed were excluded from the classes upon which citizenship was conferred, upon well-settled rules of construction those who were taxed were by implication included in the grant. In other words, those Indians who were taxed were not excepted from the class who were declared to be citizens.

Previous to the adoption of the fourteenth amendment, it had been held by high authority that congress might naturalize Indians by special act (7 Op. Attys. Gen. 746); and, of course, if this could be done by special act, it could by a general law, and the act in question would confer citizenship on the defendant. No doubt can be entertained of the power of congress to declare what persons shall be recognized as citizens of the United States, and when, by the fourteenth amendment, such citizens were declared to be citizens of the several states in which they should reside, the whole subject of citizenship was transferred to the jurisdiction of congress, and the rights of the defendant could safely rest upon the act in question. It is not necessary, however, to decide that the Indians in this state became citizens by force of the civil rights bill. I prefer to regard that act as a contemporaneous con-struction of the meaning of the fourteenth amendment. The civil rights bill was passed by the same congress which adopted the resolution to submit the fourteenth amendment to the legislatures of several states. Both the amendment and the civil rights bill dealt with the question of citizenship, and in the declaration defining the class of persons to whom it was extended language almost identical was used in each. While, primarily, these measures, originated for the protection of natives of African descent, who, by the decision in the case of Scott v. Sandford, 19 How. [60 U.S.] 393, were held not to be citizens of the United States, within the meaning of the constitution, it is not to be doubted that they were intended to confer the rights of citizenship upon such others as, owing to the peculiar condition of our national development, were not citizens in legal contemplation, though by birth and by allegiance they were or might become entitled to recognition as such.

The phraseology employed is sufficiently broad to include Indians who have abandoned their tribes and become so far integrated with the general body of citizens that the states in which they reside have subjected them to the duties of citizens and enforced over them the prerogatives of sovereignty. Prior to the adoption of the fourteenth amendment, many of the Indian tribes had become disintegrated, and the members had abandoned their tribal relations, and were distributed among and assimilated with the general body of citizens of the state in which they lived, conforming to the same usages, and their rights of person and property regulated by the same laws, which controlled the rest of the inhabitants of the state. They were natives by birth, and were not aliens in allegiance. Their status had been defined, sometimes, as that of alien residents; sometimes, as that of domestic subjects. In the case of Scott v. Sandford, 19 How. [60 U.S.] 404, Chief Justice Taney said: "If an individual Indian should leave his tribe, and take up his abode among the white population, he would be entitled to all the rights and privileges which would belong to an emigrant from any other foreign people." Accepting this as a correct statement of the law, it would follow that such an Indian was not, and in the absence of special legislation could not become, a citizen. He could not be naturalized, because the naturalization laws only apply to persons born out of the United States. The remarks of Chief Justice Taney were applicable to that class of Indians who had left their tribes, and thus abandoned their tribal relations; but instances were extant, in the history of the Indians tribes, where the tribal organization had become defunct, and where the individual Indians had so far been recognized as citizens of the state that they had been authorized to acquire and hold real estate, and subjected to taxation and to the civil jurisdiction of the courts. It had never been authoritatively decided whether or not such Indians were citizens.

In 1822 the supreme court of this state decided, in Jackson v. Goodell, 20 Johns. 187, that the Indians resident in this state were citizens, but that decision was reversed by the court of errors. Since that decision, however, great changes have taken place in the social and political relations between the Indians and the body of citizens at large, as is well illustrated by the history of the Oneidas. By treaties between the United States and the Six Nations, the Menominees, and Winnebagoes in 1831 and 1838 the Six Nations acquired extensive cessions of lands in Wisconsin near Green Bay; and about that time the main body of the Oneidas removed to these lands. Since then, the tribal government has ceased as to those who remained in this state. It is true those remaining here have continued to designate one of their number as chief, but his sole authority consists in representing them in the receipt of an annuity which he distributes among the survivors. The 20 families which constitute the remnant of the Oneidas reside in the vicinity of their original reservation. They do not constitute a community by themselves, but their dwellings are interspersed with the habitations of the whites. In religion, in customs, in language, in everything but the color of their skins, they are identified with the rest of the population. In 1843, by an act of the legislature of this state, they were authorized to hold their lands in severalty, according to a partition which had theretofore been made. Reference has already been made to the general law of this state, passed in 1843, subjecting them to taxation and to the jurisdiction of the courts in the same manner and to the same extent as other citizens. In view of the changes which have intervened in the social and political relations of the Indians of this state since the decision of Jackson v. Goodell, there is certainly fair reasons to assume that, irrespective of the fourteenth amendment, they would now be held to be citizens of the state. However that might be, those who, like the defendant, have no tribe, and are taxed, are, within the language of the fourteenth amendment, subject to the jurisdiction of the United States, as that language should be interpreted in the light of the civil rights bill. They are natives, they owe no allegiance other than to the government of the United States, and they have been placed by the state upon an equality with its citizens respecting important rights denied to aliens. As the state and the United States can impose upon them all the duties and obligations of subjects, they are entitled to the corresponding rights which spring from relation. These are the rights which a government owes to its citizens.

For these reasons, my conclusion is the defendant was entitled to vote, and was improperly convicted. The motion for a new trial is granted.

22

United States v. Boylan et al.
No. 167
Circuit Court of Appeals, Second Circuit
265 F. 165; 1920 U.S. App. LEXIS 1388
March 3, 1920

PRIOR HISTORY:

In error to the District Court of the United States for the Northern District of New York.

OPINION BY: MANTON

OPINION: Before WARD, HOUGH, and MANTON, Circuit Judges.

MANTON, Circuit Judge. The United States government instituted this action for the purpose of ejecting the defendants below from 32 acres of land situated in the city of Oneida, Madison County, N.Y. The action is brought on behalf of certain Oneida Indians, under the claim that they are the wards of the federal government, and that the government has legal capacity to intervene in their behalf and eject from the said premises the defendants below, who claim title. Their title depends upon the following alleged conveyances:

On April 1, 1885, several deeds of conveyance were made by some of the original twenty-three Indians mentioned in the treaty of 1842 made by the state of New York with the Oneida Indians. Isaac Hanyost, a descendant of Margaret Charles, mentioned as one of the tribe in the treaty of 1842, gave Philander Spalding a mortgage to secure the payment of $1,250 on a portion of the premises here in question. This mortgage was recorded April 2,

1888. On April 4, 1888, it was assigned by Spalding to Patrick Boylan and duly recorded. Shortly prior to July 3, 1897, Patrick Boylan died leaving a last will and testament, which was duly probated on July 8, 1897, and letters testamentary were issued to Joseph Beal, his sole executor named in the will. He duly qualified. The will gave the mortgage to Boylan's wife. In March, 1905, the executor commenced a statutory foreclosure of said mortgage by advertisement and, in addition, publishing and posting a copy of the notice of the sale at the office of the Hotel Brunswick at Oneida, N.Y. This notice was served on some of the Oneida Indians, but not all. The affidavits in that proceeding do not disclose who was then in occupation of the premises. The names of the persons served are given, but their relationship to the tribe is not clear. The sale actually took place on July 15, 1905, and the property was sold for $1,250 on the bid of Michael Burke of Oneida, N.Y. On August 29, 1905, Burke and his wife conveyed the premises by quitclaim deed to the defendant below, Julia Boylan. Philander Spalding and wife conveyed the same premises on July 10, 1906, by quitclaim deed, to Julia Boylan.

Julia Boylan commenced an action in the Supreme Court of the state of New York for the partition of the property here in question, and this by filing the summons and complaint and notice of pendency of action. In this proceeding, Mary George, Noah George, Henry George, Maggie, wife of Henry George, William Honyost, Mrs. William Honyost, wife of William Honyost, and Isaac Honyost, were made defendants. Chapman Schenandoah and his wife were subsequently made parties. The defendants entered an appearance through their attorneys. Such proceedings were taken that a partition of said property was had, the interests of the various defendants were determined and fixed, and the report of the referee appointed was rejected by the Supreme Court justice when the proceedings reached him on a motion for confirmation. This, however, was subsequently reversed by the Appellate Division of the Supreme Court of the state, and a final judgment was entered confirming the same, and the referee was directed to execute to the purchaser a conveyance of the property sold. Boylan v. George, 133 App. Div. 514, 117 N.Y. Supp. 573.

After deducting the costs and allowances incident to this litigation, and awarding to the plaintiff such moneys as she was entitled to in those proceedings, a deficiency judgment was awarded against the defendants for $6.05. Thus the interest of the Oneida Indians in this property was alleged to be extinguished. At the time these proceedings took place, the Oneida Indians were in possession and occupied them until they were ejected through the proceedings in the Supreme Court. By virtue of a writ of assistance, issued by that court, they were forcefully ejected and removed against their protest. The referee appointed in the state Supreme Court, partitioned the property as follows:

(1) That Julia Boylan was seized and entitled in fee simple to an undivided thirty-one fortieths of same. Her title, if any, came through such statutory foreclosure and quitclaim deeds mentioned.

(2) Mary George was seized and entitled in fee simple to an undivided three-fortieths of same.

(3) Henry George was seized and entitled in fee simple to an undivided one-fortieth of same, subject to the inchoate right of dower of his wife, Maggie George.

(4) That William Honyost was seized and entitled in fee simple to an undivided one-fortieth of same, subject to the inchoate dower right of his wife.

(5) That Chapman Schenandoah was entitled to an undivided four-fortieths of same, subject to the inchoate right of dower of his wife.

(6) That Isaac Honyost had no interest therein.

In the proceedings to partition the property, neither the United States, nor the state of New York, nor the Commissioner of Indian Affairs, nor the Oneida Indians were made parties to the suit. The lower court has found as a fact that the Oneida Tribe of Indians were actually in possession and occupation of the lands in question, together with the adjoining lands, which form a part of the original Oneida Indian reservation. In May, 1842, a treaty was made between the first and second Christian parties of the Oneida Indians and the state of New York. At this time the lands in question, together with the other adjoining lands, were set apart by this treaty to the Oneida Indians then remaining on the reservation. It is on behalf of these Indians that this action is brought. The Oneida Indians were natives of the soil lying within the limits of the state of New York when it was organized. In 1794 the United States government entered into a treaty (7 Stat. 44) with the Six Nations of Indians residing within the state of New York, and one of these was the Oneidas. That treaty provided in article 2:

> The United States acknowledge the lands reserved to the [Indians] . . . in their respective treaties with the state of New York, and called their reservation, to be their property, and the United States will never claim the same, nor disturb them . . . nor their Indian friends residing thereon and united with them in the free use and enjoyment thereof; but the said reservation shall remain theirs until they choose to sell the same to the people of the United States, who have the right to purchase.

Some of the Indians moved from the reservation in New York state to Green Bay, Wis. These immigrations took place in 1840 and 1841, under the regulations and supervision of the federal government. The right was given to the Indians as a tribe to dispose of their lands in the state of New York, if they decided to move to Green Bay and there accept other lands allotted to them. After this, the Indians remaining held a single and undivided tract reserved out of the original Oneida reservation. It was in 1842, when the commissioners of the land office of the state of New York, then constituting the Indian department of the state, arranged that the state purchase such portion of the reservation as represented the equitable share in the proportion to the number of Indians who migrated in 1842 to Green Bay, Wis. The result of this was the treaty of 1842, herein referred to, in which all of the remaining Indians joined. Some 1,110 acres were surveyed and divided into 19 lots. Article 1 of the treaty provided as follows: That the Oneidas—

> do hereby grant, bargain, sell, cede, and surrender to the people of the state of New York, all the right, title, estate, and interest

of the said party of the first part in and to all that part of their
reservation not heretofore released by said party of the first
part to the party of the second part, known and distinguished
as lots numbered 1, 3, 4, 5, 7, 10, and 15 by Nathan Burchard's
map and certificates of survey, containing 371.34 acres.

Articles 2 to 5, inclusive, provide for sales of such lands so
ceded, and for payments to the Indians named in Schedule A,
known as "Emigrating Party." Article 6 provided:

It is hereby stipulated and agreed that those members of the
first and second Christian parties of the Oneida Indians as are
included in Schedule A hereby release, quitclaim and forever
renounce to the said Indians named in Schedule B and to those
who may succeed them in their right, title and interest, claim or
demand, whatsoever in and to the said portion of land so set
apart, described, reserved and allotted for those of the first and
second Christian parties of said Indians who do not at present
intend to migrate, enrolled in Schedule B as aforesaid, all and
the residue of the said reservation not now nor heretofore
ceded to the people of the said state, known and distinguished
as lots numbered two, six, eight, nine, eleven, twelve, thirteen,
fourteen, sixteen, seventeen, eighteen and nineteen as surveyed
and allotted by Nathan Burchard. Reference is here had to the
said map and field book of the said Nathan Burchard, and to
be filed in the offices of the secretary of state and surveyor
general; when copies thereof are indorsed thereon and duly
authenticated by him, they shall for ever be deemed the metes
and bounds of the lands ceded and those reserved. And those
reserved shall be deemed the common property of all the individuals included in Schedule B.

Article [6] provided that the Indians should surrender the
lands, and, if they belong to those named in Schedule A, such
Indians should, on payment, immediately migrate and go beyond
New York; but, if they belonged to Schedule B, then such persons
were given possession of the lands so ceded. Thus the Indians in

the reservation were divided into two classes. The lots numbered seventeen and nineteen, which are involved in this litigation, came under Schedule B. Schedule B gave the names of the "tenants in common and owners of lots 17 and 19," and these did not migrate. The following are those named as tenants in common and owners:

Aaron Cooper, Hannah Cooper, Dollay Cooper, Margaret Cooper, Susan Cooper, Betsy Cooper, Jenney Cooper, Moses Cooper, Moses Charles, Caty Charles, Margaret Charles, Susan Charles, Mary Charles, Elizabeth Cornelius, Daniel Cornelius, Roderic Cornelius, Jenney Cornelius Job, alias Anthony Antone, Cornelius Antone, Thomas Antone, Mary Antone, Mary Antone, and Susan Antone.

No specific lot or parcel was attempted to be allotted or set off by the treaty to any individual Indian as his or her separate share. Under article 6 of this treaty, the migrating party, referred to in Schedule A, quitclaimed and renounced to the home party, named in Schedule B, and to those who might succeed them in interest, all of the rights in the lots reserved to them. The treaty provides for the succession in interest of their successors, and not "heirs and assigns." Both parties named in the treaty joined in ceding said lands, which were to be sold by the state and the proceeds of which were to go to the migrating party. There is nothing in the treaty which indicates a partition of lands embraced in lots 17 and 19 as between the 23 individual Indians, nor did the treaty mention or contemplate any future partition between individuals. The state Constitution (article 1, section 15) provides that no purchase or contract of sale of land in this state made with the Indians shall be valid, unless made under the authority and with the consent of the Legislature. This was attempted by the state Legislature. Chapter 185, Laws 1843. That enactment provides as follows:

Section 1. The Oneida Indians owning lands in the counties of Oneida and Madison are hereby authorized to hold their lands in severalty in conformity to the surveys, partitions and schedules annexed to and accompanying the treaties made with the said Indians by the people of this state in the year one thousand eight hundred and forty-two and now on file in the office of the secretary of state, and the lots so partitioned and designated by said survey to said Indians shall be deemed to be in lieu of all claims and interest of the said Indians in and to all other lands and property in the Oneida reservation. . . .

Sec. 2. The Governor shall appoint a superintendent of the Oneida Indians. . . .

Sec. 3. It shall be lawful for the said superintendent of the Oneida Indians, upon application made to him for that purpose, by any Indian or Indians owning lands as aforesaid, to sell and convey such lands to the person or persons so occupying. . . . A deed of an Indian shall be valid to convey the title of himself, his wife and minor children, and every deed executed by virtue of this act shall be acknowledged by the grantor before the first judge of Madison county, and the consent of the superintendent shall be indorsed thereon, and when so executed and acknowledged and certified, shall be recorded in the county in which said land shall lie, with the same effect as other deeds.

Sec. 5. The said superintendent shall, with the consent of a majority of the chiefs and head men of the said Indians, sell and convey the above mentioned lots of land, held according to Indian usages, and sanctioned by treaties with them on the part of this state, as the common property of all the Oneidas who did not cede their lands to the people of this state previous to the treaty made with them, March 8, 1841, for a fair price unto any purchaser or purchasers, by requiring from them cash payments. And the conveyances shall be made, executed, and acknowledged by the said superintendent; and the consent of the chiefs and head men in council shall also be acknowledged in the presence of an officer duly qualified to take acknowledgments of deeds. . . .

Sec. 6. The deeds and conveyances made as aforesaid shall convey all the right, title and interest of the said Indians or Indian whose lands shall have been conveyed as aforesaid

of, in and to the same, and shall vest in the purchaser or purchasers, his or their heirs and assigns, forever, an absolute
estate of inheritance in fee simple.

Later the state Legislature passed an act (chapter 420 of the
Laws of 1849), for the benefit of Indians, by the terms of which
it was provided, among other things, that as to all tribes or
bands of Indians who occupied Indian reservations within the
state or hold lands therein as a common property, such tribes or
bands may, by the acts of their respective Indian governments,
divide such common lands into tracts or lots and distribute or
partition the same in parts thereof, quantity and quality relatively
considered, to and amongst the individuals or families of such
tribes or bands, respectively, so that the same may be held in
severalty and in fee simple, according to the laws of the state;
but no lands occupied and improved by any Indian according to
the laws, usage, or custom of the nation shall be set off to any
person other than the occupant or his or her family. It was further
provided that, in the event of distribution or partition, the deeds
to be made to effect the same deed be made by such officers or
commissioners as the government shall appoint and the commissioners of the land office shall approve, but, before any such
deeds be executed, the proceedings and acts authorizing such
execution and appointing the parties so to do, shall be authenticated and approved before and to the satisfaction of the county
judge in the county in which the land to be conveyed shall lie,
and be recorded in the clerk's office of the county. It was further
provided that every deed which shall be executed under such
authority shall be acknowledged before the county judge by the
parties who executed it, and such judge shall examine the deeds
and see that they be in due form and in pursuance of the authority
under which they be executed, and indorse on such deed certificate shall authorize the county clerk to record such deeds in the
records of the deeds of the county. It was further provided that
no lands thus distributed and partitioned should be alienable by
the grantee thereof, or his heirs, and such grantee, for 20 years
after the date of the recording of the deed thereof, but they may

be partitioned amongst the heirs of any grantee who shall die, and the same shall not be subject to any lien or incumbrance by way of a mortgage, judgment, or otherwise.

This enactment attempted to provide the manner and mode of partitioning the lands of Indians, with a view of safeguarding such conveyance, and guarded against the same being subject to any lien or incumbrance by way of any mortgage or otherwise. The Indian law of the state provided this. Birdseye' Revised Statutes, vol. 2, pp. 1408 (published 1896). This record indicates clearly that these requirements of the same statute of 1849 were not followed with reference to the deeds to the property here in question.

The state subsequently, by chapter 45, Laws of 1857, § 4, prohibited taxation of Indian reservation lands so long as the lands remain the property of the tribe or band occupying the same. Likewise the state made it a misdemeanor for a person to purchase or to attempt to purchase lands from any Indian, or claiming title thereto, without authority and consent of the Legislature (section 384a, Penal Code of New York). Thus it is admitted by the state that the Indian lands within the state are exempt from the state jurisdiction, at least so far as taxation is concerned. The record title does not disclose any deed or attempt to make a deed whereby all of the twenty-three Indians mentioned in the treaty of 1842 ever conveyed or attempted to convey to any one their interest in the property. Some of the twenty-three did attempt to make such conveyance by deeds. No partition was ever made of lots 17 and 19 by the tribe or band of Indians, as required by chapter 420, Laws of 1849. Congress has in no way approved or consented to a partition or other disposition of the lands in question. But here, where an attempt was made to convey an interest of any of the Indians referred to since 1849, the provisions of the act have not been complied with; that is, the requirement for certification by the county judge of the county of the conveyance made by the Indians. The record discloses that between twenty-three and thirty-five Indians hold and enjoy the land here in question from the date of the treaty with the United States government in 1794 down to the time of the eviction above referred to.

The first question presented is the right of the United States to maintain this action. The trial judge has found that the Oneida Indians were a distinct people, tribe, or band. With this finding we agree. The record does not disclose, as contended for by the defendants below, that the people have been completely incorporated with us and clothed with all the rights and bound by all the duties and obligations of the state of New York. Since the Indians exist as a separate band or tribe, and therefore as a separate nation, the exclusive jurisdiction over the Indians is in the federal government, and the right to maintain an action in their behalf under the federal Constitution is solely vested in the federal government. Heckman v. U.S., 224 U.S. 413, 32 Sup. Ct. 424, 56 L. Ed. 820. The highest court of the state of New York has recognized this jurisdiction: Seneca Nation of Indians v. Christie, 126 N.Y. 122, 27 N.E. 275.

It is only where Congress has enacted legislation controlling the disposition of property of Indian reservations that valid conveyances may be made. In this way the restrictions imposed upon the sale of such lands are removed by the act of Congress. U.S. v. Waller, 243 U.S. 452, 37 Sup. Ct. 430, 61 L. Ed. 843. Congress alone has the right to say when the guardianship over the Indians may cease. U.S. v. Nice, 241 U.S. 591, 36 Sup. Ct. 696, 60 L. Ed. 1192; Tiger v. Western Inv. Co., 221 U.S. 286, 31 Sup. Cot. 578, 55 L. Ed. 738. Accordingly it has been held that it is for Congress to say when the tribal existence shall be deemed to have terminated, and Congress must so express its intent in relation thereto in clear terms. Until such legislation by Congress, even a grant of citizenship does not terminate the tribal status or relieve the Indian from the guardianship of the government. U.S. v. Nice, 241 U.S. 591, 36 Sup. Ct. 696, 60 L. Ed. 1192. The highest court of the state of New York has recognized that the federal government has never relinquished its suzerainty over the Indians of New York, even though the state of New York has legislated, granting powers to the Indians to regulate their own affairs and to protect their lands from invasion. People ex rel. Cusick v. Daly, 212 N.Y. 183, 105 N.E. 1048, Ann. Cas. 1915D, 367. The federal government made various treaties with the Six Nations of Indians in the state of New York, one as early as 1784, and again in 1789 and 1794. Later, in 1838, another treaty was entered into relating to their lands, and again in 1842. It appears that Congress provides funds for their support under various treaties and appropriations. See Annual Reports of U.S. Comm. of Indian Affairs, Dept. of Interior. The Court of Appeals said in People ex. rel. Cusick v. Daly, supra:

> Under our dual form of government, in which there are two distinct sovereignties, federal and state, each is supreme within its appropriate sphere. They exercise their respective powers in the same territory, each being independent of the other, and each having its separate executive, legislative, and judicial departments. This division of government, while simple in theory, frequently presents practical complexities which it is difficult to harmonize. One of our most troublesome problems has arisen over the status of the Indians in our political economy. They were the original occupants of our soil, and we have treated them as semi-independent nations, subject in some degree to both state and federal laws. Although greatly diminished in numbers, and restricted to reservations which are insignificant remnants of their former hunting grounds, they have maintained their tribal relations and customs, according to which they are to some extent permitted to govern their own affairs. Yet they are not citizens, either of the United States or of this state. The problem is further complicated by the fact that the history of some of the tribes within our own state differs widely from that of other tribes in the other sections of the country. 212 N.Y. 191, 105 N.E. 1050, Ann. Cas. 1915D, 367.

The Supreme Court, in Fellows v. Blacksmith, 19 How. 366, 15 L. Ed. 684, referred to the New York Indians as wards of the nation, and that court held that they could not be removed from their lands in New York state by the state courts, but that the power resided solely in the federal government. In an early case (Samuel A. Worcester v. State of Georgia, 6 Pet. 515, 8 L. Ed.

483) it was held that the state of Georgia, one of the original 13 colonies, could not enforce an act for the punishment of persons on the Cherokee reservation, where the provisions of the statute in question were in conflict with the treaty between the Cherokee Nation and the federal government. There the court clearly recognized that the Indian tribes, irrespective of their locality, were under the protection of the federal government. The Supreme Court held in the Case of The New York Indians, 5 Wall. 761, 18 L. Ed. 708, that the treaties entered into between the Indians and the government prevented the state from taxing such lands, and this because of the guaranty of tribal rights of the Indians by the various treaties of the United States. In United States v. Sandoval, 231 U.S. 28, 34 Sup. Ct. 1, 58 L. Ed. 107, the court said:

> Not only does the Constitution expressly authorize Congress to regulate commerce with the Indian tribes, but long-continued legislative and executive usage and an unbroken current of judicial decisions have attributed to the United States as a superior and civilized nation the power and the duty of exercising a fostering care and protection over all dependent Indian communities within its borders, whether within its original territory or territory subsequently acquired, and whether within or without the limits of a state. 231 U.S. 45, 46, 34 Sup. Ct. 5, 58 L. Ed. 107.

And in United States v. Kagama, 118 U.S. 375, 6 Sup. Ct. 1109, 30 L. Ed. 228, the court said:

> The power of the general government over these remnants of a race once powerful, now weak and diminished in numbers, is necessary to their protection, as well as to the safety of those among whom they dwell. It must exist in that government, because it never has existed anywhere else, because the theater of its exercise is within the geographical limits of the United States, because it has never been denied, and because it alone can enforce its laws on all the tribes. 118 U.S. 384, 6 Sup. Ct. 1114, 30 L. Ed. 228.

It will thus be observed that not only has the United States government the sole power to act as the guardian of the Indians of the state whose tribal relation still exists, but it has the sole power to legislate as to the distribution of their lands. Such Indian tribes or bands occupying lands in reservations have always been treated as alien nations. The Indians individually were aliens; neither as nations nor as individuals did they own any allegiance to the European governments. Cherokee Nation v. State of Georgia, 5 Pet. 1, 8 L. Ed. 25. The right of self-government has never been taken from them. It has never been questioned, and no attempt made at subjecting them as a people, and it has always been considered and recognized by the states as a right of the federal government to make provisions for the disposition of their lands, and until such was made by the federal government the right of occupancy remained in the Indians. Worcester v. State of Georgia, 6 Pet. 515, 8 L. Ed. 483. While the state has a right to make treaties with the Indians, it cannot interfere with the right and obligation of the federal government. The federal government cannot deprive the state of those governmental powers which are part of its inherent right. De Geofroy v. Riggs, 133 U.S. 258, 10 Sup. Ct. 295, 33 L. Ed. 642.

At all times the rights which belong to self-government have been recognized as vested in these Indians. Their right of occupancy has never been questioned, but the fee in the soil is in the state. This is a right of ultimate domain, with the right of present possession in the Indians. Congress has never legislated so as to permit title to pass from the Indians to the lots of land here in question. A transfer of the allotment to aliens is not simply a violation of the proprietary rights of the Indians; it violates the government rights of the United States.

If these Indians may be divested of their lands, they will be thrown back upon the nation a pauperized, discontented, and possibly belligerent people. The authority to enforce restrictions of this character is the necessary complement of the power to impose them. Heckman v. United States, 224 U.S. at page 438, 32 Sup. Ct. at page 432, 56 L. Ed. 820.

Our attention is not called to any act of Congress which permitted the Oneida Indians the right to hold the lands of that reservation in severalty or to mortgage or incumber them, nor that the state has conferred any such power, except as above referred to, which places restrictions and points out the method and manner of so doing. There is no authority which will enable one member of the tribe to sell and convey his interest in the reservation to an outsider, and to confer upon such purchaser the right to partition and sell in partition the lands held by several of the tribe in common. No law sanctions the sale of such lands so owned and held in a partition action brought by any person. Section 2116, chapter 3, of the Revised Statutes of the United States, relates to sales by Indians of their lands. It provides:

> That no purchase, grant, lease or other conveyance of lands, or of any title or claim thereto, from any Indian nation or tribe of Indians, shall be of any validity in law or equity, unless the same shall be made by treaty or convention entered into pursuant to the Constitution. Comp. St. § 4100.

A tribe could not sell, nor could the individual members, for they have not an undivided interest in tribal lands, nor alienable interest in any particular tract. Franklin v. Lynch, 233 U.S. 269, 34 Sup. Ct. 505, 58 L. Ed. 954; Gritts v. Fisher, 224 U.S. 640, 32 Sup. Ct. 580, 56 L. Ed. 928. The record here shows clearly that the Oneida Indians hold as tenants in common. Even under the state enactment, they were subject to the restrictions as to mode and manner of making conveyances, and these conditions have not been complied with in the attempted conveyance here in question. There are many acts indicating the exercise and enforcement of the jurisdiction of the federal government over the Indians in the state of New York, as is illustrated in the matters of trafficking in intoxicating liquors. The capacity of the United States to sue for the purpose of setting aside conveyances of land allotted to Indians under its care, where restrictions upon alienation have been transgressed, have been passed upon and reaffirmed. Marchie Tiger v. Western Improvement Co., 221 U.S.

286, 31 Sup. Ct. 578, 55 L. Ed. 738; Bowling v. U.S., 233 U.S. 528, 34 Sup. Ct. 659, 58 L. Ed. 1080; Heckman v. U.S., 224 U.S. 413, 32 Sup. Ct. 424, 56 L. Ed. 820. The Indian tribes are communities dependent upon the United States; dependent largely for their daily food; dependent for their political rights. They owe no allegiance to the states, and receive from them no protection. Choctaw Nation v. U.S., 119 U.S. 1, 7 Sup. Ct 75, 30 L. Ed. 306.

Affirming, as we do, the conclusion reached by the District Court, that the United States and the remaining Indians of the tribe of the Oneidas still maintain and occupy toward each other the relation of guardian and ward, and that the United States may maintain this action, we conclude that the partition action and judgment and the sale made thereunder are void, so far as they eject the Indians from the possession of the property. We do not think that the state of New York could extinguish the right of occupancy which belongs to the Indians. The state has never conferred the absolute and unrestricted right on these Indians to convey these lands, and we further approve the finding below that the attempted conveyance of the land did not comply with the act of 1849. The finding below that the attempted con-veyance of these lands and the judgment of sale and partition is null and void is approved, as is the decree restoring the ejected Indians to possession.

Decree affirmed.

DISSENT BY: WARD

DISSENT: WARD, Circuit Judge (dissenting). The right of the United States to maintain this suit in ejectment depends, as it seems to me, upon the question whether the particular Oneida Indians whom the United States undertakes to represent are or are not tribal Indians. If they are not, the United States has no concern with them. United States v. Nice, 241 U.S. 591, 36 Sup. Ct. 696, 60 L. Ed. 1192. It is true that May 23, 1842, when the treaty between the state of New York and the Oneida Indians was made, they were tribal, and it is said that for this reason the treaty is invalid; the United States not being a party to it. But this can hardly be maintained, in view of the great number of

Indian treaties which the state has made without any approval of or co-operation with the United States, and upon which the title to immense areas of valuable lands depends. See the consideration of this subject by Judge Andrews in Seneca Nation v. Christie, 126 N.Y. 122, 27 N.E. 275. A special committee appointed by the Assembly of 1888 to investigate the Indian problem of the state annexed to their report 14 treaties with the Oneida Indians alone between 1788 and May 23, 1842, in which the United States had no part; the Indians conceding their title to the state of New York and the later treaties fixing the rights inter sese of those Oneidas who wished to emigrate to the West and those who wished to remain on the reservation.

Title to all tribal lands was in the British crown, subject to the Indians' right of occupancy, which title upon the Revolution vested in the colonies, and subsequently in the original states, under the Articles of Confederation and upon the establishment of the present government. The right of pre-emption went with this title to the states. The United States never had either the title to the lands or the right of pre-emption. Harcourt v. Gaillard, 12 Wheat. 523, 6 L. Ed. 716.

By the treaty of May 23, 1842, the Oneida reservation was divided into 19 lots; the Indians known as the Emigrating Party ceded their title to the state in lots 1, 3, 4, 5, 7, 10, and 15, and their title in lots 2, 6, 8, 9, 11, 12, 13, 14, 16, 17, 18, and 19 to the Home Party. Schedule B attached to the treaty enumerates the individuals comprising the Home Party by name and states that they hold their lands in severalty as tenants in common and owners. The lands now in question were part of lot 17, and 23 individuals, comprising 4 families, are named as tenants in common and owners of that lot; in other words, their Indian title of occupancy was changed into a title in fee simple.

This treaty was subsequently confirmed by an act of the Legislature. Chapter 185, Laws 1843. Section 1 provided:

1. The Oneida Indians, owning lands in the counties of Oneida and Madison, are hereby authorized to hold their lands in severalty, in conformity to the surveys, partitions and schedules

annexed to and accompanying the treaties made with the said Indians, by the people of this state in the year one thousand eight hundred and forty-two, and now on file in the office of the secretary of state. . . .

Sections 2, 3, 4, and 5 provided safeguards for the Indians in respect to alienation. Section 6 provided:

6. The deeds and conveyances made as aforesaid shall convey all the right, title and interest of the said Indians or Indian, whose lands shall have been conveyed as aforesaid, of, in and to the same, and shall vest in the purchaser or purchasers, his or their heirs or assigns forever, an absolute estate of inheritance in fee simple.

The earliest deeds of conveyance by Oneida Indians of these lands in the chain of title to the defendants were executed in accordance with the provisions of this act. But, because the later deeds after 1865 were not so executed, the court holds them to be void, and to convey no title to the defendants. This overlooks the fact that chapter 486, Laws 1847, relieves the Oneida Indians from the restriction of chapter 185, Laws 1843, abolishes the office for them, imposes the performance of his duties for two years on the superintendent of Indians, whose office was to cease in two years from the passage of the act, viz. December 15, 1849, and thereafter "the said Indians shall have the power to sell and convey their real estate the same as if they were natural-born citizens of the United States." From that date I think that their tribal relation ceased to exist as matter of law. No wonder that the legislative committee of 1888 reported as to the Oneidas:

They have no tribal relations and are without chiefs and other officers; they as a tribe receive no money from any source, but receive a small annuity from the federal government, amount to about 11 yards of cotton cloth to each person per year.

Judge Wallace held to the same effect in *United States v. Elm*, 25 Fed. Cas. 1006, No. 15,048.

It is said that chapter 420, Laws 1849, still imposed restrictions on the right of the Oneida Indians to convey, which restrictions were not thereafter observed in the deeds in the chain of title to the defendants, and therefore they were void and conveyed no title. This contention overlooks the fact that the act of 1849 applied only to tribal Indians, and did not repeal or qualify in any way chapter 486, Laws 1847, passed for the special benefit of the Oneida Indians.

The laws of New York relating to Indians have been consolidated three times, viz.: Chapter 92, Laws 1813; chapter 679, Laws 1892 (which repealed chapter 185, Laws 1843, and chapter 486, Laws 1847, relating to the Oneida Indians); and chapter 31, Laws 1909, being chapter 26 of the Consolidated Laws. In neither of these two later consolidations are the Oneida Indians mentioned at all, whereas the Onondagas, Senecas, Tuscaroras, the Saint Regis, and the Shinnecock Tribes were and still are regulated by them. It is perfectly clear that the Legislature no longer considers the Oneidas as a tribe or their land in question part of an Indian reservation. The above considerations make inquiry into the powers of Congress unnecessary, because those powers are concerned only with tribal Indians.

The judgment should be reversed.

Afterword

Change and Continuity at Oneida

The modern history of the Oneida Nation of Indians largely begins with the New Deal in the 1930s. The nation adopted bylaws and a constitution, forming a new tribal government after congressional passage of the Indian Reorganization Act of 1934. By that date, the Wisconsin Oneidas had less than ninety acres left in tribal hands. Four years later, scholars at the University of Wisconsin, under the auspices of the federal government, established the WPA Oneida Language and Folklore Project, which lasted until federal funding dried up in the early months of 1942.

These WPA stories, along with the vast documentary record found at the National Archives in Washington, D.C. and at the Wisconsin Historical Society in Madison, clearly show that the Oneidas were not merely acted upon by outside federal, state, and local officials, boarding school administrators, railroad magnates, and land speculators. Oneidas themselves developed diverse ways to maintain tribal existence. They initiated new political strategies, learned new entrepreneurial skills, and grafted on new cultural patterns even in the darkest days of the allotment era. They sought legal action in the federal courts to secure their right to vote, to win monetary compensation under the Treaty of Buffalo Creek of

1838 to protect their tribal interests, and to reclaim lost lands in New York State.

Oneida identity persisted despite efforts to assimilate the Indians and the abusive treatment inflicted on students by some administrators, teachers, and other employees at the federal boarding schools in the United States or at the institutional schools in Canada. The editors have attempted to show that these schools had another side. While most white policy makers aimed to transform the Indian students into white men and women, Oneida parents, mostly impoverished, were more concerned about their children's basic needs and survival. These schools provided food, clothing, and housing to the children. The schools were a window to a white world that was alien to reservation existence. Learning about this world was required for the children's survival. The founding of the Oneida Boarding School, favored by a majority of Oneidas, must also be recognized as an effort by the Oneidas themselves to improve the quality of education on their reservation since the existing day schools run by missionary societies were underfunded and of poor quality.

Oneidas sent many of their children away to far-off boarding schools for reasons that made sense in the age of allotment. The curriculum at Hampton was far more advanced than what was provided in reservation day schools, and bright, highly motivated students such as Josephine Hill (Webster) excelled and brought back skills that were needed by the Oneidas to survive. The music program at Carlisle was world-class by the mid-1890s, leading to accolades for the Wheelocks, Dennison and James, both accomplished artists. Although sports programs, especially at Carlisle, were too often exploitative of Indians' athletic prowess, reservation Indians nationwide were extremely proud of the achievements of their student athletes on the gridiron, in track and field, and at the Olympic games. More important, attendance and success at these schools meant access to future employment, a steady job in Indian boarding schools or in other areas of the federal Indian service. The networking of Indian alumni of these schools made it easier for economic success and political attainments in the future. It must be pointed out that many of the Oneida tribal leaders in Wisconsin, New York, and Canada were students at the boarding or institutional schools. As late as the early 1990s, the Oneida tribal business committee was chaired by Purcell Powless (see Powless, Part II). Other post–Indian Reorganization Act Wisconsin Oneida political leaders such as Oscar Archiquette, Irene Moore, Mark Powless, and Morris Wheelock all attended these schools.

Oneida memories of what happened to them in the age of allotment did not die off and were kept alive from generation to generation. They inspired later assertions of tribal sovereignty and legal activism. The return of tribal lands by the railroad in 2003 is reflective of the great turnaround in Oneida fortunes. Yet, much of what has transpired since that date makes the problems faced by the Oneidas from 1860 to 1920 unrecognizable.

Today, more than sixteen thousand Oneidas occupy a reservation of more than sixteen thousand acres of tribal lands. Over the past forty years, the Oneidas have made their mark politically on the national scene. Robert Bennett was the first American Indian since Reconstruction to be appointed commissioner of Indian affairs, serving in that capacity during the administration of President Lyndon Johnson. In the mid-1970s, Ernest Stevens, Sr., served on the American Indian Policy Review Commission, established by the U.S. Congress. More recently, Richard Hill and Ernest Stevens, Jr., have headed the National Indian Gaming Association.

The Wisconsin Oneidas have become a major force economically as well. They fully own and operate the Radisson Hotel and Conference Center, along with their Oneida Casino, situated just across from Green Bay's Austin Straubel Airport; the Baybank, a full-service bank; the Oneida Industrial Park, a thirty-two-acre land development project with Wal-Mart as its major tenant and anchor store, and with the Oneida Mason Street Casino adjacent to the site; Oneida Printing, a state-of-the-art printing business; Oneida Nation Farms, an agricultural operation on the reservation focusing on cattle and apple raising, that provides discounted food to tribal members; Oneida Retail Enterprise, a chain of four "One Stops," four smokeshops and one gift shop that sell Pendleton blankets as well as gas and discounted cigarettes and serves as mini-marts and mini-casinos; and Seven Generations Corporation, which leases a fifty-thousand-square-foot health facility to Belin Health Systems. Moreover, the Oneida Nation of Indians is an investor, with three other Indian nations, in a Marriott Residence Inn Capitol in Washington, D.C., and is a major shareholder in the Native American Bank, N.A. Recently, during the renovation of the Green Bay Packers' Lambeau Field, the Oneidas contributed moneys to the project, which led to the naming of part of the facility as the "Oneida Nation Entrance Gate."

On August 14, 2003, the Oneida Nation of Indians of Wisconsin held a major conference on the reservation focusing on its tribal history. Attended by over two hundred people, the meeting included an evening of musical entertainment. For the first time since August 1921, Dennison Wheelock's symphony, *Aboriginal Suite,* was performed. The Grieg-inspired piece was performed by the Green Bay Concert Orchestra. The performance by this full ensemble of non-Indian musicians was followed by performances by two Oneida Indian singing societies—one from Oneida, Wisconsin, and the other comprised of Canadian Oneidas from their reserve at Southwold, Ontario. They sang Christian hymns in the Oneida language, influenced by the Presbyterian missionary Samuel Kirkland from the second half of the eighteenth century.

These two distinct performances—of Wheelock's music and of traditional singing—clearly show much about Oneida existence. To survive, the Oneidas have needed to adapt in order to survive, but they have also clung to traditions that date back to their experiences in their central New York homeland. In the age of allotment, the third major crisis in their long history, they were forced to change, but they never abandoned their sense of being Oneida, their connection to other Oneidas in Canada and New York, or their continued efforts at seeking justice, all reinforced by the elders in council, by the WPA stories, or by contemporary historical conferences.

Appendix A

Carlisle Indian School Oneida
Student Names

List of Oneida students found in the archives of the Cumberland County Historical Society [CCHS], Carlisle, Pa; the National Archives Record Group 75 [NARA], Washington D.C.; and in Barbara Landis's personal research files. For source information for the names on this listing, go to www.carlisleindianschool.org. This list is compiled from the Genevieve Bell NARA database, RG75 (310 student folders in File 1327), CCHS library holdings (365 records in manuscript/monograph holdings and 65 photographs), and Barbara Landis's Carlisle Indian School Research web pages (2 names). This information is always being updated as new names/spellings/ corrections are found.

Adams, Lavinia
Adams, Samuel
Antone, Christjohn
Antone, Gertrude
Archiquette, Belinda
Archiquette, Chauncey
Archiquette, Christine
Archiquette, Isaac
Archiquette, Joel

Archiquette, Joshua
Archiquette, Josiah
Archiquette, Libbie
Archiquette, Lillian
Archiquette, Louise
Archiquette, Martin
Archiquette, Sarah
Archiquette, Vivian
Archiquette, William

Baird, Alexander
Baird, Angeline
Baird, Charles
Baird, Elizabeth H.
Baird, Eunice
Baird, Genus L.
Baird, Isaac
Baird, Jonas
Baird, Laban
Baird, Phoebe
Baird, Rome (Roman)
Baird, William
Beechtree, Andrew
Beechtree, Julia
Beard, Daniel
Brown, Joseph
Brown, Lyman
Caswell, Benjamin
Caswell, Leila Corne
Charles, Elias
Charles, Josephine S.
Charles, Wilson
Christjohn, Alpheus
Christjohn, Louisa (Louise)
Christjohn, Martin
Christjohn, Moses
Clynch, Robert
Coates, Henrietta
Coates, Lulu
Coates, Malcolm
Conlon, Angeline
Cooper, Electa
Cornelius, Alice
Cornelius, Alpheus
Cornelius, Amy
Cornelius, Anderson
Cornelius, Briggs

Cornelius, Brigman
Cornelius, Carrie
Cornelius, Casper
Cornelius, Charles B.
Cornelius, Chester P.
Cornelius, Christian
Cornelius, Clara Alma
Cornelius, Cora
Cornelius, Cornilia
Cornelius, Cynthia
Cornelius, Deleila
Cornelius, Delia
Cornelius, Edith
Cornelius, Edwin
Cornelius, Elizabeth
Cornelius, Elsie
Cornelius, Frances
Cornelius, Fred
Cornelius, Harvey
Cornelius, Ida
Cornelius, Isabella
Cornelius, James Millard
Cornelius, Jesse
Cornelius, Joel
Cornelius, John
Cornelius, Joshua
Cornelius, Katie Powlas
Cornelius, Leila
Cornelius, Lillian
Cornelius, Lorenzo
Cornelius, Louie
Cornelius, Louisa
Cornelius (Sickles), Martha
Cornelius, Mary
Cornelius, Mary Frances
Cornelius, Matilda
Cornelius, Melissa

Cornelius, Nancy
Cornelius, Nancy O.
Cornelius, Ophelia
Cornelius, Peter
Cornelius, Phillip
Cornelius, Rose Jerusha
Cornelius, Sampson
Cornelius, Sylvester O.
Cornelius, Thomas
Cornelius, Wesley
Coulon, Angeline
Coulon, Emma Amy
Coulon, Lucy J.
Coulon, Monrow
Coulon, Sherman
Coulon, Sophia
Coulon, Sopley
Daily, George Jr.
Danforth, Antone
Delane, Robert
Denny, Cornelius I.
Denny, Delia
Denny, Elizabeth
Denny, Isabel Cornel
Denny, Joseph
Denny, Sallie (Sally)
Denny, Wallace
Doxtater (Doxtator), Andrew
Doxtater (Doxtator), Dollie
   Wheelock
Doxtater, Fred
Doxtater, Frederick
Doxtater (Doxtator), Reuben
Doxtater, Wilson
Doxtator, Abbie Jane
Doxtator (Doxtater), Alice
Doxtator, Charles

Doxtator, Chauncey
Doxtator, Earl
Doxtator, Hulda (H.)
Doxtator, Mary Jane
Doxtator, Melinda Thomas
Doxtator, Minnie
Doxtator, Phoebe
Doxtator, Robinson
Doxtator, Sophie (Sophia)
Doxtator, Truman Jr.
Doxtator, Wilson
Doxtatore (Doxtator),
   Benjamin
Elm, Andrew
Elm, Arthur
Elm, Chester
Elm, Cora T.
Elm, Fay
Elm, Guy
Elm, Horton G.
Elm, Ida
Elm, John
Elm, Lavina
Elm, Levi
Elm, Margaret
Elm, Ray
Elm, Ruth
Ferm, Celinda D. King
George, David
Green, Edward
Green, Frank
Green, Lena
Green, Mamie
Green, Melissa
Green, Vera
Ground, Norman C.
Hill, Abraham M.

Hill, Abram
Hill, Alison (Allison)
Hill, Calsey
Hill, Cecelia
Hill, Charles
Hill, Electa
Hill, Emma
Hill, Flannigan
Hill, Herman N.
Hill, Hyson
Hill, Hyson N.
Hill, Julia
Hill, Lavina
Hill, Levi
Hill, Lucinda
Hill, Maria
Hill, Marshall
Hill, Martha E.
Hill, Martin
Hill, Mary
Hill, Moses B.
Hill, Nicodemus Herman
Hill, Olive
Hill, Sophia
Hill, Suffye
Hill, Walter
Hill, Zelpha
Hillman, Levi E.
Honyoust (Honiyoust),
    Charles
Honyoust (Honiyoust), John
House, Cornelia Cornelius
House, John
House, Lizzie
House, Lucy Coulon
House, Margaret
House, Wallace

Huff, Lillie (Lily)
Huff, Sophia
Isaac, John
Island, Carrie
Island, Louis
Jacobs, Agnes
James, Hugh
James, Julia
James, Thomas
John, Amelia
John, Eliza
John, Harry
John, Hyson
John, Isaac
John, Jane
John, Jemima
John, Lydia Alida
John, Lyford
John, Nettie
Johns, Minor C.
Johnson, Elizabeth
Johnson, Florence C.
Johnson, Moses
Johnson, Willard
Jordan, Alpheus
Jordan, Elias
Jordan, Ephiram
Jordan, Eva
Jordan, Gertie
Jordan, Ida
Jordan, Peter
Kelly, Ellen
Kelly, Herman
Kelly, William
Kich, Lucinda
Kick, Albert
Kick, Ernest W.

Peters, Moses
Peters, William
Peterson, Elizabeth
Peterson, Madaline
Powias, Ophela
Powlas, Ada
Powlas, Alice E.
Powlas, Alpheus James
Powlas (Powless), Alphian
Powlas, Benjamin
Powlas (Powless), Chauncey
Powlas, Eddie
Powlas, Eli
Powlas, Emmanuel
Powlas, Hattie M.
Powlas, Ida
Powlas, Isaac
Powlas, Jefferson
Powlas, John C.
Powlas, Josiah A.
Powlas (Powless), Julia Ann
Powlas, Manuel
Powlas, Marian A.
Powlas, P. J.
Powlas, Peter
Powlas, Purcell
Powlas, Sadie
Powlas, Whitney
Powlas(s), Katharine E. (Katie)
Powlas(s), Lydia Wheelock
Powless (Powlas), Eugene
Powless, Hyson
Powless, Jesse
Powless, Josiah
Powless, Melvina
Reed, Amos
Rickman, Martha Sickles

Rockwell, Edna
Rockwell, Henry
Skanadore (Schenandore),
    Absalom
Schanondore, Alicia
Shandore, Alonzo
Skenandore, Ami
Skenandore, Annie
Skenandore (Schanandore),
    Baptiste
Skenandore, Ben
Skenadore (Skenandore),
    Darias (Derias)
Skenandore, Dorchester
    (Duncheatuea)
Schanandore (Shanandore),
    Edwin
Schanandore (Schenandore),
    Electa
Skenandore, Eli
Skenandore, Elisabeth
Skanandore (Schenandore)
    (Schenandoah), Elsie
Schanandore, Foster
Skenandore (Schenandore),
    Fred
Skenandore, Harry
Skenandore, Hilton
Schandore, Ida
Skenandore, Jacob
Schenandore (Shanandoah),
    Jane
Schanandore, Jamison
Schenandore (Shanandore),
    Jemima
Skenandore (Scanadoah),
    Jemison

Schanadore, Jenoson
Skenandore, John
Skenadore (Skenandore),
    Josephine
Schenandoah, Leila
Schenandore, Lena
Schanandore, Lillie
Schenandore (Skenandore),
    Louis
Schandore, Louise
Shanandoah, Luch
Schanandore (Schenandore)
    (Schenandore), Lucia
Shanandoah, M.
Skenandore, Madeline
Schenandore, Melissa
Skenandore, Minnie
Schandore, Nancy
Schanandore, Phebe (Phoebe)
Schenandoah (Schenandore),
    Sadie Jane
Skenadore (Schenandore)
    (Schanandore), Sylvester
Schanandore (Schenandore),
    Thomas
Skenandore (Schenandore)
    (Schanandore), Wesley
Schenandore, Whitney
Schenandoah, William Thos.
Schanandore (Schenandore),
    Willie
Schuyler, Alice
Schuyler, Cleveland
Schuyler, Electa
Schuyler, Evelyn
Schuyler, Joseph A.
Schuyler, Josephine

Schuyler, Mellond
Schuyler, Wilson
Sickles, Arthur
Sickles, Caleb M.
Sickles, Elizabeth
Sickles, Florence
Sickles, Fred(erick)
Sickles, Herbert
Sickles, Martha
Silas, Albert
Silas, Alvin
Silas, Anderson
Silas, Cynthia
Silas, Elizabeth
Silas, Fannie
Silas, Mary Louis
Silas, Roger
Silas, Sophia Metoxen
Silas, Wilson
Smith, Abraham
Smith, Abram J.
Smith, Alpheus
Smith, Cirenus
Smith, Dempster
Smith, Frank
Smith, Fred E.
Smith, Harrison B.
Smith, Henry W.
Smith, Jonas
Smith, Josephine
Smith, Juliette E.
Smith, Lillie
Smith, Loomis
Smith, Louisa
Smith, Mary F.
Smith, Nelson
Smith, Oscar

Smith, Sarah E.

Smith, Simpson

Smith, Sirenus

Smith, Thomas

Smith, Wilbough

Smith, Wilson

Somers, Abbie

Somers, Jacob

Summers, Cecilia

Summers, Emmeline

Summers, Frank

Summers, Lucinda

Summers, Richard

Summers, Susan

Summers, Wesley

Swamp, Cecilia

Swamp, Elias

Swamp, Grace

Swamp, Moses

Sweezy, Hattie Powlas

Thomas, Maggie

Thomas, Melinda

Tibbetts, George

Tibbetts, Lillian Cornelius

Two Ax, Juliet Smith

Webster, Allie M.

Webster, Cynthia

Webster, Delia

Webster, Elizabeth

Webster, Emma

Webster, Ephriam

Webster, Evalina

Webster, Harry

Webster, Isaac N.

Webster, Jemima Wheelock

Webster, Jesse

Webster, Joh

Webster, John

Webster, Johnson

Webster, Lafayette

Webster, Lena

Webster, Levi

Webster, Lewis

Webster, Louis

Webster, Lucy

Webster, Mary

Webster, Olive

Webster, Ophelia

Webster, Solomon

Welch, Florence

Wheelock, Amelia

Wheelock, Archie

Wheelock, Austin

Wheelock, Benjamin

Wheelock, Cecelia

Wheelock, Cecilia

Wheelock, Dennison

Wheelock, Dolly

Wheelock, Elizah

Wheelock, Hugh

Wheelock, Ida E.

Wheelock, Ida Powlas

Wheelock, James R.

Wheelock, Jemima

Wheelock, Joel

Wheelock, Joshua

Wheelock, Julia Powlas

Wheelock, Lida (Lidia O.)

Wheelock, Mae

Wheelock, Martha

Wheelock, Martin

Wheelock, Mary

Wheelock, Nancy

Wheelock, Olive

Wheelock, Paul
Wheelock, Percy Mae
Wheelock, Phenus
Wheelock, Phinea
Williams, Ethel M.

Williams, Edgar
Williams, John
Woodman, Thomas
Yudda (Yuda) (Yedda),
    Monteville

Appendix B

Hampton Institute Oneida
Student Names

Editors' note: This partial list was compiled from Oneida tribal records of Hampton Institute held by the records of the Oneida Indian Historical Society and the Oneida Cultural Heritage Department.

Adams, Julius
Adams, Lavinia
Adams, Louisa
Antone, Mary
Archiquette, Irene
Archiquette, Robert Smith
Archiquette, Solomon
Baird, Chauncey
Baird, Ellen
Baird, Emerson Charles
Baird, Laban
Baird, Luella Jane
Baird, Phoebe (Ya-go-win)
Baird, Reuben
Bread, Daniel
Bread, Katie
Bred, Josephine Lucy [NY]

Burning, Ida Mae [NY]
Charles, Josiah
Cooper, Electa
Cooper, Minnie
Cornelius, Cornelia
Cornelius, Eli
Cornelius, Elizabeth Louise
Cornelius, Jerusha
Cornelius, Jesse H.
Cornelius, Julia
Cornelius, Lavinia (Ojiji)
Cornelius, Mason
Cornelius, Rebecca
Cornelius, Sampson
Coulon, Lucy Jerusha
Coulon, Sherman Peters
  (Shawart)

Crisjohn, Susie [NY]
Danforth, Cecilia
Danforth, Janice [Jane]
  (Lanikien)
Danforth, Thomas (Dwnis)
Denney, Charles
Denney, Wilson
Doxtator, Chauncey D.
Doxtator, Chauncey Ruseter
Doxtator, Edward W.
Doxtator, Elizabeth (Libbie)
Doxtator, Eva
Doxtator, Hyson
Doxtator, Jane
Doxtator, Nancy
Doxtator, Peter Juno
Elm, Andrew
Elm, Edward
Elm, Elias E. [NY]
Elm, Horton G. [NY]
Elm, Ida
Elm, Jason
Elm, Lena
Elm, Moses
Elm, Nathan
Green, Augustus (Oneida &
  Sioux)
Green, Flora
Hill, Electa
Hill, Eliza
Hill, Flannigan Kay
Hill, George W.
Hill, Hiram
Hill, Inez Rachel
Hill, Isaiah
Hill, John C.
Hill, John W.

Hill, Jones
Hill, Josephine Gertrude
Hill, Lucinda (Yo-si-na)
Hill, Martha
Hill, Rose
Hill, Rosetta
Hill, Wilson J.
Honyoust, Daniel
Honyoust, William [William H.
  Rockwell] [NY]
House, Eliza
House, George
James, Mary
John, Jane
John, Joshua
John, Marshall [NY]
John, Miner
Johnson, Emma [NY]
Johnson, Stella [NY]
King, Fred
King, Martin
Laymon, Clayton Carl
Laymon, Guy
Ludwick, Lena
Metoxen, Adam
Metoxen, Claudia Clara
Metoxen, Cornelius
Metoxen, Jameson
Metoxen, Joseph
Metoxen, Joshua
Metoxen, Matilda (Tillie)
Metoxen, Minnie Ellen
Metoxen, Nelson
Metoxen, Redmond Marcellus
Metoxen, Wilson
Ninham, Christine
Ninham, John

Parker, Andrew
Parkhurst, Alexander
Parkhurst, Charles
Powless, Abbie
Powless, Alfred
Powless, Cora May
   (Scattering Flowers)
Powless, Ella
Powless, Elsie
Powless, Hattie Belle
Powless, Hyson
Powless, Lyman (Tantetolus
   or Dr. War Eagle)
Powless, Maggie
Powless, Martin
Powless, Olive Jane
Powless, Purcell
Powless, Richard
Reed, Amos
Reed, Isaiah
Reed, Joel
Reed, Melissa (Kahawani)
Scanahdoah (Skenandore),
   Chapman [NY]

Scanahdoah (Skenandore),
   Joel (Taligone) [NY]
Scanahdoah (Skenandore),
   Nicholas [NY]
Scanandore, William Thomas
   [NY]
Sickles, Samuel
Silas, Elsie E.
Silas, Lillie Esther
Silas, Mary Louisa
Skenandore, Abram
Skenandore, Amelia
Skenandore, Amy
Skenandore, Anderson (1st)
Skenandore, Anderson (2nd)
Skenandore, Edward
Skenandore, Eli
Skenandore, Elias (1st)
Skenandore, Elias (2nd)
Skenandore, Elizabeth
Skenandore, Elsie
Skenandore, James
Wheelock, Rhoda Henrietta

Bibliography

Archives and Manuscript Collections

Brown County Library Local History Room, Green Bay, Wis. Scrapbooks; vertical files.

Cumberland County Historical Society, Carlisle, Pa. (CCHS). Records of the U.S. Indian Industrial School. Students' vertical files; Carlisle school publications, curriculum, photographs.

De Pere Historical Society, De Pere, Wis.
Vertical files; photographic archives.

Dickinson College Archives, Carlisle, Pa.
Morgan, James Henry, letters to Richard Henry Pratt.
Carlisle photographs.
Dickinson College Catalogue, 1890–1900 (with Dickinson Preparatory School).

Hampton Institute Archives, Hampton, Va.
Oneida students' records; institute publications.

Library of Congress, Washington, D.C. (LC).
Hughes, Charles Evans, Papers.
LaFollette Family Papers.
Lenroot, Irvine, Papers.
Roosevelt, Theodore, Papers.

Madison County (N.Y.) Historical Society, Oneida, New York.
Oneida vertical files; photographic collection.

National Archives, Washington, D.C. (NA).
Bureau of Indian Affairs (BIA). Central Classified Files (CCF), 1907–1939. RG75.

Indian Claims Commission Records. RG279.

Kansas Claims. Special Case File No. 29. RG75.

Office of Indian Affairs (OIA). Records, 1824–1881, microcopy no. 234 (correspondence with Green Bay Agency [GBAR], 1824–1880; New York Agency Emigration, 1829–1851; New York Agency, 1829–1880); Records, 1881–1907. All in RG75.

Records of the Carlisle Indian School (U.S. Industrial School). Carlisle, Pa. Student files. RG75.

War Department Records. Civil War pension records (CWPR) of the Fourteenth Wisconsin Volunteer Infantry Companies F and G; Adjutant General's Office (appointment, commission, personnel records; compiled military service records; regimental books). All in RG94.

Neville Museum of Brown County, Green Bay, Wis.
Martin, Morgan L., Papers.
Williams, Eleazer, Journal. 1832.

New York State Archives, Albany, N.Y. (NYSA).
Division of Military and Naval Affairs, Records. Adjutant General's Office.
New York State Governor (Charles Evans Hughes), Records.
Investigation case files related to eviction of Oneida Indians, 1909–1910.

New York State Library Manuscript Division, Albany, N.Y. (NYSL).
Beauchamp, William, Papers.
Hough, Franklin Benjamin, Papers.
Parker, Arthur C., Papers.
Society of American Indians Papers (SAI Papers)

Oneida Indian Historical Society, Oneida, Wis., Records

Oneida Nation of Indians of Wisconsin, Oneida, Wis. (ONIW).
Oneida Cultural Heritage Department. Genealogical records; WPA Oneida Language and Folklore Project.
Oneida Land Management Department (OLMD). Allotment, boarding-school, railway-lease records.
Oneida Nation Museum. Photograph collection.

Public [National] Archives of Canada, Ottawa, Ont.
Indian Affairs. RG10.

[Smithsonian] Cooper-Hewitt Museum, New York City.

Sybil Carter Indian Lace Association Pamphlet Collection.

St. John Fisher College, Rochester, N.Y.

Decker, George P., Papers.

State Historical Society of Wisconsin (SHSW). See Wisconsin Historical Society, Madison, Wis. (WHS).

U.S. Military History Institute, Carlisle Barracks, Army War College, Carlisle, Pa.

U.S. Indian Industrial School, Carlisle, Pa., papers; File "Richard Henry Pratt on His Eightieth Birthday."

University of Rochester, Rush Rhees Library, Rochester, N.Y.

Morgan, Lewis Henry, Papers.

Parker, Arthur C., Papers.

University of Wisconsin Area Research Center, Green Bay, Wis.

Archiquette, John, Diary; Holy Apostles Episcopal Church (Oneida) Records; Martin, Morgan L., Papers; Powless, Joseph, Diary.

Wisconsin Historical Society, Madison, Wis. (WHS). Previously known as State Historical Society of Wisconsin (SHSW).

Blue and Red Regimental Books F. Co., Fourteenth Wisconsin Volunteer Infantry

Draper, Lyman, Papers (Frontier Wars Papers Series 11U)

Jones, William, Papers.

Kemper, Jackson, Papers.

Martin, Morgan Lewis, Papers.

McLaughlin, James, Papers.

Montezuma, Carlos, Papers.

Seymour, John F., Papers.

Yale University, New Haven, Conn. (YU).

Collier, John, Papers. Sterling Library.

Pratt, Richard Henry, Papers. Beinecke Library.

MISCELLANEOUS MANUSCRIPTS ON MICROFILM

Iroquois Indians: A Documentary Record of the Six Nations and Their League. Edited by Francis Jennings et al. Woodbridge, Conn.: Research Publications, 1985. Fifty microfilm reels.

The Papers of Carlos Montezuma, M.D. Edited by John W. Larner. Wilmington, Del.: Scholarly Resources, 1883. Nine microfilm reels.

The Papers of the Indian Rights Association. Glen Rock, N.J.: Microfilm Corporation of America, 1975.

The Papers of the Society of American Indians. Edited by John W. Larner. Wilmington, Del.: Scholarly Resources, 1987. Ten microfilm reels.

Newspapers and Magazines

Appleton Crescent

Baltimore Sun

Brown County Democrat (De Pere, Wis.)

Chicago Inter-Ocean

Chicago Journal

Chicago Tribune

De Pere Journal-Democrat

De Pere News

Evening Sentinel (Cumberland County, Pa.)

Gazette-Record-Jeffersonian (Lawrence, Kan.)

Green Bay Advocate

Green Bay Intelligencer

Green Bay Press-Gazette

Indian Helper (Carlisle Indian Industrial School)

Metronome

Milwaukee Journal

Milwaukee Sentinel

Morning Star (Carlisle Indian Industrial School)

New York Herald

New York Sun

New York Times

New York Tribune

Philadelphia Public Ledger

Quarterly Journal (Society of the American Indians)

Red Man (Carlisle Indian Industrial School)

Rocky Mountain Times

Southern Workman (Hampton Institute)

Syracuse Herald

Tulsa Daily World

Court Cases

New York Indians v. United States. U.S. Court of Claims. Doc. No. 17861 (1905).

United States v. Boylan et al. 265 F. 165 (2nd Cir. 1920); appeal dismissed 257 U.S. 614 (1921).

United States v. Cook. 86 U.S. 591 (1873).

United States v. Elm. U.S. District Court, Northern District of New York— Albany. Case No. 15,048, 25 Fed. Cas. 1006–1008, December 24, 1877.

Dissertations and Theses

Basehart, Harry S. "Historical Changes in the Kinship System of the Oneida Indians." Ph.D. diss. Harvard University, Cambridge, Mass., 1952.

Bell, Genevieve. "Telling Stories out of School: Remembering the Carlisle Indian Industrial School, 1879–1918." Ph.D. diss. Stanford University, Palo Alto, Calif., 1998.

Brunhouse, R. L. "A History of the Carlisle Indian School: A Phase of Government Indian Policy, 1879 to 1918." M.A. thesis, University of Pennsylvania, Philadelphia, 1935.

Campisi, Jack. "Ethnic Identity and Boundary Maintenance in Three Oneida Communities." Ph.D. diss. SUNY, Albany, 1974.

Geier, Philip Otto. "A Peculiar Status: A History of the Oneida Indian Treaties and Claims: Jurisdictional Conflict within the American Government, 1775–1920." Ph.D. diss. Syracuse University, New York, 1980.

Gilchrist, Everett A. "Richard Henry Pratt and American Indian Policy, 1877–1906." Ph.D. diss. Yale University, New Haven, Conn., 1967.

Ricciardelli, Alex. "Factionalism at Oneida: An Iroquois Community." Ph.D. diss. University of Pennsylvania, Philadelphia, 1961.

Ricciardelli, C. H. "Kinship Systems of the Oneida Indians." Ph.D. diss. Philadelphia: University of Pennsylvania Press, 1961.

Stovey, Patricia. *Parallel Souls: Studies on Early Twentieth-Century Native American Leaders in Relation to Black Activists W. E. B. Du Bois and Marcus Garvey, 1900–1934.* M.A. thesis. University of Wisconsin, Eau Claire, 2000.

Trosper, Ronald. "The Economic Impact of the Allotment Policy on the Flathead Indian Reservation." Ph.D. diss. Cambridge, Mass.: Harvard University Press, 1975.

Government Publications

Donaldson, Thomas, comp. *The Six Nations of New York.* Extra Census Bulletin of the 11th Census [1890] of the United States. Washington, D.C.: U.S. Census Printing Office, 1892.

Godfrey, Anthony. *A Forestry History of Ten Wisconsin Indian Reservations under the Great Lakes Agency.* Salt Lake City: U.S. West Research, for BIA Branch of Forestry, 1996.

Kappler, Charles J., comp. and ed. *Indian Affairs: Laws and Treaties.* 5 vols. Washington, D.C.: GPO, 1903-1941. Vol. 2, reprinted as *Indian Treaties, 1778–1883.* Mattituck, N.Y.: Amereon House, 1972.

New York State Legislature Assembly. Document No. 51. *Report of the Special Committee to Investigate the Indian Problem of the State of New York.* Appointed by the Assembly of 1888. 2 vols. Albany: Troy Press, 1889. [Popularly known as the Whipple Report.]

————. *Report of the Indian Commission to Investigate the Status of the American Indian Residing in the State of New York, . . . March 17, 1922.* [Popularly known as the Everett Commission Report.]

Reel, Estelle. *Course of Study for the Indian Schools of the United States.* Washington, D.C.: GPO, 1901.

Richardson, James D., comp. *A Compilation of the Messages & Papers of the Presidents, 1789–1897.* 10 vols. Washington, D.C.: GPO, 1896–1899.

Royce, Charles C., comp. *Indian Land Cessions in the United States. 18th Annual Report* of the Bureau of American Ethnology, 1896–1897. Part 2. Washington, D.C.: GPO, 1899.

U.S. Bureau of the Census. Census nos. 1–15, 1790–1920.

U.S. Congress. *Congressional Record,* 1860–1920.

————. House of Representatives. Document No. 251. *Oneida Indians: Letter from the Secretary of the Interior Transmitting Report of Negotiations with Oneida Indians for Commutation of Their Perpetual Annuities as Provided for by the Act of March 3, 1911.* 62nd Cong. 2nd sess. Washington, D.C., 1911.

————. Senate. Subcommittee of the Committee on Indian Affairs. *Hearings on S. Res. 79: Survey of Conditions of the Indians in the United States.* 43 Parts. 70th–76th Cong. Washington, D.C.: GPO, 1928–1943.

U.S. Indian Claims Commission. *Decisions of the Indian Claims Commission.* New York: Clearwater, 1973–1978. Microfiche edition.

U.S. Interior Department. Commissioner of Indian Affairs. Annual Reports 1849–1933.

U.S. Statutes at Large (Stat.). 1871–1906.

U.S. War Department. *The War of the Rebellion: A Compilation of the Official Records of the Union and Confederate Armies.* 128 vols. Washington, D.C.: GPO, 1880–1901.

General Sources

Abernethy, Byron R., ed. *Private Elisha Stockwell, Jr., Sees the Civil War.* Norman: University of Oklahoma Press, 1958.

Adams, David Wallace. *Education for Extinction: American Indians and the Boarding School Experience, 1875–1928.* Lawrence: University Press of Kansas, 1995.

————. "Education in Hues: Red and Black at Hampton, 1878–1893." *South Atlantic Quarterly* 76 (Spring 1977): 159–76.

————. "From Bullets to Boarding Schools: The Educational Assault on American Indians." In Weeks, *"They Made Us Many Promises,"* 154–74.

————. "More than a Game: The Carlisle Indians Take to the Gridiron, 1893–1917." *Western Historical Quarterly* 32 (Spring 2001): 25–54.

Ambrose, Stephen, ed. *A Wisconsin Boy in Dixie: The Selected Letters of James K. Newton.* Madison: SHSW, 1968.

Andrews, Thomas G. "Turning the Tables on Assimilation: Oglala Lakotas and the Pine Ridge Day Schools." *Western Historical Quarterly* 33 (Winter 2002): 407–30.

Antone, Eileen M. "The Educational History of the Onyota'a:ka Nation of the Thames." *Ontario History* 85 (December 1993): 309–20.

Antone, Eileen M., and Nicholas G. Antone. *History of the Oneida Homemakers.* Brantford, Ont.: Woodland Indian Cultural Education Centre, 1978.

Antone, Grafton, ed. *Oneida 1990 Sesquicentennial: In Our Own Stories along the Thames River.* Brantford, Ont.: Woodland Publishing, 1990.

Armstrong, M. F., and Helen W. Ludlow. *Hampton and Its Students.* New York: G. P. Putnam's Sons, 1874.

Barsh, Russel. "American Indians in the Great War." *Ethnohistory* 38 (1991): 276–303.

Beauchamp, William M. *A History of the New York Iroquois.* New York State Museum Bulletin 78. Albany, 1905.

Bieder, Robert E. *Native American Communities in Wisconsin, 1600–1960: A Study of Tradition and Change.* Madison: University of Wisconsin Press, 1995.

Bloom, John. *To Show What an Indian Can Do: Sports at Native American Boarding Schools.* Minneapolis: University of Minnesota Press, 2000.

Bloomfield, Julia K. *The Oneidas.* 2nd ed. New York: Alden Brothers, 1907.

Britten, Thomas. *American Indians in World War I: At Home and at War.* Albuquerque: University of New Mexico Press, 1997.

Campisi, Jack. "Oneida." In *Handbook of North American Indians,* vol. 15, *The Northeast,* ed. Bruce G. Trigger. Washington, D.C.: Smithsonian Institution, 1978, 481–90.

————. "The Wisconsin Oneidas between Disasters." In *The Oneida Indian Journey: From New York to Wisconsin, 1784–1860,* ed. Laurence M. Hauptman and L. Gordon McLester III, 70–84. Madison: University of Wisconsin Press, 1999.

Campisi, Jack, and Laurence M. Hauptman, eds. *The Oneida Indian Experience: Two Perspectives.* Syracuse, N.Y.: Syracuse University Press, 1988.

————. "Talking Back: The Oneida Language and Folklore Project, 1938–1941." *Proceedings of the American Philosophical Society* 125 (December 1981): 441–48.

Carlson, Leonard A. *Indians, Bureaucrats, and Land: The Dawes Act and the Decline of Indian Farming.* Westport, Conn.: Greenwood, 1981.

Castel, Albert. *Decision in the West: The Atlanta Campaign of 1864.* Lawrence: University Press of Kansas, 1992.

Child, Brenda J. *Boarding School Seasons: American Indian Families, 1900–1940.* Lincoln: University of Nebraska Press, 1998.

Christjohn, Amos, and Marie Hinton. *An Oneida Dictionary.* Edited by Clifford Abbott. Oneida, Wis.: ONIW, 1998.

Cohen, Felix S. *Handbook of Federal Indian Law.* Washington, D.C.: U.S. Department of the Interior, 1942; reprint, Albuquerque: University of New Mexico Press, 1972.

Coleman, Michael C. *American Indian Children at School, 1850–1930.* Jackson: University of Mississippi Press, 1993.

Controneo, Ross R., and Jack Dozier. "A Time of Disintegration: The Coeur d'Alene and the Dawes Act." *Western Historical Quarterly* 5 (October 1974): 405–19.

Current, Richard N. *The History of Wisconsin. Vol. 2, The Civil War Era, 1848–1873.* Madison: SHSW, 1976.

———. *Pine Logs and Politics: A Life of Philetus Sawyer, 1816–1900.* Madison, Wis.: SHSW, 1960.

———. *Wisconsin: A Bicentennial History.* New York: W. W. Norton, 1977.

Dean, Eric T., Jr. *Shook over Hell: Post-Traumatic Stress, Vietnam and the Civil War.* Cambridge, Mass.: Harvard University Press, 1997.

Deloria, Vine Jr., and David E. Wilkins. *Tribes, Treaties and Constitutional Tribulations.* Austin: University of Texas Press, 1999.

Duncan, Kate L. "American Indian Lace Making." *American Indian Art* 5 (Summer 1980): 28–35, 80.

Ellis, Albert G. "Fifty-four Years' Recollections of Men and Events in Wisconsin." *Wisconsin Historical Collection* 7 (1876): 207–68. Reprint, Madison: SHSW, 1908.

Episcopal Church Mission to the Oneidas. Oneida: The People of the Stone: The Church's Mission to the Oneidas. Oneida, Wis.: Episcopal Church of the Holy Apostles, 1899.

Fries, Robert F. *Empire in Pine: The Study of Lumbering in Wisconsin, 1830–1900.* Madison, Wis.: SHSW, 1951.

Fritz, Henry Eugene. *The Movement for Indian Assimilation, 1860–1890.* Philadelphia: University of Pennsylvania Press, 1963.

Geary, James W. *We Need Men: The Union Draft in the Civil War.* DeKalb: Northern Illinois University Press, 1991.

Graymont, Barbara. *The Iroquois in the American Revolution.* Syracuse, N.Y.: Syracuse University Press, 1972.

Greenwald, Emily. *Reconfiguring the Reservation: The Nez Perces, Jicarilla Apaches and the Dawes Act.* Albuquerque: University of New Mexico Press, 2002.

Grinnell, George Bird. "Tenure of Land among the Indians." *American Anthropologist* 9 (January 1907): 1–11.

Hagan, William T. *The Indian Rights Association.* Tucson: University of Arizona Press, 1985.

————. "Private Property: The Indians' Door to Civilization." *Ethnohistory* 3 (Spring 1956): 126–37.

————. "Reformers' Images of the American Indians." In Weeks, *"They Made Us Many Promises,"* 145–54.

————. *Taking Indian Lands: The Cherokee (Jerome) Commission.* Norman: University of Oklahoma Press, 2003.

————. *Theodore Roosevelt and Six Friends of the Indian.* Norman: University of Oklahoma Press, 1997.

Haller, John S. *Outcasts from Evolution: Scientific Attitudes of Racial Inferiority, 1859–1900.* Urbana: University of Illinois Press, 1971.

Harmon, Alexandra. "American Indians and Land Monopolies in the Gilded Age." *Journal of American History* 90 (June 2003): 106–31.

Hauptman, Laurence M. *Between Two Fires: American Indians in the Civil War.* New York: Free Press, 1995.

————. "Designing Woman: Minnie Kellogg, Iroquois Leader." In *Indian Lives: Essays on Nineteenth and Twentieth Century Native American Leaders,* ed. L. G. Moses and Raymond Wilson, 159–88. Albuquerque: University of New Mexico Press, 1985.

————. "Governor Theodore Roosevelt and the Indians of New York." *Proceedings of the American Philosophical Society* 119 (February 1975): 1–7.

————. *The Iroquois and the New Deal.* Syracuse, N.Y.: Syracuse University Press, 1981.

————. *The Iroquois in the Civil War: From Battlefield to Reservation.* Syracuse, N.Y.: Syracuse University Press, 1993.

————. *The Iroquois Struggle for Survival: World War II to Red Power.* Syracuse, N.Y.: Syracuse University Press, 1986.

————. "Senecas and Subdividers: Resistance to Allotment of Indian Lands in New York, 1875–1906." *Prologue* 9 (Summer 1977): 105–16.

Hauptman, Laurence M., and L. Gordon McLester III. *Chief Daniel Bread and the Oneida Nation of Indians of Wisconsin.* Norman: University of Oklahoma Press, 2002.

————, eds. *The Oneida Indian Journey: From New York to Wisconsin, 1784–1860.* Madison: University of Wisconsin Press, 1999.

Hertzberg, Hazel W. *The Search for an American Indian Identity: Modern Pan-Indian Movements.* Syracuse, N.Y.: Syracuse University Press, 1971.

Hinton, Maria, transcriber and translator. *A Collection of Oneida Stories.* Oneida, Wis.: Oneida Nation of Wisconsin, 1996.

Holford, David M. "The Subversion of the Indian Allotment System, 1887–1934." *Indian Historian* 8 (Spring 1975): 11–21.

"A History of the [Carlisle Indian Industrial School] Band." *Red Man* 13 (Feb. 1896).

Horsman, Reginald. "Scientific Racism and the American Indian in the Mid-Nineteenth Century." *American Quarterly* 27 (May 1975): 152–68.

———. "The Wisconsin Oneidas in the Preallotment Years." In Campisi and Hauptman, *The Oneida Indian Experience,* 65–82.

Hosmer, Brian C. *American Indians in the Marketplace: Persistence and Innovation among the Menominees and Metlakatlans, 1870–1920.* Lawrence: University Press of Kansas, 1999.

Hoxie, Frederick E. *A Final Promise: The Campaign to Assimilate the Indians.* Lincoln: University of Nebraska Press, 1984.

———, ed. *Talking Back to Civilization: Indian Voices from the Progressive Era.* New York: Bedford Books, St. Martin's Press, 2001.

Hurst, James Willard. *Law and Economic Growth: The Legal History of the Lumber Industry in Wisconsin, 1836–1915.* Cambridge, Mass.: Harvard University Press, 1964.

Indian Rights Association. Annual Reports, 1883–1920. Philadelphia Indian Rights Association, 1883–1920.

Iverson, Peter. *Carlos Montezuma and the Changing World of the American Indian.* Albuquerque: University of New Mexico Press, 1982.

Jennings, Francis, et al., eds. *Iroquois Indians: A Documentary History of the Six Nations and Their League.* Woodbridge, Conn.: Research Publications, 1985. Fifty microfilm reels, Newberry Library, Chicago.

Johnston, Basil H. *Indian School Days.* Norman: University of Oklahoma Press, 1988.

Jordan, Judy, comp. "Descendants of Cornelius Dockstader." Genealogical Records, Oneida Cultural Heritage Department, ONIW.

Keller, Robert H., Jr. *American Protestantism and United States Indian Policy, 1869–1882.* Lincoln: University of Nebraska Press, 1983.

Kellogg, Laura Cornelius. *Our Democracy and the American Indian: A Comprehensive Presentation of the Indian Situation as It Is Today.* Kansas City, Mo.: Burton, 1920.

———. "Some Facts and Figures on Indian Education." *Quarterly Journal of the Society of American Indians* 1 (April 1913).

Kennedy, Frances H., ed. *The Civil War Battlefield Guide.* 2nd ed. Boston: Houghton Mifflin, 1998.

Kickingbird, Kirke, and Karen Ducheneaux. *One Hundred Million Acres.* New York: Macmillan, 1973.

Kinney, J. P. *A Continent Lost, a Civilization Won: Indian Land Tenure in America.* Baltimore: Johns Hopkins University Press, 1937.

Klement, Frank L. *Wisconsin and the Civil War.* Madison: SHSW, 1963.

Kvasnicka, Robert, and Herman Viola, eds. *The Commissioners of Indian Affairs, 1824–1977.* Lincoln: University of Nebraska Press, 1979.

Lake Mohonk Conference of Friends of the Indian (and Other Dependent Peoples). *Annual Reports of Proceedings,* 1883–1916, 1929.

Lampard, Eric E. *The Rise of the Dairy Industry in Wisconsin: A Study in Agricultural Change, 1820–1920.* Madison: SHSW, 1963.

Leupp, Francis E. *The Indian and His Problem.* New York: Scribner, 1910.

———. "Indian Lands: Their Administration with Reference to Present and Future Use." *Annals of the American Academy of Political and Social Science* 33 (1909): 620–30.

———. "The Indian Land Troubles and How to Solve Them." *American Monthly Review of Reviews* (October 1910): 468–72.

Lewis, Bonnie Sue. *Creating Christian Indians: Native Clergy in the Presbyterian Church.* Norman: University of Oklahoma Press, 2003.

Lewis, Herbert S., ed. *Oneida Lives: Long-Lost Voices of the Wisconsin Oneidas.* Lincoln: University of Nebraska Press, 2005.

Liebhardt, Barbara. "Allotment Policy in an Incongruous Legal System: The Yakima Indian Nation as a Case Study, 1887–1934." *Agricultural History* 65 (Fall 1991): 778–803.

Linderman, Gerald. *Embattled Courage: The Experience of Combat in the American Civil War.* New York: Free Press, 1987.

Lindsey, Donal F. *Indians at Hampton, 1877–1923.* Urbana: University of Illinois Press, 1995.

Locklear, Arlinda. "The Allotment of the Oneida Reservation and Its Legal Ramifications." In Campisi and Hauptman, *The Oneida Indian Experience,* 83–100.

Lomawaima, K. Tsianina. *They Called It Prairie Light: The Story of Chilocco Indian School.* Lincoln: University of Nebraska Press, 1994.

Love, William De Loss. *Wisconsin in the War of the Rebellion.* . . . New York: Love Publishing, 1866.

Lurie, Nancy O. *Wisconsin Indians.* Madison: SHSW, 1987; rev. ed. 2002.

Malcolm, Jan, ed. "The Oneida Veterans Pentagon Project." Oneida Nation Museum, ONIW.

Manypenny, George W. *Our Indian Wards.* Cincinnati: R. Clarke & Co., 1880.

Marten, James. "Exempt from the Ordinary Rules of Life: Researching Postwar Adjustment Problems of Union Veterans." *Civil War History* 47 (2001): 57–70.

Martin, Deborah B. *History of Brown County, Wisconsin: Past and Present.* 2 vols. Chicago: S. J. Clarke, 1913.

Mason, Carol I. *Introduction to Wisconsin Indians: Prehistory to Statehood.* Salem, Wis.: Sheffield, 1987.

McDonnell, Janet A. "Competency Commissions and Indian Land Policy, 1913–1920." *South Dakota History* 11 (Winter 1980): 21–34.

———. *The Dispossession of the American Indian, 1887–1934.* Bloomington: Indiana University Press, 1991.

———. "Land Policy on the Omaha Reservation: Competency Commissions and Fee Patents." *Nebraska History* 63 (Fall 1982): 399–412.

McLaughlin, James. *My Friend the Indian.* 1910. Reprint, Lincoln: University of Nebraska Press, 1989.

McLester, Thelma. "Josephine Hill Webster, 1883–1978: Supervisor of Oneida Lace Industry and First Woman Postmaster." In Campisi and Hauptman, *Oneida Indian Experience,* 116–18.

———. "Oneida Women Leaders." In Campisi and Hauptman, *Oneida Indian Experience,* 109–11.

McVitty, S. R. "The Story of Seventy Years of Progress." *Missionary Bulletin* 16 (1920): 160–208.

Meriam, Lewis, et al. *The Problem of Indian Administration.* Baltimore: Johns Hopkins University Press, 1928.

Meserve, Frederick. *Historical Portraits: A Collection of Photographs.* 28 vols. New York: Privately printed, 1913.

Meyer, Melissa L. *The White Earth Tragedy: Ethnicity and Dispossession at a Minnesota Anishinaabe Reservation, 1889–1920.* Lincoln: University of Nebraska Press, 1994.

Miller, John R. *Cumberland Justice: Legal Practice in Cumberland County, 1750–2000.* Carlisle, Pa.: Cumberland County Bar Foundation, 2001.

Milner, Clyde A. II, and Floyd A. O'Neil, eds. *Churchmen and the Western Indians, 1820–1920.* Norman: University of Oklahoma Press, 1985.

Mitchell, Reid. *Civil War Soldiers: Their Expectations and Their Experiences.* New York: Viking Penguin, 1988.

Murdock, Eugene C. *One Million Men: The Civil War Draft in the North.* Madison: SHSW, 1971.

Nesbit, Robert C. *Wisconsin: A History.* Madison: SHSW, 1973.

Oberly, James W. *A Nation of Statesmen: The Political Culture of the Stockbridge-Munsee Mohicans, 1815–1972.* Norman: University of Oklahoma Press, 2005.

O'Grady, Terence J. "The Singing Societies of Oneida." *American Music* 9 (Spring 1991): 67–91.

Oneida Nation of Indians of Wisconsin. *Oneida Land Returned.* Oneida, Wis.: ONIW, 2003.

Onondaga Historical Association. *Official Record of the Indian Conference Called to Determine the Status of the Indians of the Six Nations, March 6–7, 1919.* Syracuse, N.Y.: Onondaga Historical Association, 1919.

Otis, D. S. *The Dawes Act and the Allotment of Indian Lands.* Edited by Francis Paul Prucha. 1934. Norman: University of Oklahoma Press, 1973.

Oxendine, Joseph B. *American Indian Sports Heritage.* Champaign, Ill.: Human Kinetics Books, 1988.

Parker, Arthur C. *Parker on the Iroquois.* Edited by William N. Fenton. Syracuse, N.Y.: Syracuse University Press, 1968.

Peabody, Francis G. *Education for Life: The Story of Hampton Institute.* Garden City, N.Y.: Doubleday, Page, 1918.

Peffer, E. Louise. *The Closing of the Public Domain: Disposal and Reservation Policies, 1900–1950.* Palo Alto, Calif.: Stanford University Press, 1951.

Pernin, Peter. *The Great Peshtigo Fire.* 2nd ed. Madison: SHSW, 1999.

Philp, Kenneth R. *John Collier's Crusade for Indian Reform, 1920–1954.* Tucson: University of Arizona Press, 1977.

Pilkington, Walter, ed. *The Journals of Samuel Kirkland.* Clinton, N.Y.: Hamilton College, 1980.

Pisani, Donald J. "Irrigation, Water Rights and the Betrayal of Indian Allotment." *Environmental Review* 10 (Fall 1986): 157–76.

Porter, Joy. *To Be Indian: The Life of Iroquois-Seneca Arthur Caswell Parker.* Norman: University of Oklahoma Press, 2001.

Pratt, Richard Henry. *Battlefield and Classroom: Four Decades with the American Indian, 1867–1904.* Edited by Robert M. Utley. New Haven, Conn.: Yale University Press, 1964.

———. *The Indian Industrial School, Carlisle, Pennsylvania: The Origin, Purposes, and Progress and the Difficulties Surmounted.* Carlisle, Pa.: Hamilton Library Association, 1908; CCHS Publications, 1979.

Prevost, Toni Jollay. *Indians from New York in Wisconsin and Elsewhere.* Bowie, Md.: Heritage Books, 1995.

Priest, Loring Benson. *Uncle Sam's Stepchildren: The Reformation of United States Indian Policy, 1865–1887.* New Brunswick, N.J.: Rutgers University Press, 1942.

Prucha, Francis Paul. *American Indian Policy in Crisis: Christian Reformers and the American Indian, 1865–1900.* Norman, Okla.: University of Oklahoma Press, 1976.

———, ed. *"Americanizing" the American Indian: Writings by the "Friends of the American Indian," 1880–1900.* Cambridge, Mass.: Harvard University Press, 1973.

———. *The Churches and the Indian Schools, 1888–1912.* Lincoln: University of Nebraska Press, 1979.

———. *The Great Father: The United States Government and the American Indians.* 2 vols. Lincoln: University of Nebraska Press, 1984.

Quiner, Edwin B. *Military History of Wisconsin; a Record of the Civil and Military Patriotism of the State, in the War for the Union.* Chicago: Clarke Publishing, 1866.

Reyhner, Jon, and Jeanne Eder. *American Indian Education: A History.* Norman: University of Oklahoma Press, 2004.

Ricciardelli, Alex F. "The Adoption of White Agriculture by the Oneida Indians." *Ethnohistory* 10 (Fall 1963): 309–28.

Richards, Cara E. *The Oneida People.* Phoenix: Indian Tribal Series, 1974.

Riney, Scott. *The Rapid City Indian School, 1898–1933.* Norman: University of Oklahoma Press, 1999.

Ritzenthaler, Robert E. *The Oneida Indians of Wisconsin.* Public Museum of the City of Milwaukee Bulletin 19 (Nov. 1950).

Schafer, Joseph. *A History of Agriculture in Wisconsin.* Madison: SHSW, 1922.

School Days: An Exhibition on the History of Indian Education. Brantford, Ont.: Woodland Indian Cultural Education Centre, 1984.

Shattuck, George C. *The Oneida Land Claims: A Legal History.* Syracuse, N.Y.: Syracuse University Press, 1991.

Smith, Alice E. *The History of Wisconsin.* Vol. 1, *From Exploration to Statehood.* Madison: SHSW, 1973.

Smith, Burton M. "The Politics of Allotment: The Flathead Indian Reservation as a Test Case." *Pacific Northwest Quarterly* 70 (July 1979): 131–40.

Smith, Donald B. *Sacred Feathers: The Reverend Peter Jones (Kahkweaquonaby) and the Mississauga Indians*. Toronto: University of Toronto Press, 1987.

Smith, Robert, and Loretta Metoxen. "Oneida Traditions." In Campisi and Hauptman, *Oneida Indian Experience*, 50–51.

Society of American Indians (SAI). *Report of the Executive Council on the Proceedings of the First Annual Conference, October 12–17, 1911*. Washington, D.C.: SAI, 1912.

Soltow, Lee. *Patterns of Wealthholding in Wisconsin since 1850*. Madison: University of Wisconsin Press, 1971.

Souvenir Program of the Oneida Indian Centennial, August 5–7, 1921. Pamphlet file, SHSW.

Stevens, Paul L. "Wheelock Dennison." In *The Heritage Encyclopedia of Band Music Composers and Their Music*, ed. Paul E. Bierly, supplement 3, 837. Westerville, Ohio: Integrity Press, 1991.

Stuart, Paul. *The Indian Office: Growth and Development of an American Institution*. Ann Arbor, Mich.: UMI Research Press, 1978.

Tanner, Helen Hornbeck et al., eds. *Atlas of Great Lakes Indian History*. Norman: University of Oklahoma Press, 1987.

Thwaites, Reuben Gold, ed. "Sketch and Narrative of Morgan L. Martin," *WHC* 11 (1888): 380–415.

Treat, James. *Native and Christian: Indigenous Voices on Religious Identity in the United States and Canada*. New York: Routledge, 1995.

Trigger, Bruce G., ed. *Handbook of North American Indians*. Vol. 15, *The Northeast*. Washington, D.C.: Smithsonian Institution, 1978.

Vecsey, Christopher, and William A. Starna, eds. *Iroquois Land Claims*. Syracuse, N.Y.: Syracuse University Press, 1988.

Viola, Herman, J. *Diplomats in Buckskin: A History of Indian Delegations in Washington City*. Washington, D.C.: Smithsonian Institution Press, 1981.

Walker, Francis Amasa. *The Indian Question*. Boston: J. R. Osgood & Co., 1874.

Washburn, Wilcomb E. *The Assault on Indian Tribalism: The General Allotment Law (Dawes Act) of 1887*. Philadelphia: J. B. Lippincott, 1975.

Weeks, Philip, ed. *"They Made Us Many Promises": The American Indian Experience, 1524 to the Present*. 2nd ed. Wheeling, Ill.: Harlan Davidson, 2002.

Welsh, Herbert. *Allotment of Lands: Defense of the Dawes Land in Severalty Bill*. Philadelphia: Indian Rights Association, 1887.

Whaley, Elizabeth J. *Forgotten Hero: General James B. McPherson, the Biography of a Civil War General*. New York: Exposition Press, 1955.

Whipple, Henry B. *Lights and Shadows of a Long Episcopate*. New York: Macmillan, 1899.

Witmer, Linda. *The Indian Industrial School: Carlisle, Pennsylvania, 1879–1918*. Carlisle, Pa.: CCHS, 1993.

Wonderley, Anthony. *Oneida Iroquois Folklore, Myth, and History: New York Oral Narrative from the Notes of H. E. Allen and Others*. Syracuse, N.Y.: Syracuse University Press, 2004.

Contributors

Eileen Antone, a member of the Oneida Band of the Thames and assistant professor of education at the University of Toronto, has written articles and booklets on the history of the Canadian Oneidas.

Carol Cornelius is director of the Oneida Cultural Heritage Department of the Oneida Nation of Indians of Wisconsin. An Oneida, she is the author of two books on Iroquoian culture.

Judy Cornelius was the librarian at the Oneida Library for eighteen years and has served on the Oneida Gaming Commission. An Oneida, she has been awarded a D'Arcy McNickle Fellowship from the Newberry Library in Chicago. Recently she served as treasurer of the Oneida Nation of Indians of Wisconsin.

Prudence Bennett Doxtator, an Oneida elder, attended the Guardian Angel Boarding School as well as Tomah and Flandreau Indian boarding schools.

Laurence M. Hauptman is SUNY Distinguished Professor of History at the State University of New York at New Paltz. He is the coeditor of *The Oneida Indian Experience: Two Perspectives* (1988) and *The Oneida Indian Journey* (1999). He and L. Gordon McLester III are the authors of *Chief Daniel Bread and the Oneida Nation of Indians of Wisconsin,* published by the University of Oklahoma Press (2002). In 1987 and in 1998, he was awarded the Peter Doctor Indian Fellowship Award by the Iroquois in New York for his research and writings on American Indian history.

Marie Hinton is an Oneida elder and language teacher who has worked to preserve the Oneida language over the past three decades. A graduate of the University of Wisconsin–Green Bay at the age of sixty-nine, she translated and transcribed *A Collection of Oneida Stories* (1996), which is used today by the Oneidas in their language program.

Barbara Landis is the Carlisle Indian School biographer for the Cumberland County Historical Society in Carlisle, Pa. She maintains a website devoted to the Carlisle Indian School's history: http://www.carlisleindianschool.org.

L. Gordon McLester III, an Oneida, is the coordinator of the Oneida history conferences and founder of the Oneida Historical Society. A former tribal secretary of the Oneida Nation of Indians of Wisconsin, he is the president of Bear Claw and Associates. Besides writing a children's book on Oneida history, McLester is the coauthor of *Chief Daniel Bread and the Oneida Nation of Indians of Wisconsin* (2002) and coeditor of *The Oneida Indian Journey* (1999).

Thelma McLester is the director of the Oneida Education Department for the Oneida Nation of Indians of Wisconsin. An Oneida, she has been awarded a D'Arcy McNickle Fellowship from the Newberry Library in Chicago and has written articles on the Oneidas' history for several scholarly presses and an encyclopedia. She has served as a trustee of Haskell Junior College and on the editorial board of *Voyageur* magazine.

Mary Schuyler Metoxen, an Oneida elder, is a graduate of Flandreau Indian Boarding School.

James Oberly is professor of history at the University of Wisconsin–Eau Claire. He is the coeditor of *Many Trails of the Mohican Nation* and the author of several articles on American Indian history. He has served as a historical consultant to both the Stockbridge-Munsee Band of Mohican Indians and the Oneida Nation of Indians of Wisconsin. His book, *A Nation of Statesmen: The Political Culture of the Stockbridge-Munsee Mohicans, 1815–1972,* was published by the University of Oklahoma Press in 2005.

Purcell Powless, an Oneida elder, served for over two decades as tribal chairman of the Oneida Nation of Indians of Wisconsin. Chairman Powless attended Pipestone Indian Boarding School and was graduated from Flandreau Indian Boarding School.

Patricia Stovey wrote her M.A. thesis on Laura Minnie Cornelius Kellogg at the University of Wisconsin–Eau Claire. She is a Ph.D. candidate in the educational policy studies program at the University of Wisconsin–Madison.

Loretta Webster, an Oneida, is the former attorney for the Office of Land Management of the Oneida Nation of Indians of Wisconsin.

WPA Storytellers: Oscar Archiquette, Chauncey Baird, Levi Baird, Filmore Cooper, Guy Elm, Lavinia Elm, Moses Elm, Thomas Elm, Albert Hill, Mark Powless, John Skenandore, Rachel Swamp Josephine Hill Webster. The WPA Oneida Language and Folklore Project, administered by Dr. Morris Swadesh, Dr. Floyd Lounsbury, and later Dr. Harry Basehart, collected hundreds of stories from Oneida elders between 1938 and 1942, which are today part of the curriculum in the Oneida schools. Unlike other WPA projects of the time, these stories provide a unique portrait of an American Indian community because they were collected, translated, and transcribed by the Oneidas themselves.

Index